ANNE OF DENMARK

ANNE OF DENMARK

Wife of James VI of Scotland: James I of England

ETHEL CARLETON WILLIAMS

LONGMAN

LONGMAN GROUP LIMITED
LONDON

Associated companies, branches and representatives throughout the world

First published 1970
ISBN 0 582 12783 1

Printed in Great Britain by
W. & J. Mackay & Co Ltd, Chatham

CONTENTS

ILLUSTRATIONS

ACKNOWLEDGEMENTS

In writing this book I have tried to reconstruct the life of Anne of Denmark from the letters and diaries of her contemporaries, who wrote while the events they mentioned were fresh in their minds rather than from memoirs and histories written many years later. I have quoted extensively from the letters of John Chamberlain (edited by N. E. McClure and published by the American Philosophical Society in 1939) who was both shrewd and accurate as being well placed for getting early news of coming events. The originals of most of the letters quoted are in the Public Record Office amongst the State Papers Domestic for the reign of James I.

I am most grateful to Mr J. Anthony Williams and Dr Doyle of the History department of Endsleigh College of Education, Hull for reading the typescript and making valuable comments and criticisms, and to Dr Barratt of the Division of Western manuscripts in the Bodleian Library, Oxford, for help in the early stages of the book. I am indebted to the staffs of the Kongelige Bibliotek and Rigsarkiv in Copenhagen, the British Museum, the Public Record Office, and the National Library of Scotland in Edinburgh for their help in dealing with elusive books and manuscripts. Above all I wish to thank the staff of the Bodleian Library, both in the manuscript and reading rooms, for the great kindness they have shown me.

I

GIRLHOOD
1574-1589

The birth of Anne of Denmark was not an occasion of universal rejoicing. When she was born at Skanderborg Castle[1] in Jutland on 12 December 1574 her father, King Frederick II of Denmark, was so mortified on hearing the news that he burst into his wife's bedroom and upbraided her for giving him another daughter when he so ardently desired a son. Fortunately both for herself and for her children, Queen Sophie possessed great strength of character and, young as she was,[2] three years of married life had already taught her to discount her husband's irascible outbursts.

Although King Frederick may have had many admirable qualities, as a ruler,[3] there is no denying that he left much to be desired as a husband. He was so restless that it seemed as if he were bent on demonstrating the laws of perpetual motion. The King was always rushing about in the open air, spending days and even weeks hunting. He would journey from one to another of his seven royal castles, moving from Kronborg to the cramped accommodation of Frederiksborg,[4] and thence to his favourite hunting seat at Skanderborg, where he pulled down Valdemar Atterdag's old castle and built for himself a Renaissance palace. Even here his unquiet spirit could not rest. Soon he was travelling south to Koldinghus, then to Haderslev, and on to Antvorslev, where the monastery founded by Valdemar I had at the Reformation become a royal residence. Finally he returned to Kronborg,[5] where he was planning a great fortress castle to command the Sound. It was all extremely exhausting and utterly futile, but

Queen Sophie wisely insisted on accompanying her husband on his travels, for she knew that he had a roving eye and that, should the opportunity offer, he would return to his mistress Anna Hardenberg,[6] whom he had passionately desired to marry.

Amongst Queen Sophie's most pressing problems was the care of her two daughters. They were too young to be subjected to the ceaseless round of travel, but fortunately a solution soon presented itself. After the Reformation and the dissolution of the monasteries, the upper classes in Denmark could no longer send their children to be educated in cloister schools, so they parted with them as infants to be brought up by their grandparents. They did not return to their families until they were fourteen or fifteen years of age. Queen Sophie decided to follow the prevailing fashion and sent Anne and her elder sister Elizabeth to be brought up by their grandparents, the Duke and Duchess of Mecklenberg, at Güstrow.

So for the next four years the two little girls settled down to live in a small provincial German town. It was a happy time, with a well-organised routine and much loving care and affection. Their grandfather, Duke Ulric III of Mecklenberg, was a shrewd, benevolent old man, whose advice was sought by his subjects from all parts of the Duchy. It was considered to be so valuable that he became known by his contemporaries as the German Nestor.[7] Their grandmother, Duchess Elizabeth, daughter of King Frederick I of Denmark, was practical rather than intellectual. She was deeply devout, austere in her ways, and exacting in her demand for unquestioning obedience from her grandchildren; but she was essentially kindhearted, and was able to give them that feeling of security which is so necessary for a happy childhood.

Life at Güstrow was frugal, orderly and virtuous; very different from the hectic conditions prevailing at the Danish Court, where gargantuan meals and heavy drinking were the order of the day. King Frederick was sometimes known to spend as long as seven hours over a meal, and his capacity for drink may be gauged by his drinking glass, holding three quarts of wine, which can be seen at Rosenborg Castle.

On 12 April 1577, to the great joy of the Danish people, Queen Sophie gave birth to a son—the future King Christian IV—at Frederiksborg Castle. King Frederick was overjoyed. At last he had the child of so many hopes; for although Denmark was not a hereditary monarchy, there was little doubt that his son would be elected to succeed him on the throne of Denmark.

Anne was too young to remember much of her brother's christening on Trinity Sunday, but she must have heard about it from her grandparents, who travelled from Mecklenberg to Copenhagen, Duchess Elizabeth in March and Duke Ulric in May. For them it was a memorable day which began with the pealing of bells, the playing of bands and the thunder of cannon. The burghers of Copenhagen lined the streets and cheered wildly as the state carriage drawn by eight white horses drove slowly past with the baby prince seated on his grandmother's lap. After the ceremony at the church of Our Lady, the procession re-formed and returned to Fredriksborg Castle, where rich offerings were made to the new heir. In the evening the royal guests and the citizens of Copenhagen were entertained at a banquet on a colossal scale. Tables groaned beneath the weight of 1,250 chickens, 8,000 eggs, 700 lambs, 400 pigs, 100 smoked boars' heads and 1,600 dried flounders.

Only a week later, before the citizens of Copenhagen had fully recovered from the effects of the revelry, the infant Christian was sent to Güstrow to be brought up by his grandparents. For the next two years the three children lived happily together and Anne developed that deep devotion to her brother which was to remain with her throughout her life—an affection which neither time nor absence could weaken.

It seemed as if life would continue in the same unbroken pattern for many years, but suddenly there came a rude awakening. The Rigsraad demanded the immediate return of the infant Prince to his native land.[8] The Councillors had become aware that their future king was surrounded by German influences and was receiving a German education. As Christian was only two years of age, these influences could not have penetrated very deeply, but the Rigsraad was thoroughly alarmed and determined to remove the child from such dangerous contacts as speedily as possible. King Frederick, who had no wish to offend his father-in-law, tried to present the case to Duke Ulric in as favourable a light as possible.

But now our faithful Council so often assembled by us [wrote the King] *desires us to take our eldest son to us and keep him at home in our kingdom. Not that our dear son and the other children should enjoy less good upbringing with your affectionate care than with us. Experience shows that our children stand in your affection as they do in ours and that your affection gives them just as good care as we ourselves could give them, but by a father's longing desire our children and the Council wish for their return.*[9]

Anne and her sister Elizabeth accompanied their brother on his return to Denmark and for the next four years were under their mother's care. Queen Sophie was one of the most remarkable women of the age. She was a daughter of the sixteenth century, but with the qualities of that age intensified. She was beautiful in the style admired at that time, with long hair of a rich shade of gold, deep blue eyes and innate grace of movement, which she inherited from her parents. Moreover, Sophie possessed the virtues dear to the heart of all Danes. She was a gifted cook, a redoubtable housewife and above all a devoted mother. She was the pillar which supported the whole family and the wise counsellor to whom they could turn in time of trouble.

The Queen had very high standards and was in many ways a martinet. She ruled her ladies in waiting with an iron hand, making them rise at daybreak to spend hours at their spinning wheels and forbidding them to wear jewels or to eat any but the plainest food. What was even more remarkable was her tolerant attitude towards her husband. In spite of King Frederick's many failings, she was devoted to him. Even when he insisted on excluding her from any part in the affairs of government, her devotion did not weaken.

So Anne found life with her mother was stimulating. The

Queen provided a happy childhood for Anne and her sister, taking great care of their health, tending them herself in their childish illnesses and being their confidante in their troubles. She trained her children in the virtues she herself prized most highly, and from her mother Anne learnt two lessons which were to be invaluable in later life; one was to be self-reliant and never depend on other people and the other—and more important—was to fight for what she believed to be right and to struggle on, even when all seemed lost. Well might one of Cecil's agents tell his master that Queen Sophie was 'a right virtuous and godly princess which with motherly care and great wisdom ruleth her children'.[10]

When Anne was nine years old a welcome break came in the daily routine of lessons and domestic training. Her father, Frederick II, had decided that the time had come to have her brother Christian duly elected as his successor to the throne of Denmark. Notices were dispatched to all parts of the country to send representatives to vote, and on Sunday, 14 June 1584, the royal family assembled at Viborg, the old capital of Jutland. Next day seven-year-old Christian appeared holding his father's hand in the market place and took his place on a dais, where he listened to the Chancellor, Niels Kaas, telling the people of the solemnity of the occasion and the sanctity of the oath they were about to swear. Then the act of homage began. First the Queen and her daughters, then the members of the Rigsraad, the nobles, the university professors, the bishops, the provosts, the clergy, the mayors, the burghers and the peasants knelt before the young Prince, repeated the oath and shook his hand. Anne might well be proud of her brother with his upright carriage and dignity. Young as he was, Christian rose to the occasion and showed a poise worthy of a future monarch.

When the act of homage came to an end the proceedings became more lighthearted. The King and his son left the tribune and according to custom the scarlet cloth with which it was covered was thrown to the people to be scrambled for as a souvenir. Later an original Danish play with a topical theme,

King Solomon's Homage, was performed in the courtyard of Viborg Castle. In it King David, as an old man, recognised his son Solomon as his successor, but the spectators noticed that Christian seemed to enjoy the antics of the fool more than the acting of the players. A banquet brought the day to a close, during which King Frederick drank himself under the table as a mark of respect to the players.

After three days of festivities the Court moved to Odense, then to Ringsted and finally to Lund, and in each place further acts of homage were received by the young heir apparent. By the end of July these ceremonies were over and the girls returned to their lessons, while Christian with his young brother Ulric was sent to Sorø Academy, the Eton of Denmark, one of the country's two public schools.

New Year's Day 1588 opened with gloomy forebodings for King Frederick. His health was beginning to fail and portents such as a sword and shield in the sky foretelling death and destruction heightened his unrest. In April, while on a sailing holiday, he was seized with such severe stomach pains that he was taken ashore to his castle of Antvorslev, where he died on 4 April at the early age of fifty-three—a premature death accelerated by overeating and excessive drinking. As the clergyman said at his funeral service, 'had the King drunk a little less, he might have lived many a day yet', a remark which was all the more tactless because of its indubitable truth.

King Frederick had been a popular monarch. He had given his people peace for the greater part of his reign. The King encouraged learned men such as Henrik Rantzau and Tycho Brahe, the astronomer, and he took a keen interest in education. Yet at his death he left many problems to his son. Chief among these was the power he had allowed to the nobles, who reached the peak of their ascendancy in his reign.

With King Frederick's death, the position of his widow was completely changed. It was at once stronger and more difficult. Sophie of Mecklenberg was a forceful woman. Her direct, rather challenging, manner inspired confidence. She was intelligent, interested in science and astronomy, and a capable administrator. The fact that she had been excluded by her husband from any part in public affairs merely made her more determined than ever to assert herself. She was a devoted mother to her seven children, just as she had been a faithful and loving wife. For if in public King Frederick addressed her as 'my Sophie', in private he often ignored and humiliated her. So Sophie determined to repair the humiliations of the past and exercise real power in Denmark as Regent during her son's minority.

Yet Queen Sophie was well aware that her position was far from secure. On his deathbed King Frederick had given his wife no real powers. He had merely commended her and the children to the care of God and the Danish people. 'What the Rigsraad will do, time will show. I hope they will prove amenable',[11] wrote Sophie to her father soon after her husband's death. She was determined to control her children's education, to see that her daughters made advantageous marriages and that her younger sons, Ulric and Hans, did not infringe their brother's royal rights. Queen Sophie cared for few people, but for her children no sacrifice was too great.

It was not long before she was engaged in a struggle with the Rigsraad, above all with two of its powerful members, Jørgen Rosenkranz and the Chancellor, Niels Kaas. To her dismay she heard that she was to be presented with the castle of Nykøbing as a suitable place of retirement for her widowhood. As she was a woman of dynamic energy, only twenty-eight years of age, the prospect was not alluring. Meanwhile there was the King's funeral to be arranged and here the Queen Mother scored her first victory over the less imaginative Councillors. They had planned it as a very simple affair, but Queen Sophie had very different ideas. Her husband, she insisted, must be buried as befitted a great monarch, and his funeral must impress the world with the might and power of the Danish people.

Anne, from her place in the rear of the funeral procession, could watch the vast cortège wending its way to Roskilde

Cathedral, the burial place of the kings of Denmark. Far away in the distance at the head of the procession walked sixty students singing psalms, for whom Frederick had provided maintenance and tuition. They were followed by the royal bands with trumpets and kettledrums draped in black. Then came the distinguished guests, foreign noblemen and representatives of the diplomatic corps, and after them twelve led horses, their attendants carrying standards representing various states of the Danish Empire. This was an imaginative touch in which the hand of Queen Sophie could be seen. They were followed by the late King's charger with its empty saddle and immediately in front of the royal bier the four chief Councillors of State carrying the royal regalia: Jørgen Rosenkranz with the orb, Peder Munk with the sceptre, Peder Gyldenstjerne with the sword and Niels Kaas carrying the crown. Then came the coffin supported on the shoulders of thirty-two noblemen, while eight more carried the canopy and thirty more paced alongside. Behind walked eleven-year-old King Christian with his grandmother, followed by his brothers Ulric and Hans. Next came three hundred ambassadors, nobles, and members of the Council marching three abreast; bringing up the rear Anne walked with her mother and her sister Elizabeth, followed by the ladies of the Queen's household and Danish noblewomen.

The cortège entered the great red-brick cathedral with its roofs and spires of weathered copper to the tolling of bells and the mournful strains of the organ. Slowly it made its way along the nave to the choir, where the coffin was placed in the sanctuary and the regalia laid on the altar. After a sermon in Latin and a discourse in German the King's body was taken for burial to the Chapel of the Three Kings, which occupies two bays of the nave and has fine fifteenth-century paintings of the Magi presenting their gifts, Saint Anna and the Infant Christ.

No sooner was King Frederick buried than strife between Queen Sophie and the Council of State broke out afresh. The Queen insisted on having a share in the government and the Councillors were equally determined to banish her to Nykøbing.[12]

In the end a compromise was reached. The Council invited Queen Sophie to advise them on her son's upbringing during Christian's minority, and to do so she would live in Copenhagen with her daughters. The Queen was delighted, for this meant she and her family would be living at the public expense and not on their own resources. Perhaps the Council would have benefited from Queen Sophie's advice, for she had a flair for finance and much sound common sense, but it must be admitted that she was quick-tempered, obstinate and apt to be intolerant of the opinion of others. As it was, the quarrel with the Rigsraad was never wholly healed and throughout her life she was the bitter enemy of Henrik Rantzau.[13]

Suitors from all parts of Europe were appearing to seek the hands of Anne and her sister in marriage. They had inherited their mother's fine carriage, her grace of movement and her lovely golden hair. Perhaps Anne was not so good-looking as her sister, but she was taller and well developed for her fourteen years. In fact, she was a very attractive girl.

One of the first suitors to urge his claims was King James VI of Scotland. He sought Anne's elder sister Elizabeth as his bride, for his ministers had been urging him to marry and provide Scotland with an heir. He was never an ardent wooer, for as he told his people, 'God is my witness, I could have abstained longer than the weal of my country could have permitted [had not] my great delay bred in the breasts of many a great jealousy of my inability, as if I were barren stock.' Such zeal as James had was tempered by the fact that two obstacles stood in his way. One was that Queen Elizabeth frowned upon the match. She feared that Scotland would become too powerful by gaining increased trade in the Baltic and at the same time having the protection of the Danish navy. At this period of his life James was desperately afraid of doing anything which might offend Queen Elizabeth. His heart was set on succeeding to the throne of England and he had no intention of endangering his prospects by making a marriage of which she disapproved.

In addition to this there was the thorny question of the Orkneys. These islands had been part of the dowry of the Danish Princess Margaret when she married King James III of Scotland on 8 September 1469, but there was a proviso that when the money for the dowry was paid in full the islands should be returned to Denmark. But the arrears were never paid, so the Orkneys remained linked with Scotland, though the islanders never ceased to look upon Norway as their mother country. Frederick tried to regain his lost heritage by requesting the return of the Orkneys and at the same time offering the redemption money. He went so far as to send an envoy to Scotland with a message that if King James sought a Danish bride 'the claim of Orkney should go right'.

In the autumn of 1587 James sent his old tutor Peter Young and Sir Patrick Vaus to Denmark to make discreet inquiries about the Danish princesses and, if the outcome were favourable, to ask for the hand of Princess Elizabeth. In the meanwhile King Frederick had been having second thoughts. He no longer felt any desire to have King James as a son-in-law. For one thing he felt that James's demands for his daughter's dowry were exorbitant, and what was even worse the negotiations had dragged on so long that he was convinced the King was a faint-hearted wooer. King Frederick, who believed in action, decided that Henry Julius, Duke of Brunswick, would be a more reliable suitor, so he promptly betrothed his eldest daughter to the young German, at the same time softening the blow by assuring the Scottish envoys that 'for the second [daughter] Anna, if the King did like her, he should have her'.[14]

So the envoys returned in a jubilant mood 'well rewarded and well contented with all they had seen especially the fair young princess'. But matters seemed once again to have reached a deadlock, for James felt that it was beneath the dignity of a reigning monarch to marry any but the eldest daughter, and whatever her charms, Anne was only the younger sister. Then suddenly came the news of King Frederick's death at Antvorslev and everything was changed.

2

THE COURTSHIP OF KING JAMES 1589-1590

As guardian to the eleven-year-old King Christian IV of Denmark, Queen Sophie was enabled to fulfil two aims dear to her heart. One was to ensure that her younger sons were provided with large grants of lands and substantial sums of money, and the other was to find eligible husbands for her four daughters. King Frederick's fumbling attempts at matchmaking had nearly driven her demented. This time, she was determined, King James should not slip through her fingers.

When the envoys sent by King James seemed about to return empty-handed Queen Sophie salvaged the negotiations by sending with them to Scotland a charming portrait of Princess Anne.[1] She had seen the admiring glances which Peter Young and Colonel Stewart had cast towards her second daughter and she believed the miniature would prove equally attractive to King James. It was a shrewd stroke. The King's interest was aroused, and even if the would-be bridegroom's demands for a dowry remained as exorbitant as ever, Queen Sophie believed that she could whittle them down. A much greater cause for anxiety was her belief that King James was by no means single-hearted in his quest for a Danish bride.

The Queen's suspicions were well founded. For while King James was considering marriage with Princess Anne, he was at the same time negotiating for the hand of Princess Catherine of Bourbon, the sister of Henry of Navarre. As James was well aware, the French match had much to recommend it. There was the traditional friendship, dating back hundreds of years, between France and Scotland, and in James's veins ran the blood of his French grandmother, Mary of Guise. Moreover, Queen Elizabeth was less opposed to the match. Perhaps she looked upon Henry of Navarre as a pillar of Protestantism, little guessing that one day he would decide that Paris was worth a Mass.

On the other hand, there were grave disadvantages. James had to acknowledge that Henry of Navarre was not yet King of France and it was by no means certain that he ever would be. Worse still, Catherine was eight years older than her suitor and admittedly no beauty. A contemporary had gone so far as to describe her as 'old, and cracked and something worse if all were known'.[2] As Catherine was only thirty-one, this was an unduly harsh judgment. But what King James found even more disturbing was the fear that the Navarre marriage might involve him in war with Spain and lead him into a head-on conflict with the Catholic League.[3]

Yet James continued his courtship of Catherine on paper, writing to Henry of Navarre in September 1588: 'Have me commended to the Princess of Navarre with apologies that I had not the leisure to write a dainty letter fitted for a lady.' The idea of King James with his coarse language and liking for bawdy jokes writing a dainty letter to a lady strikes a humorous note. However, a little later he did find time to write to Catherine assuring her of his steadfast affection.

Madame [wrote James], *the well known and true report of your virtues having long since reached my ears, and filled me with so much admiration . . . that I deem those men too happy who had the good fortune to be eyewitnesses of the same. But since, alas, Heaven has hitherto not allowed me even one such hour, I was unwilling to lose the opportunity of waiting upon you by letter as a proof of my great desire to visit you in person, but I shall take the first opportunity to make you understand my intentions more particularly. Meanwhile I beg you, Madame, to look on me as one who hopes to make known to you the love he bears you and remains Your ever most affectionate . . .*[4]

In spite of these loving words, King James could not make up his mind. The praises of his old tutor, Peter Young,[5] for Anne of Denmark's charms, lingered in his mind, for the King had a high opinion of his tutor's judgment. Then in May 1589 politics played their part on behalf of Anne. The Scots were strongly in favour of a Danish marriage and riots broke out in Edinburgh against Chancellor Maitland, who favoured the Navarre match. The Scottish merchants feared they would lose the Danish markets. It was whispered that the riots had been engineered by Peter Young and Colonel Stewart, and it was evident that they had been actively supported by the Provost and burgesses of Edinburgh, who were indulging in rosy daydreams of getting exemption for their goods from the dues paid by all ships passing through the Sound.[6]

James had no wish to lose his throne as his mother had done and he came to the conclusion that a Danish marriage was the safer course. So in June 1589 he sent Lord Keith, the Earl Marischal, Lord Dingwall and John Skene to Denmark to seek the hand of the Princess Anne. When Queen Elizabeth learnt of the mission she was highly displeased. In the opinion of the Virgin Queen, the ideal solution would be to keep James from marrying at all. Nor was the Queen's displeasure lessened when she discovered that the thousand pounds she had sent him for other purposes had been used to finance the mission.

As Queen Sophie had foreseen, James's demands for a dowry were as exorbitant as ever. He actually asked for 'ten hundred thousand pounds Scots to be delivered into our hands immediately after completing the marriage'.[7] In addition to this, he sought favourable terms of trade for the Scottish merchants, naval and military support in case Scotland was invaded, the sovereign possession of the Orkneys, and help in forming an anti-Catholic league. Even Lord Keith felt these demands were rather excessive and he sailed to England to tell King James that the Danes found his conditions 'a little strange',[8] adding that he was convinced that they would not accept them without some modification. Finally James was persuaded to drop his demand for an enormous dowry, which he did with the characteristic remark that he would not be a merchant for his bride,[9] and the Danes agreed to abandon all claim to the Orkneys during King Christian's minority. By July the match was made.

Yet all was not plain sailing. Soon Queen Sophie was embroiled in a violent quarrel with the Rigsraad, who wished to exercise the utmost economy over the royal wedding. Queen Sophie's ideas were very different. She was determined that regardless of expense the ceremony should be staged with the utmost magnificence. There should be colour, pageantry and lavish display. She remembered how the Rigsraad had tried to make the King's funeral a parsimonious affair and how she had vanquished them. So she entered the battle full of confidence. Spending was to be the order of the day.

Messengers were sent to shop in Paris and other cities of Europe, while in Denmark three hundred tailors were soon at work making Princess Anne's wedding gown. Embroiderers toiled day and night working on her trousseau, while bales of cloth and silk awaited their attention piled up in the royal palace. They were skilled in their craft and soon the most stylish dresses appeared from their workroom. One dress of peach and parrot coloured damask with fishboned skirts lined with wreaths of pillows round the hips was especially admired. Nor was this all. New liveries were provided for Anne's servants, fresh trappings for her horses, and a special coach, all silver with no ironwork, was ordered for her. Meanwhile Anne was engaged in the more mundane task of embroidering shirts for her fiancé.

For the first time in her life Anne found that she had become a person of importance. Her wishes were honoured, her opinions sought, her orders swiftly obeyed. Human nature being what it is, Anne could not avoid a feeling of triumph, not only because she would be married before her elder sister but also because her husband was a King and Elizabeth was only marrying a duke.

Anne was living in an enchanted world, where everything was radiant, harmonious and beautiful. She believed King James would prove to be the most perfect of husbands. True she had

had other suitors, one of whom was Prince Maurice of Nassau. No one could call him a Prince Charming, but Queen Sophie was deeply disappointed that his suit proved to be short-lived. For when the Danes insisted that Princess Anne must have her own Lutheran chaplain, Prince Maurice hastily withdrew his offer, without any hearts being broken.

'The young lady is so far in love with the King's Majesty as it were death to her to have it broken off and hath made good proof divers ways of her affection which his Majesty is apt in no way to requite',[10] Thomas Fowler informed William Asheby, the English ambassador to Denmark on 28 July 1589, and a fortnight later Asheby was sounding the same note in his report to Walsingham. 'The King is but a cold wooer. He is not hasty of marriage';[11] a remark which merited more attention than it received. All his life, except perhaps for six short months, King James disliked women, regarding them as inferior beings. All his interest was centred on the attractions of personable young men.

As yet this was hidden from the fourteen-year-old girl, eagerly awaiting her wedding day, which was brought a stage nearer when at the end of July the Danes sent three commissioners to London to receive further instructions.

The Earl Keith arrived in Copenhagen to act as proxy for King James in the wedding ceremony. The royal family moved into Kronborg Castle. Few brides can have had a more romantic setting for their wedding than Kronborg, with its copper-sheathed spires and grey sandstone walls mirrored in the waters of the Sound. There Earl Keith, dark, handsome, saturnine, went through the marriage service, according to Lutheran rites, with the youthful Princess. After the contract had been signed and the great seal affixed, he led her to the west wing, where rooms had been furnished for King James and his bride. Then, according to Danish marriage custom, the Earl seated himself beside Princess Anne on the bridal bed in the royal bedchamber.

All too soon farewells had to be said. On 1 September Anne sailed for Scotland in the *Gideon*, the flagship of Admiral Peter Munk, which was escorted by thirteen war vessels. Great preparations had been made to make the vessel worthy of a Queen of Scotland. The largest cabin, which was set apart for her use, was hung with tapestries and furnished with a bed for the Queen and a pallet for her personal maid Anna.

The North Sea is always a treacherous piece of water and that autumn it was at its most temperamental. Howling north-west winds whipped up huge seas. The *Gideon* was unduly light through carrying too little ballast. Her timbers leaked, and huge waves breaking over the ship soon flooded the hold with two feet of water. Anne was tossed from side to side and her spirits were not made lighter when Admiral Munk, crawling on all fours to her cabin, as dawn broke, informed her 'there is water in the hold and all the prayers of the learned doctors Knibbe and Niels Krage were proving of no avail'. The escorting vessels, with torn sails, broken masts and leaky timbers had been scattered, and two of them, the *Parrot* and the *Fighting Cock,* were far astern.

It was a terrifying ordeal for a fourteen-year-old girl who had led a very sheltered life. Anne was deeply attached to her family and even the discourses of the learned doctors, Knibbe and Krage, proved a poor substitute for her mother's loving care. The intense loneliness was even harder to bear than the grave peril. Three times the ships were driven back by contrary winds; once when they were within sight of Scotland. The pitching and rolling of the *Gideon* threw the unfortunate girl from side to side. Anne was unable to stand upright and all she could hear was the howling of the wind and the lapping of water in the hold. Once indeed, when three cannon broke loose on the deck, Anne narrowly escaped being crushed to death.

Admiral Munk was a deeply worried man. Never in all his days had he known such storms. Good seaman though he was, he found it impossible to reach the coast of Scotland. By the terms of his commission, he could not return to Denmark without his full complement of ships. It seemed as if the forces of evil were working against him. Then one day, sitting in his storm-tossed cabin, the answer came to him. It must be the work of witches and ruefully he remembered how he had given a cuff or a blow to a Copenhagen citizen whose wife was a notable witch. Undoubtedly the storms must have been caused by the lady to avenge the insult to her husband.[12]

When after a third storm the *Gideon* could barely keep afloat, Admiral Munk decided to abandon the attempt to reach Scotland and sail instead to Norway,[13] where he could land Queen Anne and her attendants in an inland fjord. There the Queen could stay in Norway until the spring brought the promise of better weather and calmer seas. This he accomplished successfully, and much to her relief Anne at last set foot on dry land.

In Scotland King James was waiting with ever-growing anxiety for the arrival of his bride. As the days passed and no sign of the *Gideon* could be seen, his fears increased, and he ordered national fasting and public prayers to be said for Queen Anne's safe arrival. From Seaton he moved to Craigmillar Castle,[14] two miles from Edinburgh, where his mother Mary Queen of Scots, had taken refuge for several weeks after the murder of Rizzio. It cannot have been a place likely to raise the spirits of a neurotic king, and while there James could neither sleep nor rest, so he sent out a small convoy to seek for news.

At length on 10 October a Danish ship, battered and storm-tossed, arrived from Norway bringing letters from Queen Anne with details of her terrible voyage.

One Stephen Beale, a Dane [reported Fowler to Burghley], *brought letters from the young Queen and from such Councillors and great men about her, and they were all indeed tragical discourses, pitiful, for the said Queen was in extreme danger of drowning; in her own ship a cannon brake and slew eight men afore her, and shook the ship that hardly could keep her above water, but with extreme labour; and being a ten huge ships, they were all brosed and weather-beaten, that having taken a Sound in Norway twenty miles within the land, they abode there and dare not stir because such is the preciseness of the Danish commissions determined in Council that they dare not bring the young Queen hither, what wind soever they have, with fewer ships than they brought out; and eleven of the great ships are gone home to repair, being lightened of their heavy ordinance, so there is but five small ships with the Queen, who lies in a miserable place for victual or any good thing; and they have been seven weeks at sea, and twice or thrice, within sixty miles of their coast, and yet driven back again.*[15]

James, reading the despatch 'with tears and with heavy deep drawn sighs,' decided that something must be done to rescue his bride from such appalling conditions. He sent for the Earl of Bothwell, Admiral of Scotland, nephew of Mary Queen of Scots' third husband, and ordered him to sail to Norway with six ships and bring back Queen Anne to Scotland. It was a mission after Bothwell's own heart in which his adventurous spirit could find an outlet. Alas for his hopes! When he presented an estimate of the cost of the expedition to the Council they flatly declared that it was out of the question to incur such expense.

Chancellor Maitland, who had been one of the main critics of Bothwell's estimate, suddenly came forward with a suggestion that 'if his Majesty would be contented with such ships as he and some other loyal subjects could furnish, he would go and seek the Queen himself'. Perhaps this was a shrewd attempt on Maitland's part to regain the royal favour. For James blamed him for opposing his marriage to a Danish princess and also for delaying to send envoys to Denmark to negotiate the marriage until the stormy weather had set in.[16]

At length the King made up his mind. At this period of his life he was full of romantic dreams, seeing himself as a knight errant about to rescue a maiden in distress. He would go to Norway and bring back his bride. It was a courageous choice, for braving the North Sea in Maitland's small ship of 130 tons involved no little danger. In vain Maitland and the Duke of Lennox implored him not to embark on such a perilous enterprise, but James would not listen to their warnings. Yet not even this romantic voyage robbed the King of his political sense. Knowing that it would be dangerous to leave the Chancellor in Scotland to his own devices while he was absent from the kingdom, James insisted that Maitland must sail with him. At the same time he appointed a Regency Council in which the opposing parties were carefully balanced to rule in his absence. On one side there was Lennox and Hamilton and on the other Bothwell and Maxwell.

Before sailing James wrote a long letter to Anne on 8 October in French. As James knew no Danish and Anne could not speak English, this was their only means of communication. Anne was reported to be working hard to learn French to please her future husband. It was a long letter, which being translated reads:

Only to one who knows my inmost heart could I express my fear and anxiety on account of the storms since you embarked; and specially since some ships, which set sail later, have arrived without news of you. My feelings constrain me to send a messenger in all diligence to discover your whereabouts, both to bring me back news of you and to give you news of me. For this purpose I can think of no more suitable messenger than the bearer, the Prior of Pittenweem, who has often shown alacrity in this affair, and is devoted to the service of us both.

Praying you then to believe all that he will say on my behalf, I will end praying with all my heart the Creator, (my only love) gives you a safe, speedy and happy arrival in these parts so that you can have proof of the entire affection of one who to you alone has vowed his entire life.

JACQUES R.[17]

Small as it was, the ship in which James sailed must have been very overcrowded. There were on board, in addition to the officers and attendants appointed to serve Queen Anne, 'all the minions of the King's stable and bedchamber'. James tried to insist that Thomas Fowler should go with them, but prudently he replied: 'I was yet but weak, and durst not venture to sea in this cold time of the year.'

There was no fear that the seafarers would be short of food on the voyage, 'for these ships, specially the Chancellor's, is so furnished and fraught with good and delicate victual as it was thought strange of so many live cattle and pulleyn, so much banquetting stuff, so much wine of all sorts'.[18]

The King kept his intention to sail to Norway a closely guarded secret.[19] Not even Bothwell nor his close friend, the Duke of Lennox, were allowed to know about it. Indeed, when they 'laid it sorely to his charge that he meant to undertake this dangerous voyage, he mocked and gibed at them'. Certainly they did not exaggerate the hazards, for the squadron consisted of five ships, of which the largest, in which King James intended to sail, was only 130 tons.

On Sunday, 22 October, James meant to slip stealthily on board this vessel in Leith harbour, but the ship was washed from her mooring by a storm. When a day or two later James did embark[20] he was more fortunate than his bride in having four days of fair weather, but on the fifth a storm arose and a day later he landed at Flekkefjord in Norway. From there he made his way overland to Tønsberg on the Oslo Fjord, where he stayed for several days. On Sunday James attended service in Tønsberg church, where he heard a sermon preached by David Lindsay, the Presbyterian minister at Leith, as is recorded on a tablet set in the wall of the church.[21]

The winter of 1589–90 was unusually severe, even for those northern regions. The fjords were frozen over early and so was the sea near the coast, while the roads were sheets of ice. Slowly and laboriously James made his way by road to Oslo, where he lodged in the house of the Shoemakers' Guild. As soon as he arrived he hastened 'with boots and all' to see his bride.

Anne was waiting, with mingled excitement and trepidation, in the Bishop's palace, for the coming of her bridegroom. When she saw a man of medium height, with protruding eyes and a square-cut brown beard, advancing towards her with an unsteady gait, she realised that it was not the Prince Charming of her dreams but a complete stranger. When the stranger bent down to embrace her, she shrank back in dismay and declared in a faltering voice that it was not the custom in Denmark to kiss on first meeting.[22] It must be remembered that Anne had been very well brought up. Soon they were conversing amicably together, probably in French, and before King James left Anne allowed herself to be kissed.

Next day James came in state to pay his respects to his bride, preceded by six heralds in red velvet coats and sable-lined cloaks. James himself wore an elegant blue velvet suit. He greeted Anne with a kiss and this time there were no protests. Then he told her that they must be married without delay. In fact, their wedding day was to be tomorrow and the place St Halvard's church.

So on 23 November 1589 King James went in procession from his lodgings to the church, where Anne, wearing her wedding dress, which had survived all the perils of the sea, met him. She looked very young and appealing, with her golden hair and ivory complexion. David Lindsay, the King's favourite Minister, was touched by her youth and described her, a little later, as 'a princess both godly and beautiful, as appeareth by all that know her. I trust she shall bring a blessing to the country like as she giveth great content to his Majesty.'

The service was in French and when it was over King James remained behind to receive the congratulations of the Norwegians, to which, not knowing the language, he replied in Latin. Meanwhile Anne had retired for a short rest. As they drove from the church James arranged a curious spectacle for the entertainment of the people of Oslo. By his orders four young Negroes danced naked in the snow in front of the royal carriage, but the cold was so intense that they died a little later of pneumonia.

The wedding feast was held in the great hall at Akerhus, the grim fortress which stands on a rocky promentory in Oslo fjord. The rigours of a northern winter had made food very scarce, but 'the banquet was made after the best form they could for the time'.

It was not altogether a happy occasion, as a furious quarrel broke out between the Earl Marischal and Chancellor Maitland over a point of precedence. Keith claimed that as the King's envoy he should be given precedence, but Maitland insisted that when the King was there in person his commission had lapsed. James did his best to pacify them, but the quarrel flared up again, this time over money. The Earl Marischal wanted to use part of Anne's dowry to defray his expenses, while the Chancellor maintained that for the time at least the dowry must be kept intact.[23] Perhaps Archbishop Spottiswoode's comment best sums up the situation. 'It is hard', he said, 'for men in drink, at which they were continually kept, long to agree.'[24]

On the day after the wedding King James gave his bride 'as a morrowing gift,'[25] a grant of the abbey lands of Dunfermline with its rich endowments. James's original intention had been to return to Scotland immediately after his wedding. In this idea he was heartily supported by Chancellor Maitland, who dreaded the mischief the Council, presided over by the Duke of Lennox with the Earl of Bothwell as his principal adviser, might be hatching. Also he had no wish to see further expense incurred on the marriage journey in view of the straitened financial position.[26]

But the Fates were against him. The King received a letter from his mother-in-law, Queen Sophie, inviting him and his bride to visit her in Copenhagen and meet the twelve-year-old King of Denmark. James accepted with alacrity. He had no wish to hasten back to the hectoring ministers of the Kirk, the quarrelsome Councillors and the penury of Scotland. Another reason for delay was the unprepared state of the Scottish royal palaces to receive his bride. The English ambassador, Asheby, had described the situation to Walsingham in August saying: 'Surely Scotland was never in worse state to receive a Queen than at this present, for there is neither house in repair but all most ruinous and want furniture and the time so short as this defect can not be helped if she come before winter.'[27] A month later he wrote: 'None of the King's houses can be fit to receive her, he must borrow Dalkeith which is the nighest fair house to Edinburgh for the Queen to stay in.'[28]

So Christmas was spent in Oslo. As the fjords were frozen over and travel by sea impossible, the King and Queen set out on an overland journey by sledge through Bohuslan, along the coasts of Norway and Sweden. They were welcomed by the King of Sweden's brother and feasted on New Year's Day with a banquet followed by dancing enlivened by volleys of artillery fire. At length they reached Halsingborg, and as the Sound was frozen over, they made the crossing to Elsinore in horsedrawn sledges.

At Kronborg they were greeted by salvoes of guns and the castle was blazing with lights. Anne was overcome with joy to see her mother and brother Christian again, and receive a warm welcome from a family group consisting of her sister Elizabeth and her fiancé Henry Julius, Duke of Brunswick, her brothers Hans and Ulric and her younger sisters Augusta and Hedwig.

Then followed three months of undiluted happiness. For the only time in his life King James was in love and he insisted that once again he must be married to Queen Anne, this time by Lutheran rites. So on 21 January 1590 the ceremony took place, in the chapel, and the reception in the Riddersal at Kronborg, a magnificent room running the whole length of the south wing. The walls were hung with rich tapestries, and the silver statues in the niches gleamed in the light of hundreds of wax candles. Next day Anne received another morrowing gift, this time Falkland Palace, which stood in the centre of Fife to the east of the Lomond hills.

Meanwhile King James was in his element. The young King Christian arranged a round of gaieties for his entertainment. There was running the ring, hunting with hounds and hawking by day and feasting and heavy drinking by night. Comedies were staged in Danish and Latin, and what James enjoyed even more, taking part in discussions with learned members of Copenhagen University. One memorable day King James visited Roskilde, where he met Dr Niels Hemmingsen, one of the most famous Danish scholars of the age, who lived in retirement in the cathedral city on account of his extreme Calvinist opinions. Together they discussed predestination. Another day the King made a speech lasting three hours in Latin to the doctors of theology at Copenhagen University and was presented with a silver cup.

Night after night the halls of Kronborg resounded to the sounds of drinking, dancing and merry-making, to the delight of King James, who in spite of his scholarly tastes revelled in such carousals. So greatly was he enjoying himself that when he wrote to Alexander, Lord Spynie, he ended his letter 'From the castle of Cronenburg quhaire we are drinking and dryving [killing time] in the auld manner'.[29]

Anne, too, was utterly content. As month after month slipped by and the bitter weather showed no sign of breaking, she rejoiced that her mother insisted that they must stay for her sister Elizabeth's wedding, which was to take place at Easter. In March, when the days were lengthening, Anne went with her husband to visit Tycho Brahe's observatory on the island of Hveen. Tycho Brahe was then at the height of his fame. He was the first astronomer to win an international reputation. Scholars flocked from all parts of Europe to visit him. Frederick II had thought so highly of the distinction he conferred on Denmark that he had given him Hveen,[30] an island in the Sound, where he built Stjerneborg, an underground observatory in which his delicate instruments were free from vibration, as well as Uranienborg, which was both a residence and a research centre. In the observatory were Tycho's sextants and quadrants and his great globe covered with parchment.[31] In addition he had a fine library, his own printing press and a vast open-air aviary.

A visit to Hveen was an exhausting experience, as Anne must have found as she threaded her way through workshops, chemical laboratories, the printing press where Brahe's great book on astronomy was being set up in type, and the desk were he was compiling the first reliable list of fixed stars. After the visit James wrote to his host:

We have seen with our own eyes and heard with our own ears in your residence at Uraniborg and I have learnt from your very agreeable and learned discourses, things which still occupy my mind to such a degree that it is difficult to say whether I recollect them with greater pleasure or admiration when we think it over ourselves.[32]

Above: Skanderborg Castle, Denmark, in the 16th century. *Left:* Anne of Denmark as a girl.

Queen Anne in hunting dress with her greyhounds.

King James, 1621. Portrait by D Mytens

Tycho Brahe was a difficult man. He was brilliant but irascible and could be extremely overbearing. His devotion to science was so great that to obtain money for his research and apparatus he oppressed the peasants on his estate and made their lives a misery.[33] Fortunately on the day of the royal visit he was in the best of humours, and when James was leaving he begged for one of his hunting dogs. The King at once gave him two of his own English mastiffs. It was one of these dogs, according to popular belief, which was the cause of Tycho's enmity with Walkendorp, which ultimately led to his downfall.

At Easter the long-awaited wedding of Princess Elizabeth to the Duke of Brunswick took place. Like Anne's wedding, it was at Kronborg, and to her great joy her grandfather, Duke Ulric, travelled from Mecklenberg to be present. The twelve-year-old King Christian escorted his sister from her chamber to the chapel, with his brothers Ulric and Hans walking in front, while Anne and her mother, Queen Sophia, came behind.

It was the last family reunion that Anne was ever to know. In the difficult days that lay ahead for her it must have lingered in her mind as one of her happiest memories. It seems strange that Anne never returned to Denmark to visit her family, but her experiences at sea had been such as to make her a confirmed landswoman for the rest of her life. Not even to see her mother or her much-loved brother Christian would she brave the North Sea again.

3

QUEEN OF SCOTLAND
1590

On Tuesday, 21 April 1590, Queen Anne embarked, for the second time, on her voyage to Scotland. Once again she experienced the agony of saying farewell to her mother and sisters and brothers and setting out to sail into the unknown. It was true that the parting was softened a little by the presence of two hundred fellow countrymen and countrywomen who were coming to Scotland for her coronation, and by her two maids of honour, Katrine Skinkell and Anna Kaas, close friends who were to remain with her in Edinburgh. But nevertheless for a girl of fifteen it was no small ordeal.

Again Anne sailed in Admiral Peter Munk's flagship and, as before, her journey was beset with storms. On 1 June she arrived at Leith, where she found an uproarious welcome awaiting her. Her loyal subjects lined both sides of the streets and the air re-echoed to their shouts of greeting.

The new Queen was tall for her age and had an innate dignity. The citizens of Leith took her to their hearts as she smiled and bowed to them. King James led her to a platform where seated they listened to James Elphinstone making a speech congratulating them on their safe arrival in Scotland. Fortunately he spoke in French, as otherwise his speech would have been incomprehensible to Queen Anne, for to add to the language difficulty his words were punctuated by salvoes from the guns of the ships in the harbour.

Then a number of eminent Scots were presented to the Queen.

First as President of the Council came Ludovic, Duke of Lennox, whose father Esmé had done so much to alleviate the bitterness of James's unhappy boyhood. He was followed by Francis, Earl of Bothwell and other members of the Council. Then came James Erskine, Earl of Mar, King James's closest friend and companion from boyhood. Noblemen and a bevy of noble ladies followed, some of whom were of especial interest to Queen Anne, as they were to be the ladies of her household. First and foremost was Annabelle, Countess of Mar,[1] mother of the present Earl, a stern, autocratic lady who was destined to be the Queen's unyielding enemy. Lady Mar looked on James as a son, so she subjected Anne to the disapproval usually meted out to daughters-in-law. Then came Chancellor Maitland's wife and the younger maids of honour. But one important person was missing. Jane Kennedy,[2] who was to have been the first lady of the Queen's bedchamber, was not there to greet the young sovereign. She had been tragically drowned when crossing by ferry to Leith in a violent storm. Had she lived she might have been adviser to Queen Anne. Andrew Melville attributed her death to the influence of witches, 'who in conjunction with their sisterhood in Norway, had brewed the storm to drown the harmless young Queen, but their malice fell thus upon her lady in waiting'.[3]

As soon as the presentations had been made Anne was taken to her lodging in the Old Custom House at Leith, then known as the King's Work,[4] to rest. James remained behind to take 'the chief of the dames by the hand, every one after another', before going to a service of thanksgiving for his safe return to Scotland. For five days the King and Queen remained in Leith, while Holyroodhouse was being made habitable for them.

This had already given King James no little cause for anxiety. After the solid comfort of the palaces where he had stayed in Denmark, he was extremely anxious to provide accommodation worthy of his bride. But the Crown was desperately poor and financial stringency was the order of the day. We have already seen what the English ambassador to Scotland and Fowler, Queen Anne's secretary, thought of conditions in Scotland. The task which faced the worried bridegroom was a wellnigh hopeless one.

Yet James rose to the occasion. While still in Denmark he had sent orders for hundreds of yards of red velvet to be cut up and made into hangings to cover the wall of Holyroodhouse. Colonel Stewart hurried to Scotland to announce the coming of the King and Queen to the Council, and to request them to have two horses, one with a saddle of black velvet fringed with gold and the other in silver lamé, in readiness for the Queen's use when she landed at Leith.

On 6 May Anne made her state entry into the city of Edinburgh. She was the centre of attraction as she rode in her silver coach, which she had brought from Denmark, drawn by eight white horses. As the cavalcade passed along Canongate and turned into the Royal Mile, the citizens lining the streets cheered as they caught their first glimpse of the young Queen with her flawless complexion and sparkling eyes. King James on horseback rode beside the coach,[5] accompanied by the Duke of Lennox, the Earl of Bothwell and Lord Hamilton.

To Anne it was a happy occasion, but her husband viewed it with very different feelings. King James had a morbid fear of assassination and wore bulky, padded garments to ward off the assassin's blow. When he saw the great crowds and the futile efforts of the guards 'to hold off the press of the people' he decided that never again would he allow himself to be in such close proximity to his loyal subjects. When they arrived at Holyrood House, King James took Queen Anne's hand, led her through the inner courtyard to the great hall and then to her bedchamber, which was resplendent with hangings of gold and silver cloth.[6]

Preparations for the Queen's coronation were going on apace. So many foreign guests were expected that fifteen feather beds were hired at the cost of two shillings a night from the fourth of May until the eighteenth of July for use in Holyroodhouse. Even so, accommodation there was very limited and extra rooms were taken in Edinburgh, each provided with a feather bed, coal and a candle for six shillings and eightpence a night.

King James was full of plans for a league of Scotland, England, Denmark and the Protestant states of Germany to keep the peace in Europe, but at the same time he brooded dolefully over the cost of entertaining the Danish guests who had accompanied Queen Anne, whose upkeep amounted to twelve thousand marks a day.

King James was a complex character. He was a mass of contradictions. While spending lavishly on his stables, his horses, his hunting dogs and hawks, he would plead poverty to such an extent that he would beg the loan of silver spoons from one of his subjects, borrow a thousand marks from another and ask his friend the Earl of Mar to lend him a pair of silk stockings to wear when he received the Spanish ambassador, on the ground that 'Ye wad not that your King should look like ane scrub on sic an occasion.'

At least for the Queen's coronation King James was determined that no expense should be spared. Anne's coronation robe was of purple velvet lined with Spanish taffeta, and the pages and footmen who attended her had new liveries of crimson velvet, while the Danish noblemen had scarlet broadcloth for their tablecloths and stool covers in the royal chapel.

The coronation took place on Sunday, 17 May, in the Abbey church of Holyrood. It was the first coronation by Protestant rites that had ever been held in Scotland, and as might be expected it gave rise to fierce controversy. The ministers of the Kirk were watching like hawks for any trace of Catholicism in the service. They even objected to the anointing on the grounds that it was a pagan custom. King James, however, was determined that no part of the coronation service should be omitted as a result of Presbyterian pressure. He told the malcontents that anointing with holy oil dated from the Old Testament and warned the ministers that if they would not perform the rite, he would call upon one of the few remaining bishops.[7] His choice of Robert Bruce to crown the Queen also caused much discontent; his fellow ministers promptly denounced him as an episcopalian, but in the end they had to give way, which they did with a bad grace.

Two processions were formed which made their way to the Abbey church[8] from Holyroodhouse. In the first walked King James, resplendent in purple velvet and ermine robes, followed by the members of his household, Scottish nobles, knights and ministers. In the second was the fifteen-year-old Queen, preceded by Danish noblemen in magnificent robes with chains set with diamonds round their necks, and after them came the Scottish lairds and burgesses and Lyon King at Arms with his heralds in yellow and scarlet. Immediately in front of the Queen walked the Earl of Angus, carrying the sword of state, the Duke of Hamilton with the sceptre and Chancellor Maitland, who had recently been created Lord Thirlstane, bearing the cross 'betwixt his twa hands'.[9]

Then came Queen Anne with Robert Bowes, the English Ambassador on her right and Admiral Peter Munk on her left, followed by Lady Bowes and Annabel, Countess of Mar, and behind them Lady Seton and Lady Thirlstane. Next came the ladies of the Queen's household and the maids of honour, amongst whom were Katrine Skinkell and Anna Kaas. Slowly the procession wound its way along the nave to the sanctuary, where Queen Anne took her seat on a dais beside King James.

The service lasted seven hours. This included sermons in English, Latin and French as well as two short orations. It began with a sermon by the Rev. Patrick Galloway, and when that had ended the Duke of Lennox, Lord Hamilton, Robert Bruce and David Lindsay mounted the dais and asked the King's permission to proceed with the coronation. Robert Bruce, turning to the congregation, announced 'that he was directed by his Majesty to crown the Queen'. Then the anointing took place, the Countess of Mar, opening the neck of the Queen's gown and the minister pouring 'a bonny quantity of oil'[10] on her arm, forehead and neck. Anne then withdrew to a cabinet in the Abbey escorted by her ladies, where she put on her coronation robes and returned to her seat on the dais.

King James asked for the crown to be brought to him, which he handed to Lord Thirlstane, the Chancellor, who placed it on the Queen's head, while Lord Hamilton handed her the sceptre and Lord Angus the sword of state. Then Queen Anne took an oath to defend the rights of the Church, saying:

I, Queen of Scotland, profess and before God and His angels wholly promise that during the whole course of my life, as far as I can, I shall sincerely worship the same eternal God according to His will revealed in the Holy Scriptures. That I withstand and despise all papistical superstitions and ceremonies and rites contrary to the word of God and I will procure peace to the kirk of God within this kingdom. So God, the Father of all Mercies, have mercy upon me.

The trumpets sounded, the heralds shouted 'God save the Queen', which was re-echoed by the congregation. Then Andrew Melville gave an oration in Latin of two hundred verses, which was followed by an address by Robert Bruce in which he asked the congregation to hold up their hands as a sign of their obedience, which they did.[11] Next came the act of homage. One by one the nobles knelt before the Queen and took the oath. At length the service ended, the procession re-formed. Queen Anne, wearing her crown and preceded by the Chancellor, left the Abbey to return to Holyrood House.

The city of Edinburgh wished to show their loyalty by giving the Queen of Scotland a civic welcome. Her entry was to have been on coronation day, but as that was Sunday, in deference to the protests of the Kirk, it was postponed for two days. On 19 May Queen Anne stepped into the Danish coach and escorted by Scottish and Danish nobles drove from Holyroodhouse along the south side of Canongate to Westport, where the magistrates greeted her and a boy dressed as an angel was lowered in a globe and handed her the keys of the city.[12]

It was a gay scene. The coach was drawn by eight white horses and a canopy of purple velvet was held over it by noblemen. At Edinburgh Cross the fountains ran with wine. At the

Butter Cross girls played on organs. Then the Queen went to St Giles, where Robert Bruce preached a sermon, which fortunately lasted only half an hour. At Nether Bow the Queen's coach stopped so that she could watch a pageant depicting her marriage. When it ended a purple box containing jewels worth 20,000 crowns, and with the letter A in diamonds on the lid, was handed to Anne, a munificent gift for a fifteen-year-old girl. The most exotic touch of all was the forty-two young men, dressed in white taffeta and cloth of silver, with gold chains round their necks and visors over their blackened faces, who danced the whole way in front of the Queen's coach.[13]

At length the day for which King James and Chancellor Maitland had been longing so impatiently dawned. On 25 May the Danish visitors who had come for the coronation embarked at Leith. In spite of Scotland's poverty, King James distributed gold chains and medals bearing his effigy as parting gifts[14] and gave them a sumptuous feast. The winds were favourable, the sea calm and speeded by a volley of guns from Edinburgh Castle, they set sail for Denmark.

With the coming of the young Queen to Scotland changes were introduced into King James's Court, which was notorious for its coarseness and licence. To a girl strictly brought up as Queen Anne had been, it was intolerable to be subjected to scurrilous remarks by one of the King's gentlemen in waiting while walking from her own apartments to the King's at Linlithgow Palace. A fresher, purer air blew through the whole Court, which was felt by everyone in the royal circle. As early as June 1590 William Dundas wrote to his friend Archibald Douglas:

Things are beginning to be greatly altered here; the Court wondrous solitary, for the patron of the Court of Denmark is greatly before the King's eye and of our reformatours by whom the King's house is diminished of the best of his old servants. Our Queen carries a marvellous gravity, with her patrial solitariness, contrary to the humour of our people, hath banned all our ladies clean from her.[15]

In July Anne paid her first visit to Dunfermline, crossing the Firth of Forth by ferry with her Danish ladies, Katrine Skinkell and Anna Kaas, and eight Danish gentlemen who were remaining in Scotland. After disembarking Anne rode the five miles to Dunfermline, but when she arrived at the Palace accommodation fell far short of her expectations. Yet King James had done his best. In May he had spent £400 in 'reparation of the house of Dunfermline before the Queen's Majesty passing there'. Her royal bed, which had been sent from Denmark, was set up in readiness for her. At this period of his life James treated her with camaraderie and consideration.

It could not be denied that Anne had grounds for disappointment with her morrowing gift. Dunfermline Palace had originally been the Abbot's lodging and the Abbey guest house. With the dissolution of the monasteries it had fallen into a bad state of repair through neglect. Not even the sight of her walnut bedstead carved with antique figures could raise her spirits.[16] Anne decided that she must build a new house for her own use. Building was in her blood. Her father had built the great sea-girt fortress of Kronborg and her brother Christian was to transform the skyline of his capital and make Copenhagen one of the most beautiful cities in Europe.

Anne planned to place her new house lower down the hill and link it to the older building by a gallery on the north-east. In the years to come the Queen became very fond of Dunfermline. She enjoyed its pleasant air and green fields which reminded her of Denmark, and above all because she felt the new house was peculiarly her own. On this, her first visit, she passed her time hunting and hawking with her husband, for James was passionately fond of the chase and even the most urgent business had to give way for it.

From Dunfermline the King and Queen moved to the royal palace of Falkland which, with its Renaissance façade, classical columns and medallions, was the work of King James's grandfather, James V. Here Anne spent several weeks before returning to Dunfermline at the end of September, where she remained while James went further afield on hunting expeditions. Later she moved to Edinburgh for the winter.

Soon Queen Anne found herself becoming involved in the feuds of the Scottish nobles. Even while she was in Denmark there had been bitter quarrels amongst the Scots who accompanied King James.

The Company who were with his Majesty put him to great trouble to agree their continual janglings, strife, pride and partialities. The Earl Marischal, by reason that his was an ancient earldom, and had been first employed in this honorable commission thought to have the first place next unto his Majesty. . . . The Chancellor, by reason of his office, would needs have pre-eminence. There were also contentions betwixt him and the justice clerk. The constable of Dundee and my lord Dingwall could not agree about place. George Hume did quietly shoot out William Keith from his office of master of the wardrobe. At length they were all divided into two factions; the one for the Earl Marischal, the other for the Chancellor, who was the stronger, because the King took his part.[17]

In Scotland the acrimony was even worse. Factions of the Catholic lords were forming against the Protestant lairds. Inevitably Anne was drawn into the conflict. She began a bitter feud with Chancellor Maitland. The memory of his support for a marriage for James with Catherine of Navarre did not predispose her in his favour, nor did her dislike of Lady Maitland[18] improve matters. But worse was to come. When James granted his bride the abbey lands of Dunfermline as a morrowing gift, the lordship of Musselburgh was specially excluded, as the King had granted this to Maitland in 1587.[19]

This was a gnawing grievance to Anne, which time did nothing to minimise. Like all her generation, she was profoundly conscious of the importance of land. It meant not only wealth but security; coinage might be clipped or debased, but land remained stable. So to see part of the lands which she believed to be hers given to another aroused her furious resentment.

In June 1591 the Danish Government requested the Chancellor to ensure that all grants of land made to the Queen were actually in her possession. So Anne's fury can be imagined when she found that Maitland was selling part of his property, as a precaution in case he was made to give up the lordship of Musselburgh.[20] Anne continued to insist that the Chancellor must abandon all claim to the lordship of Musselburgh, and when he refused she stirred up violent opposition. On 30 March 1592 King James dismissed Maitland, ordering him to stay away from the Court until he was summoned. With a heavy heart the Chancellor retired to his estate at Lethington and from there he wrote to King James seeking permission to leave the country, for to remain at home and live deprived of His Majesty's presence was to him a very hell, which he could hardly endure, promising to return at 'such time as your Majesty should think convenient to call me again to your service'.

The King realised that the quarrel must be ended. Maitland was one of his few able statesmen, and he owed many lessons in stratecraft to him. So he begged Queen Anne to forget her grievances and urged Maitland to make concessions to the Queen, in the cause of peace. The ministers of the Kirk played their part in insisting that the Queen should end the quarrel and Queen Elizabeth wrote to her 'dearest sister' suggesting that she should look more kindly on the Chancellor.[21]

With victory almost within her grasp, Anne would accept no half measures. Like many modern politicians, she believed that success covers a multitude of errors. So she refused to compromise and continued hostilities. In 1593 came victory.

The visit King James paid to Maitland at Lethington in the closing days of April may have led to his change of mind. Whatever the cause, on 30 April Maitland wrote a conciliatory letter to Queen Anne asking her the reason for her displeasure with him and pleading to be heard in his defence.[22]

Finally, in June 1593 Parliament ratified the Queen's right to the abbey lands of Dunfermline including the lordship of Musselburgh,[23] and on 15 July Maitland formally surrendered his rights to Queen Anne, receiving the sum of £20 in repayment for the money he had paid King James for them. Queen Anne was to hold the lordship of Musselburgh during her lifetime, then it was to return to members of the Maitland family.[24]

This was to lead to trouble in the future. Later Queen Anne was granted all the Dunfermline abbey lands, Musselburgh not being excluded, and twenty years after the Queen's death the Chancellor's family were complaining that they had received no income for Musselburgh.[25]

Equally unfortunate were the Queen's relations with Sir James Melville. Young as she was, Anne had an iron will and a determination which verged on obstinacy. Nothing would make her yield, if she believed she was right. Very unwisely, while she and her husband were staying at Falkland Palace, the King sent for Melville and entrusted him with the task of initiating the Queen in the customs of the country and the ways of the Court.

From the first Anne resented Melville's dictatorial manner. She found his homilies and proferred advice intensely distasteful. James might argue that Melville 'was the fittest man to commit that charge to', but Anne held a very different opinion. To make matters worse, the King praised Melville publicly to her for his popularity and great experience. When Anne heard that he was to be appointed a gentleman of her bedchamber she received the news coldly, and matters were not improved when a few days later she asked him 'if he was set to be her keeper'.[26] Sir James tried to disarm her by flattery, telling her that she 'was known to be descended of so noble and princely parents and so well brought up that she needed no keeper, albeit her dignity required to be honourably served, with men and women, both young and old, in sundry occasions'. Anne refused to be appeased and merely replied that she had been ill used.

Besides Sir James's strictures the Queen had to endure the stinging reprimands of the Presbyterian ministers. Soon after she landed in Scotland they censured her for non-attendance at the kirk, and for spending her nights 'waking and balling'. Not infrequently she was publicly denounced from the pulpit. One minister, the Rev. David Black, openly questioned her beliefs and said that the religion of Scotland was but the show of a religion.

Soon it was evident that the Queen's popularity with her Scottish subjects was beginning to wane. This may have been partly because there was no sign that she was giving Scotland an heir, but undoubtedly some of King James's unpopularity, due to his uncouth manners and dislike of any contact with his humbler subjects, may have fallen upon Queen Anne.

4

THE EARL OF BOTHWELL
1590-1593

One of King James's most absorbing interests was the study of witchcraft, which he regarded as 'a branch of theology',[1] He enjoyed holding lengthy discussions on the subject, and while he was in Denmark his interest quickened when he heard that Admiral Peter Munk attributed to the malevolence of witches, the storms which had so harassed Queen Anne's voyage. It is true that the Admiral believed that much of his misfortune had a more mundane reason: that it was due to the parsimony of the treasurer, Christopher Walkendorp, in sending the ships to sea in an unseaworthy condition.[2] A furious quarrel ensued between the two Danes, but to the end the Admiral remained convinced that the storms were the work of witches.

In the summer of 1590 a great witch hunt was instituted in Copenhagen. One of the first victims was Anna Koldings, who under pressure divulged the names of five other women, one of whom was the wife of the burgomaster of Copenhagen. They all confessed that they had been guilty of sorcery in raising storms which menaced Queen Anne's voyage and that they had sent devils to climb up the keel of her ship. In September two women were burnt as witches at Kronborg.

It occurred to King James that there might be witches in Scotland who had helped to produce the storms. He would have been better advised to ponder over Reginald Scott's book *A Discovery of Witchcraft*, published in 1584, which cast doubts on the widely held belief in witches. But instead, as soon as he landed in Scotland, a witch hunt was set in progress, which yielded surprising results. A coven of witches was found at North Berwick. Chief among them was Agnes Sampson, who after torture confessed that she had been guilty of raising storms to endanger the Queen's ship.

Agnes Sampson was not one of the poor helpless old women who were the usual victims of witch hunts. She was a person of standing and some strength of character, but under the pressure of thumbscrews her courage failed and she incriminated Richard Graham and several other women. Graham in his turn declared that no less a person than the Earl of Bothwell had consulted him about the date of King James's death[3] and bribed him to raise a storm to endanger the King's voyage from Denmark.

By means of 'a conjuring of cats', he claimed to have produced so great a storm that King James and his bride had narrowly escaped death. The spell was cast by taking a cat, christened Margaret, tying four joints from a dead man to each of its feet and at midnight throwing it into the sea, crying 'See there be no deceit among us.' As the cat Margaret swam safely ashore in spite of its handicap, the witches interpreted this as a sign that Queen Anne would reach Scotland unharmed.

Nothing could have pleased King James more than this unexpected accusation of Bothwell. Of all his subjects the one he most feared was Francis Hepburn, fifth Earl of Bothwell.[4] Now Fate seemed to have played into the King's hands. A charge of witchcraft was fraught with infinite danger to anyone, however powerful, against whom it was made. Bothwell was brought before a secret meeting of the Council, at which King James was present, and ordered to be detained in Edinburgh Castle until a further trial could be arranged. King James believed that he would be safe from the menace of his unruly kinsman for many years to come, but events were to prove him wrong. Within a week Bothwell had managed to make his escape over the wall of Edinburgh Castle.

Bothwell's escape reduced King James to a state of panic. He feared his kinsman's ruthless nature, which had no respect for either the law or the sanctity of royalty, but above all he believed the Earl possessed supernatural powers and communed with warlocks. So alarmed was he that he spent the summer and autumn dodging from one of his palaces to another in the hope of escaping from his pursuer, for Bothwell had taken refuge in Caithness, where he had gathered a band of some four hundred men.

Queen Anne's feelings towards the rebel Earl were very different from those of her husband. She had a lurking admiration for his swashbuckling bravado, his witty tongue and pleasant manners. For Bothwell was gifted, dynamic and endowed with the Stuart charm. He treated the Queen with deference and consideration in contrast to the behaviour of the Earl of Mar and his autocratic mother, Countess Annabel. Anne found him a stimulating companion, for, as the Earl spoke several languages, they could converse in French, which was a welcome relief for the Queen, after struggling with the broad Scotch of most members of King James's Court. So when news came of Bothwell's escape Anne did not share her husband's fears. She little guessed that for the next two years her life was to be overshadowed by apprehension and insecurity.

The second Christmas was spent by Queen Anne with her husband at Holyrood House. It cannot have been a festive time, for tension was in the air and three days after Christmas Day what James most dreaded happened—the Earl of Bothwell struck.

About seven o'clock on a dark December evening Bothwell and his followers entered Holyrood House through an old stable. His main aim was to repay a grudge on Chancellor Maitland, who had accused him of witchcraft. Pandemonium reigned as the intruders raced through the building shouting 'Justice, Justice! A Bothwell, a Bothwell.' Snatching the keys from a porter, they tried to set fire to the door of the King's bedchamber and hack down the door of Maitland's apartment.[5]

Nor did the Queen escape from the ordeal. For the invaders, believing that the King was sheltering in her apartments, battered on her door with 'certain great forehammers', and as the

Henry, Prince of Wales, *circa* 1610. Portrait attributed to Robert Peake

Princess Elizabeth. Portrait by M. J. Van Miereveldt

Negotiation of the Spanish Treaty at Somerset House, 1604. *Left*, Spaniards. *Right:* Robert Cecil with paper and inkpot, Lord Henry Howard, The Earl of Devonshire, Lord Howard of Effingham (Earl of Nottingham) and The Earl of Dorset. Painting attributed to M. Gheeraedts II massive oak panels began to splinter she thought that every moment would be her last. Although the master of her household, Harry Lindsay, put up a brave defence, it seemed as if nothing could save them.[6]

Then the alarm sounded. The common bell of the city of Edinburgh pealed its warning, the citizens ran to the Palace carrying their pikes, only to find that the intruders had fled down the stairs, killing as they ran John Shaw, the Master of the King's Stable, and two other servants. After being repulsed from the Chancellor's hiding place, Bothwell and four of the ringleaders leapt on their horses and made good their escape in the darkness.[7] In his absence Bothwell was publicly proclaimed a traitor from the Mercat Cross in Edinburgh, and a reward was offered for his head.

Chancellor Maitland was so shaken by the terror of that December night that he insisted that the King and Queen must leave Holyroodhouse and lodge in Nicol Edward's house in Niddry's Wynd, a damp, grey alley which still further depressed Queen Anne's spirits. Maitland himself took up his quarters in Alexander Clarke's house near by.

Time did not weaken the Queen's dislike and distrust of the Chancellor, and when at the end of February King James suggested that they should go to Linlithgow Palace for a change of scene, Anne definitely refused to stay there if Maitland was to be one of the party. At every opportunity she urged her husband to dismiss him from his office.

James was extremely neurotic and worry over Bothwell was reducing him to a nervous wreck. Nor were matters improved by a sinister incident which occurred in February 1591. King James's closest friend, the Earl of Huntley, the leader of the Catholic earls, was concerned in the murder of the Earl of Moray, who was not only a Stuart but a close friend of Bothwell. The 'bonny Earl of Moray', who was the son-in-law of Regent Morton, was an extremely personable man of great stature; and rather unwisely Queen Anne commented on his good looks and lovely golden hair, to the intense annoyance of her husband. Nor were his feelings soothed when ballads were sung about the Queen's love for the bonny Earl, and not even the fact that there was no substance in such an accusation did anything to lessen the royal rage.

Meanwhile Bothwell remained at large, always on the move, sometimes on the Border, now in Leith, later, it was rumoured, in Dundee. Suddenly, on 28 June 1592, the rebel Earl struck again. This time his objective was Falkland Palace, where King James had gone for the hunting and Queen Anne for a change of air. The King's apartments were on the first floor in the east range and a winding stair led to Queen Anne's bedroom on the floor above. The Earl with three hundred followers tried to force his way into the Palace by the little postern in the east range which gave access to the King's bedchamber. The marks of bullets fired to distract the attention of the main guard can still be seen on the flanking towers of the gatehouse.

It was 2 a.m. when Bothwell led his Borderers from Annandale and Liddesdale to the King's apartments, but James was not taken unawares. He had barricaded himself in the Tower and was watching the artillery barrage which finally drove the invaders away. At 7 a.m. Bothwell retreated, taking all Queen Anne's horses with him to make pursuit impossible.[8]

Bothwell had fled, but the tension continued. It was not long before Queen Anne again incurred her husband's displeasure. James, who had a good deal of the schoolmaster in his make-up, enjoyed instructing the young and censuring their faults, and his wife was an easy victim. In August, when they were in residence at Dalkeith, John Wemyss, the young laird of Logie, a staunch supporter of Bothwell, and suspected of complicity in the attack on Falkland Palace, was a prisoner in the guardroom at Dalkeith. He had an ally in one of the Queen's Danish maids, who is variously called Margaret Vinster or Twynstoun. She was deeply in love with him and planned to set him free. When it was her turn to sleep in the Queen's bedchamber she waited until the King and Queen were asleep before going to the Captain of the Guard to tell him that Logie was wanted for questioning by King James.

He was brought by an armed guard to the Queen's bedchamber, Margaret met them at the door, told the soldiers to wait and taking Logie by the hand, led him through the royal bedroom and lowered him by a cord from the window 'and so by her good charitable help he happily escapit by the subtletie of love'.[9]

Logie might be free, but Anne did not escape so easily. James was convinced that she knew about the plot. He insisted that Margaret should be sent back to Denmark. When the King was angry his language was both coarse and menacing. Anne was only seventeen and his hectoring tones soon reduced her to tears. But she was staunchly loyal and no amount of bullying could make her incriminate Margaret. The girl was her friend and fellow countrywoman and she would not betray her.[10]

It may have been this Margaret who later in 1603 involved Queen Anne in further trouble, which caused her to lose much of her newly won popularity with her English subjects. There were loud-voiced complaints at Court that the Queen was being remiss in signing documents and tradesmen were bewailing her slackness in paying their accounts. The trouble seems to have arisen because Anne placed too much trust in her Danish maid Margaret 'who usurping too much authority commands and directs in her Majesty's name with insolence which with reason can not and shall not in anywise be obeyed'.[11]

Bothwell struck again, for the last time, on 24 July 1593, and even more dramatically than before. He came between 8 a.m. and 9 a.m. to Holyrood and waited near the kitchen entrance until the door was opened for him by the Countess of Athol, the daughter of Lady Gowrie. He entered quietly with his friend John Colville and hid behind the hangings in the King's anteroom until it was time for James to dress. When he heard signs of movement Bothwell entered the room with the Duke of Lennox and the Earl of Athol holding a drawn sword in his hand. The sight of bare steel always unnerved King James and uttering a cry of terror he rushed for refuge to the Queen's bedchamber, but found the door locked.

When Anne realised that she was a prisoner she was filled with desperate fear. Through the door she could hear her husband shouting and other male voices. Could the Queen but have seen what was happening a strange sight would have met her eyes. Bothwell, like all the Stuarts, loved to dramatise himself. He had thrown himself on his knees, laid his sword upon the ground and placed his long hair beneath the King's foot crying: 'We came not to murder you nor to do you any hurt. We came as loyal subjects to protect you from those who would do you harm. I swear it by this sword.'

Bothwell handed his sword to the King, telling him to strike; thus showing that though it was in his power to kill it was his intention to submit.[12] This, says Sir James Melville, who was in Holyrood at the time, 'moved his Majesty to have pity and compassion upon him and granted him pardon freely without compulsion: as his Majesty told me that same day and the whole manner of his in coming'.[13]

Soon bells were pealing, alarms were sounding and Queen Anne, locked in her bedchamber, was the prey to a thousand fears. The Danish envoys who were in Edinburgh on a goodwill mission to negotiate the interminable problem of the Queen's dowry became so alarmed for her safety that they hurried to the Palace and begged Sir James Melville to go to the royal apartments and see that all was well with the Queen.

Then Queen Anne to her great relief heard the door of her bedchamber being unlocked, and King James entered. He had realised that Bothwell's intentions were by no means so lethal as he had feared. Feeling that the time had come to reassure the public, he took his wife by the hand and led her to a balcony overlooking the street, where they bowed and James assured his people 'that they were well and that things were fully agreed'.[14]

This proved to be an overoptimistic estimate of the situation. The King might claim that all was well, but in reality his promise to Bothwell had been more politic than sincere. For Bothwell's victory was by no means as durable as he could have wished. He was declared a traitor and fled to the north of Scotland. When

James managed to rally the Catholic Lords to his side Bothwell took refuge in France and died in poverty in Naples in 1624.

Perhaps the only person who gained from Bothwell's attack was Queen Anne. For when the young Duke of Lennox, the son of Esmé Stuart, returned to his allegiance to King James, he brought his sister the Countess of Huntley to court with him. Henrietta Stuart was lively, very French in outlook and a firm supporter of the Jesuits.[15] Queen Anne found her a delightful companion and made her a member of her household. Soon she was one of Queen Anne's closest and most trusted friends.

5

THE BIRTH OF PRINCE HENRY
1594

The year 1594 brought both intense happiness and bitter suffering to Queen Anne. It changed her from a romantic girl, who believed that marriage was the gateway to perpetual bliss, into a withdrawn, enigmatic woman. She realised that King James was far from being a perfect husband. In addition to the drawback that he seldom washed and frequently smelt of drink, his table manners were disgusting. For his tongue being overlarge, his food dribbled out of the sides of his mouth as he ate.

Moreover, he spoke in a thick hectoring voice, delighted in using coarse language and telling risqué tales. He talked interminably and Anne suffered hours of unspeakable boredom listening to his discourses on theology and philosophy. She also learnt to speak broad Scots and even to write it, as her earliest surviving letter to George Heriot shows. Yet James, in spite of his indolence, was extremely astute. He had secured greater power than any king of Scotland since the time of his ancestor James I, by playing off the Presbyterians against the Catholic lords; the Kirk against the State. James was a past master at keeping both sides in a state of suspense, and being totally devoid of scruples, he would switch his support from one side to the other, whenever either party showed signs of becoming too strong. In this way James succeeded in keeping his crown, which neither his mother nor his son Charles were able to do.

When in October 1593 it became known that Queen Anne was going to have a child there was intense joy throughout Scotland.

The Queen's childlessness had long made her a target for disapproving tongues. King James shared in the general joy. He knew that the birth of a son and heir would strengthen his position and make Queen Elizabeth more likely to name him her successor.

James had a romantic attachment to Stirling Castle, where he had spent his childhood, and he decided that the child should be born there. It is unlikely that Queen Anne had any such leanings, for the castle was the home of her enemies the Countess Annabel and the Earl of Mar, whom James regarded as a mother and brother. The royal apartments, which lay on the west side of the castle, were built round a quadrangle known as 'the lion's den', because James IV kept his pet lion there. The principal apartments were on the first floor. Certainly Anne, if she had been consulted, would have preferred her palace at Dunfermline or Falkland.

Great preparations were made for the birth of an heir. A proclamation was made from the Mercat Cross that the foreign ambassadors were to be entertained by the nobility and gentry—a step which while it saved the royal coffers certainly did not endear King James to his Scottish lairds. The King continued to indulge in nostalgic dreams of the days gone by. He had the oak cradle brought out in which he had been rocked to sleep and his old nurse Helen Little installed as head of the nursery, while the formidable Countess Annabel was placed in charge of the situation. The wishes of the seventeen-year-old Queen seem never to have been consulted.

Two days after Christmas Anne rode with her husband to Stirling and there on a cold February day she gave birth to a son who was called Frederick Henry after his two grandfathers, King Frederick II of Denmark and Henry Stuart, Lord Darnley. There was great rejoicing. Bonfires were lit in the streets, and there was dancing 'as if the people had been daft for mirth'.

Queen Elizabeth was invited to act as godmother—a diplomatic move on James's part, as it ensured that she would send a valuable christening present, and there was little likelihood that she would come in person. The chapel royal at Stirling where James himself had been baptised was much too small for a christening on such a scale and the King set to work to enlarge it.[1]

Month after month the ceremony was delayed. As King James had hoped, Queen Elizabeth declined to undertake such an arduous journey, but promised to send the Earl of Cumberland as her representative. However, the Earl fell ill and was unable to travel. As usual on royal occasions, there was friction amongst the guests. Both Anne's grandfather, Duke Ulric of Mecklenberg, and her brother-in-law, the Duke of Brunswick, were deeply affronted because King James had not sent a special envoy with their invitation. They refused to ride from Leith with Peter Young, the Scottish ambassador to Denmark, as their companion.[2]

While carpenters and stonemasons were hard at work watched by King James, a disturbing thought struck the expectant father's mind; a thought which was to haunt him for many years. Suppose the infant prince should become the rallying point for the dissident nobles, who would use him to deprive King James of his throne just as he had been the means of replacing his mother Mary Queen of Scots. It was a disquieting thought. Worse even than losing the Crown of Scotland was the prospect of missing the Crown of England, on Queen Elizabeth's death. That was a chance James was in no circumstances willing to forgo.

Meanwhile the work went on apace. No detail was overlooked. Even the captive lion was brought from Holyrood and installed in a den at Stirling. Splendid pageants and rich banquets were planned with which James hoped to dazzle the world. It was by no means easy. James was so poor and his plate so scanty that when he invited Sir Walter Dundas to the christening he begged him to bring 'his silver spoons'.

After several postponements Queen Elizabeth's representative arrived, not the crotchety Earl of Cumberland but the young Earl of Sussex. At length on 30 August the ceremony took place —the first royal christening by Protestant rites that Scotland had ever known. Even so there was an embittered protest from the ministers of the Kirk when David Cunningham, Bishop of Aberdeen, anointed the baby's forehead with holy oil.

It was a long ordeal for the baby Prince and it cannot have been made any easier by the twenty-three ells of white wool which he wore beneath his purple velvet christening robe embroidered with pearls. A procession was formed in the Queen's presence chamber. The signal honour of carrying the Prince was given to the Earl of Sussex; Lord Home bore the coronet, for the baby was Duke of Rothesay, Lord Livingstone the towel, Lord Seaton the basin and Lord Sempill the ewer. Then, followed by the ladies of the Queen's household and the chief nurse, the procession slowly wound its way to the chapel royal.

Queen Anne watched with interest as the baby was baptised by the Bishop of Aberdeen, who preached a lengthy sermon, and Lyon King of Arms cried in a loud voice, 'God save Frederick Henry by the grace of God Baron of Renfrew, Lord of the Isles, Earl of Carrick, Duke of Rothesay, Prince and Great Steward of Scotland.' Then the Queen and the rest of the company adjourned to the King's Hall, where the baby was knighted, the Earl of Mar touching his cheek with a spur while his father placed the ducal coronet on his tiny head.

Queen Anne held an audience for the foreign envoys who had come for the christening and received the gifts they brought. Sir James Melville, who was an interested spectator, noted:

I was appointed to stand a little behind and next unto her Majesty. To the English, Danish and Dutch ambassadors her Majesty made answer herself. But though she could speak seemingly French yet she sounded in my ear, to declare her answer to the ambassador of the states of Holland. Thus every-one of them, by order, gave their presents. The jewels of precious stones the Queen received in her own hand and then delivered them unto me, to put them again in their cases and lay them upon a table which was prepared in the midst of the chamber to set them upon.[3]

Queen Elizabeth, who was notoriously parsimonious in present-giving, did not realise King James's worst fears. For she gave 'a cupboard of silver overgilt, cunningly wrought' as well as some massive gold cups. The King of Denmark sent a gold chain for his sister in addition to the one for his baby nephew, but the Dutch ambassador surpassed them all. He offered a gold box containing a parchment bestowing the sum of 5,000 guilders a year on the Prince and a number of gold cups, two of which were so heavy that Sir James Melville had difficulty in lifting them. 'I leave it to others to set down their weight and value' he commented. 'But I say these which were of gold, which should have been kept in store for posterity, were soon melted and disposed: but if they had been preserved, as they ought to have been, but those who advised to break them would have wanted their part as they had of the Queen's tocher [dowry].'[4]

The events of the day were not yet at an end. There was the state banquet to attend. Queen Anne sat at the central table in the Great Hall, while the ambassadors and royal guests were seated at a table on the east side of the Hall, and the nobility on the west. As they were finishing the first course trumpets sounded, the doors of the great hall were flung open to admit a chariot drawn by the Queen's Moorish attendant, which was propelled from beneath by hidden men, just as the Paseos in Holy Week are in Spain today. In it the ladies of the Court representing Ceres, Fecundity, Concord, Liberality and Perseverance, were sitting at a table covered with fruit and sweetmeats, which were handed round to the spectators.

Then came the *pièce de résistance* of the show: a ship, eighteen feet long with lofty masts and white taffeta sails, steered by a helmswoman dressed in cloth of gold, while Neptune held his trident in the stern. The motion of the ship was 'so artificially devised within herself that none could perceive what brought her in'.[5] A choir sang the 128th psalm 'For thou shalt eat of the labours of thine hands', which was appropriate, as crabs, clams, lobsters, limpets, whiting and flukes made of sugar, 'a most lively represent in their own shape', were being distributed in the hall.[6]

Anne was delighted with this pageantry. She was young and

unsophisticated enough to enjoy the somewhat crude devices and romantic enough to see in the great ship a symbol of her momentous voyage to Scotland. Young as she was, Anne had great strength of character. She was not subtle. To her everything appeared in terms of black and white with no shades of grey. Nor did she see expediency as a reason for dishonesty. Unlike her husband, who was notorious for his cowardice, Anne had great courage and a high sense of loyalty. She would never desert a friend, whatever the cost to herself, and all her life she tried to cover up for her husband's sexual aberrations.

The Scots liked their young Queen, in spite of temporary phases of unpopularity. She was tall and good-looking with a graceful figure and was at the same time both dignified and affable, which appealed to their innate loyalty. Moreover, Anne had learnt to speak the same broad Scots that they did, which further endeared her to them. There were only two things they would have preferred to be otherwise, one was the Queen's fondness for dancing, which offended their Puritan minds, and the other was her love of finery and rich jewels.

Four or five days after Prince Henry's christening the special ambassadors from Denmark, the Low Countries and the German duchies took their departure, much to the relief of the Treasurer, who was appalled at the cost of entertaining these foreign guests. Owing to the delay in the arrival of the English ambassador, they had been lodged and feasted at the country's expense for several weeks. Before they left King James, who always showed a reckless disregard for money, presented each of the envoys with a long gold chain, and the Danish ambassador also took back with him ten deerhounds as a present for King Christian.

In September Anne wrote a letter of thanks to Queen Elizabeth for her christening presents. The hand of King James can be clearly seen in the wording, especially in the tactful allusion to 'our son, so near in blood belonging to yourself'. It runs:

Madame and dearest sister

Having understood both by your letters and the report of your ambassador, the Earl of Sussex, together with your liberal present and gift, the tokens of your kindness, how lovingly and worthily you have conceived of us and of our son, in whom God has blessed us. We are moved by the greatness of such courteous affection to discover our thankful acknowledging thereof, not only by mouth to your ambassador, but by writ unto yourself, that as you have had hitherto the causes of such favourable disposition towards us, flowing from the merits and amitie of the king of Denmark, our unwhile dearest father, so we doubt not hereafter, by our deserts and behaviour to enlarge the same and to procure a longer continuance thereunto, and rather the more seeing it has pleased God to bless us in our son, so near in blood belonging to yourself, in whose birth we perceive you to be so well contented that in the universal gladness of other nations, your joy not only has more appeared but surpassed theirs. For the which we render you such worthy and infinite thanks as our mind can conceive, or our letters may discover. Assuring you, if it lies in our power to occur to such honourable deserts by our friendly affection, we shall endeavour ourselves, if not fully to requite, yet at least by discharging us, by one way or another, to prove ourselves thankful.

Thus remitting the rest to the report and sufficiency of the Earl of Sussex, your ambassador, we commit you, Madame, and dearest sister to the good protection of God.

From our palace of Holyrood the 9 of September 1594.

Your most loving and affectionate sister and cousin. . . .[7]

Suddenly Anne's mood of contentment was shattered, and she was engaged in a struggle with her husband of such bitterness that it wrecked her married life. It is worth considering the quarrel in some detail, as it had repercussions which no one could have foreseen. It changed Anne from a lively, warmhearted girl, eager to meet her husband's wishes into a cold, embittered woman whose one desire was to see as little of her husband as possible. Although in public they maintained a façade of a happily married couple and James would refer to his wife as 'our Annie' and praise her golden hair, from that moment all pleasure in each other's society was ended.

The breach came when James informed his wife that their son was to be placed in the custody of the Earl of Mar at Stirling Castle. Anne was heartbroken when she heard her baby was to be taken from her. She was a woman with deep maternal instincts, and like her mother, Queen Sophie, she would have brought up her children well. So her grief can be imagined when she knew that she would never watch her son grow from infancy to childhood, that she could not guide his first stumbling steps or listen to his baby chatter. Anne wept, she pleaded, she stormed and raged, but all to no purpose. James was adamant, declaring that it was customary for the Earls of Mar to be the hereditary custodians of the heir to the throne at Stirling Castle and that he himself had been brought up by the present Earl of Mar's father.[8]

This argument had little weight with the unhappy mother, who saw clearly that the circumstances were entirely different. Mary Queen of Scots, was in no position to bring up her son, as she was either engaged in civil war or was a prisoner in England. Anne was naturally irritated by James's profound but misplaced belief in the Earl of Mar's loyalty and integrity. When he assured her that 'the Erskine family was most worthy of high trust', Anne, remembering hearing of the part the Earl played in the plot to kidnap King James at Ruthven in 1582, took leave to doubt his statement.

King James's action had consequences which surprised no one as much as himself. It not only increased Anne's enmity to the Earl of Mar and his mother, but it healed her long-standing quarrel with Chancellor Maitland. Once the dispute about the lands at Musselburgh had been settled, much of her bitterness ceased, and when she realised that Maitland's feelings towards the Erskine family were as hostile as her own, she saw in him a valuable ally. For the Queen was devising a plan to regain possession of her baby, in which the Chancellor's help would be vitally necessary.

Once she was sure of Maitland's support, Anne besought King James that 'she may have the keeping of the Prince and the castle of Edinburgh',[9] of which Mar was the custodian. This request enraged the King, who believed Maitland had suggested it to the Queen. With difficulty he effected a reconciliation between Mar and Maitland in his presence. It must have been an uneasy peace, for 'neither of them spoke to [the] other but both directed their speech to his Majesty'.[10]

Throughout the remaining months of 1594 until August 1595, Anne's quarrel with her husband raged with growing intensity. The Queen wept so long and so bitterly and gave way to such outbursts of hysterical rage that she became seriously ill. James, wearied of tears and scenes, retired to Falkland Palace to seek solace in hunting. He refused to see Maitland, whom he suspected of encouraging Anne's resistance.

On 25 May 1595, when Anne was with her husband at Linlithgow Palace, the quarrel flared up again with even greater acrimony. One of Cecil's agents gleefully reported that he had overheard Queen Anne desperately pleading to be allowed to have the care of her child, reminding King James 'how she had left all her dear friends in Denmark to follow him', that her brother King Christian had always been his loyal friend and 'it was an ill return to refuse her suit, founded on reason and nature, and to prefer giving the care of her babe to a subject who neither in rank nor deserving was the best his Majesty had'.[11] This nettled the King and he retorted that 'his infant, he knew, to be safe in Mar's keeping and though he doubted nothing of her good intentions yet if some faction got strong enough, she could not hinder his boy being used against him, as he himself had been against his unfortunate mother'.

In vain Anne urged that the matter should be referred to the Council; James was not to be moved. All he would do was to tell his wife that she might go to Stirling to see her son, who was now fifteen months old. This offer was much less magnanimous than it appeared. It meant that the Queen would be the guest of the Earl of Mar and Countess Annabel at Stirling Castle. Not unnaturally she refused 'lest it be supposed she went thither as a compliment to the Earl of Mar to grace the wedding of Lord Glamis, besides she was not well'.

James insisted on his wife's going to Stirling, and very reluctantly on 30 May Anne set out on horseback with her ladies. Before they had gone far she was taken ill and had to return to Linlithgow and retire to bed. When the Earl of Mar came to pay his respects Anne would not even look at the side of the room where he was standing and he was obliged to return to Stirling the same day. 'And she says she is not faminded to go to Stirling for fear they give her a possit, but makes motion to go to Dundee, to make her interest there, all to defer her never going to Stirling'.[12]

During the summer, while James was away hunting, Anne perfected her plans for gaining possession of her son. She was obliged to rely upon Maitland's help, although she knew he left much to be desired as an ally. For while posing as one of the Queen's supporters, he was secretly urging King James not to give way to her. Sir Robert Ker of Cessford and Lord Home were also helping the Queen in her scheme, but their hopes were rudely dashed, for King James learnt what was happening and returned suddenly to Falkland in a furious temper and carried off the Queen to Stirling. There Queen Anne was able to enjoy her son's company for a few hours, but James remained unyielding. Prince Henry must remain in the charge of the Earl of Mar and he put his order in writing.

My Lord of Mar

Because in the surety of my son consisteth my surety and I have concredited unto you the charge of his keeping upon the trust I have of your honesty, this I command you out of my own mouth, being in company of those I like, otherwise for any charge or necessity that can come from me, you shall not deliver him. And in case God call me at any time see that neither for the Queen nor Estates, their pleasure, you deliver him till he be eighteen years of age, and that he command you himself.

This from your assured friend

JAMES R[13]

Round one of the contest had gone to King James. Anne was so bitterly upset that at the end of July she had a miscarriage. Hitherto James had attributed the Queen's low spirits and frequent illness to hysteria, but now he was seriously alarmed. If Anne should bear him no more children and if Prince Henry should die, for he was but a weakly child, then his hopes of succeeding to the throne of England would receive a considerable setback.

Attempts on James's part to patch up the quarrel met with only partial success. On 4 September Roger Aston informed Robert Bowes that Anne 'frames herself to follow the King's will in all things' and would spend most of the winter at Linlithgow, but ten days later he was writing 'the King abides all the winter at Linlithgow to the Queen's displeasure',[14] while towards the Earl of Mar she remained as hostile as ever, refusing to speak to him.

Towards her husband Anne's attitude softened a little because she had two definite objects in view. One was to have Alexander Seton, Prior of Pluscardine, appointed Chancellor instead of Maitland, who was critically ill,[15] and the other was to gain the support of the Earls of Huntley and Errol in her attempt to snatch her son from the Earl of Mar.

The injury done to Queen Anne by depriving her of her son was too great for even the most skilled mediator to heal. What Miss Strickland calls Anne's 'indulging the mere instincts of maternity'[16] was the rock upon which King James's marriage foundered. James with his cold, fishlike nature could never understand the depths of mother love. He looked on his son as a pawn to help him gain the crown of England, or as a potential danger, serving as a rallying point for his foes. He himself, a homosexual, could never love any woman distinterestedly.

On 15 December Anne paid another visit to Prince Henry, 'who is noted to be but a weak child',[17] at Stirling Castle. For the young mother, who only three days before had celebrated her twenty-first birthday, it must have been a poignant meeting and not altogether a reassuring one. Henry, nearly two years old, was lively and alert for his age. Every day saw some new advance, but Anne was desperately worried about his health. She could not blame Countess Annabelle for neglect; indeed she had shown herself to be a conscientious if strict guardian, but she felt that what the child needed was a mother's care.

6

LIFE IN SCOTLAND
1596-1600

King James's anxiety about his succession to the throne of England increased with every passing month. Queen Elizabeth was growing feebler and yet no news came that she had named her successor. Anne, too, was keenly interested in the future, for as Queen of England she would have wealth and prestige such as she had never known. The suspense was more than King James could endure. Most unwisely he tried to form a group amongst the English parliamentarians to press his claims, while at the same time he urged Queen Elizabeth to grant him the lands his grandfather, as Earl of Lennox, had held in England. This would prevent his enemies arguing that as an alien he had no claim to the English throne. James might be erudite, but he was a poor judge of human nature or he would have known that nothing was likely to antagonise Queen Elizabeth more than any allusion to her successor on the throne. He even went so far as to send embassies to the Netherlands and other Protestant rulers in Europe, asking for troops to support his claim to the throne of England.

In the summer of 1596 an invitation arrived from Denmark for Queen Anne and her husband to attend the coronation of King Christian IV in August. The boy king had come of age. In spite of the long separation the links between Anne and her brother were still very close and it was a very real grief to her that she could not be present on the great day, as she was expecting the birth of her second child. It is probable that James had fewer regrets. He had no wish to face the perils of the North Sea again, but as he did not want to offend the Danes he sent an ambassador with a retinue of sixty. Denmark was a valuable ally. In addition to Norway, King Christian ruled over Skaane, Halland and Blekinge in southern Sweden, controlled the Sound, and possessed the rich island of Gotland. The richest and most fertile districts of Sweden were Danish, but Denmark's trade was hampered by lack of shipping. Given the support of Scottish ships, the trade of both countries could expand significantly.

On 19 August 1596 Queen Anne gave birth to a daughter at Dunfermline Palace. The child was called Elizabeth after her godmother, Queen Elizabeth of England. In spite of this distinguished sponsor, little attention was paid to the royal baby. King James was absorbed in a struggle with the Presbyterian ministers, in which Andrew Melville, coming uninvited to Falkland, went so far as to call his sovereign 'God's sillie vassal'.[1] The Edinburgh ministers not only offered no congratulations on the birth of the Princess, but attacked the King for his treatment of their champion, the Reverend David Black.[2]

A special target for their censures was Queen Anne. She was to harvest the grapes of wrath as rumours that she was a Catholic circulated, and her growing friendship with the Countess of Huntley did nothing to dispel their displeasure. David Black went so far as to call her an atheist, while other ministers refused to mention her in their prayers. This was better than Minister Black's prayer: 'Guid Lord we must pray for our Queen, for the fashion's sake, but we have no cause, for she will never do us any good.'[3]

The christening was shorn of the splendour and pageantry which had marked her elder brother's. Finances were too strained, the Kirk too hostile, the country too disturbed: the ceremony was postponed until 28 November, possibly in the hope that the inclemency of the weather would keep many of the guests from attending. Those who accepted were asked to bring haunches of venison and wild boars to eke out the christening feast. Even so it was hardly a festive occasion, for to quote David Moysie, 'little or no triumph was made both in good fare and cheer because it was in winter season and ill weather'.[4] The simple ceremony was held in the Chapel Royal at Holyrood House. The English ambassador, Sir Robert Bowes, held the baby and showed her to the congregation, while the Lyon Herald proclaimed her Lady Elizabeth, first daughter of Scotland. The chief citizens of Edinburgh presented Anne with a gold casket containing a scroll giving the baby princess a thousand Scots marks 'to be paid on her marriage'.

Once again King James insisted that the Queen must not be allowed to keep her daughter. When the child was a few weeks old she was handed over to Lord and Lady Livingstone. The Kirk did not approve of this choice of guardians. Andrew, seventh Lord Livingstone, was the nephew of one of Mary Queen of Scots' four Maries, and his wife, the daughter of the eighth Earl of Errol, was a Catholic. However, she proved to be an excellent guardian, showing both patience and affection for her charge. Elizabeth spent seven happy years at Linlithgow Palace under her care and so did her younger sister Margaret during her short life.[5]

It was some compensation to Queen Anne for the disappointment of not being able to attend King Christian's coronation when she had a visit from her brother Ulric, Duke of Holstein, in the spring of 1598. Ulric liked Scotland, especially the banquets given in his honour, and he used every means in his power to prolong his stay. He was a rather dull, heavily built youth of twenty, who enjoyed the material things of this world, such as eating, drinking and hunting, but he lacked the charm and popular appeal which endeared King Christian to his subjects. Young as he was, Duke Ulric was already showing signs of being a heavy drinker. An eyewitness in England noted: 'As for news there is nothing but quietness and great carousing with the drunken Duke of Holstein'.[6] Ulric was the first member of her family to visit Anne since she left Denmark, and although he was less close to her than his elder brother Christian, he brought first-hand news of the family and she gave him a warm welcome. For Anne was often desperately homesick! 'Many times she falleth into tears, wishing herself either with her mother in Denmark or else that she might see and speak with her Majesty.'[7]

Events in the summer of 1600 cast a shadow over the Queen's life, less sinister than the deprivation of her son but sufficiently disquieting to cause still greater distrust of her husband and a further widening of the breach between them. This was the tragic deaths of the young Earl of Gowrie and his brother Alexander Ruthven. What happened had never been satisfactorily explained.[8] The two principal characters were dead, the evidence of eyewitnesses was destroyed and only King James's version remained. To Anne the news of their deaths came as a heavy blow. She had been on friendly terms with the Ruthvens and had enjoyed the companionship of Lord Gowrie and his brother, for their good manners and breeding were a welcome change from her husband's uncouthness, just as she found their quick wit infinitely preferable to James's pedantic erudition. Three of the sisters were Queen Anne's ladies in waiting and for the eldest Beatrice she had a deep affection.

James, for his part, bore no goodwill to the Ruthvens. Patrick, their grandfather, had forcibly restrained Mary Queen of Scots, when she tried to prevent him from murdering Rizzio; and their father had kidnapped James and kept him a prisoner for ten months at Gowrie House, making him sign a paper declaring he was there of his own free will.

Coming events cast their shadows before and in July 1600 Lady Beatrice Ruthven was teasing an episcopalian minister, Dr Herries, about the handicap of having a clubfoot, when he took her hand and studying the palm said earnestly: 'Mistress, leave laughing, for I see ere it be long sad disaster shall befall you.'[9] No hint of tragedy was in the air. Her eldest brother, the Earl of Gowrie, who was twenty-one, had just returned to Scotland after a long absence abroad, a month of which he had spent at the English Court, where Queen Elizabeth had received him as an honoured guest. This was probably to annoy King James, who had irritated her by intriguing with the Earl of Essex.[10] But the family were happy to be united again and the future seemed set fair.

When Anne heard her husband's explanation of the murders, which bristled with improbabilities, like the ministers of the Kirk, she did not believe a word of his story. What happened, according to the official version which James sent to Robert Cecil,[11] was that while the King was stag-hunting at Falkland young Alexander Ruthven arrived and told him that a pot full of gold coins had been discovered on a man. James abandoned the hunt and set off for Gowrie House with young Ruthven, the Duke of Lennox, the Earl of Mar, and a royal page, John Ramsay.[12]

The arrival at Gowrie House was quite unexpected. After dinner James went with Alexander Ruthven to a room in a turret, where he remained for an hour and a half. Then the King's voice was heard shouting, 'Treason, treason. I am betrayed. They are murdering me.' Ramsay, the page, finding an unlocked door, burst into the room and slew the Master of Ruthven. His brother, the Earl, dashing upstairs to see what was happening, was also killed. James ran from the house by a back gate, went by water to Inch and then rode to Falkland Palace, where he asked the ministers of the Kirk in Edinburgh to hold thanksgiving services for his providential escape. This they declined to do.

It is difficult to understand why the King, with his neurotic fear of assassination and his addiction to padded waistcoats, ever went to Gowrie House, and even stranger why he allowed himself to be alone locked in a turret room with the Master of Ruthven. The mystery may never be solved, but probably the tragedy was unpremeditated. One explanation seems to fit the case. The King was a homosexual and Ruthven was a good-looking young man. He may have repulsed James's advances and in the ensuing struggle the King became panic-stricken and shouted for help. Ramsay rushed in, entering by an inner door, of which he could only have learnt from James himself, who knew the house well, as he had been a prisoner there for ten months. Then the boy killed the Master of Ruthven.

The Queen was deeply troubled. She remarked bitterly that 'she hoped that Heaven would not visit her family with the vengeance for the sufferings of the Ruthvens'. Being in poor health—the birth of her fourth child was near—the shock was nearly as great as the murder of Rizzio had been for Mary Queen of Scots. She not only grieved for the Earl of Gowrie and his brother Alexander, who had been so young, so charming and so gay, but she was also haunted by fears for the future of their sister Beatrice, whom James had dismissed from the Queen's service.

Anne had not many weapons, but those she had she employed to the best advantage. For two days she lay motionless in bed, not speaking to anyone, declining all food and refusing to be dressed, unless her lady in waiting, Beatrice Ruthven, were there to attend her. When James visited her she told him bluntly to beware how he treated her, for she was not the Earl of Gowrie. James Melville, who was an interested spectator, commented:

Foremost amongst those refraining to believe in the guilt of the two brothers was the Queen herself. She remained in her apartments and refused to be dressed for two days. . . . Although the King receiving full information of his wife's conduct and of the consequences to be drawn from it, he could not be persuaded to take up the matter right, but sought by all means to cover his folly.[13]

One of the strangest aspects of the matter was that James did not resent his wife's behaviour. Usually when Anne opposed him he would storm and bluster and not yield an inch. This time he tried by every means in his power to appease her. It may be that he feared another miscarriage, but probably the reason lay far deeper. Whatever the cause, James hired a famous acrobat to entertain his wife, paying no less than £333 *6s 8d* for his services, in the hope that it would divert her thoughts into pleasanter channels. Melville, who saw the performance, noted: 'Being in Falkland [I] saw a funambulous Frenchman play strenge and incredible practicks upon stented tackle in the Palace Close before the King, Queen and hale the Court.'[14] But even expensive acrobatics will not mend broken hearts.

Even more irksome to King James than his wife's opposition was Queen Elizabeth's refusal to find the King's account of the Gowrie tragedy credible. She tartly remarked that as the Earl 'had a thousand spirits, his familiars, she supposed there were more left in hell'. Nor had he more success at the French Court, where his account was treated as 'une bonne bourde'.

Parliament, however, supported the King, and on 15 November declared the Earl of Gowrie and his brother to be guilty of treason and ordered that their bodies be hanged, drawn and quartered and the name of Ruthven abolished. Eight days later the Master of Grey wrote to Robert Cecil:

Gowrie's forfeiture is passed without appropriation to the crown, the dead bodies escartelet with cruelty, all woman and man of the surname of Ruthven charged to change their surname before Whitsunday next under pain of treason which is done in prejudice of the ladies, Gowrie's sisters.[15]

King James's vengeance was complete. The head of the house and the heir were murdered, their mother and her two youngest sons were fugitives, their sisters were nameless and destitute, the family lands and money were confiscated. Could any sovereign wish for more thorough revenge?

Yet even so Queen Anne would not give up without a struggle. Loyalty to her friends was one of her outstanding virtues. James Melville, who was no champion of the Queen, admitted: 'If ever the Queen found that the King had, by wrong information, taken a prejudice against any of his faithful subjects or servants, she always exerted herself to obtain information of the truth that she might speak with the more firmness in their favour.'[16]

In this case she was firmly determined that Beatrice Ruthven should be reinstated at Court, for through no fault of her own the young girl was practically destitute. So in September 1602 with the help of Lady Paisley and Lady Angus, Beatrice was smuggled into the Queen's apartments at Holyrood and hidden in 'a chamber prepared for her by the Queen's direction, where her Majesty had much conference with her'. Beatrice stayed in the Queen's apartments for a day and a night and departed laden with gifts.

The mischief-maker Sir Thomas Erskine, Captain of the Guard, came to hear of the visit and promptly informed King James that the Queen was plotting with the Ruthvens. Perhaps his motive was revenge, for Anne had done all she could to prevent Sir Thomas being appointed Captain of the King's Guard. Cecil's agent reported that Erskine was 'one she loveth worst. She is very desirous to prevent this matter but her insecrecy makes all men flee dealing.'[17]

James stormed at his wife and cross-examined her household, but had to admit that he could find no evidence of a plot and that Beatrice Ruthven[18] 'had shown no malicious design'. Finally, in September 1603, James acknowledged defeat and granted Beatrice a pension of £200 'because though her family is hateful on account of the abominable attempt against the King, she has shown no malicious disposition'.[19]

Of all the royal palaces Dunfermline was Queen Anne's favourite. The green fields and the peaceful countryside reminded her of her childhood in Denmark. So she retired there to await the birth of her fourth child. The royal wing of the Palace was being restored, the decorators were still at work, but Queen Anne decided that it was fit for habitation.

Great preparations were made for the coming birth. Sir Dudley Carleton reported: 'Here is much ado about the Queen's lying down and great suit made for the offices of carrying the white staff, holding the back of the chair, door keeping, cradle rocking, and such like gossip's tricks which you should understand much better than I do.' While Samuel Calverts reported 'the great preparations of nurses, rockers, midwives and other officers of forty or more'.[20]

When on 19 November Queen Anne gave birth to her second son,[21] the baby was so weakly that he was baptised the same day, as no one thought he would live. Anne had been under great strain, for the horror of the Gowrie tragedy had deeply affected her. James hurried to Dunfermline to see her and found both his wife and son desperately ill. He rewarded midwife Janet Kinloch with the sum of £26 13*s* Scots pounds with his own hand.[22]

A month later the baby had gained sufficient strength to be taken in a litter to Holyroodhouse and to be christened in the Chapel Royal. He was called Charles, his father's first Christian name and also the name of his great-uncle, Charles Earl of Lennox, Darnley's younger brother. As a New Year's gift King James gave his wife a jewel for which he paid George Heriot £1,333 Scots pounds.[23]

Fortunately for Queen Anne her antagonist the Earl of Mar was no longer the power he had been in royal favour and the infant Prince was not placed in his custody. Instead he was entrusted to Lord Fyvie, Constable of the Palace, whose wife proved to be both kind and understanding, but Charles continued to be weakly with a tenuous hold on life. Even when he was four years old he could not walk and could only stand with difficulty because his legs were so weak. Attempts to teach him to speak proved unrewarding; he was indeed 'a very silent, melancholy baby'.

The fate of Anne's third son, Robert, born on 27 May 1602, was an even more unhappy one. The child was christened Robert Bruce after Scotland's national hero and he lived long enough to have a magnificent baptism. Entries in the Lord Treasurer's account show that £96 Scots pounds were distributed to the populace and his nurse Isabel Colt was given 10½ ells of Tours taffeta for a gown and 4½ ells of black velvet for a skirt.[24] King James again gave Anne a piece of jewellery after the birth of her son; this time a pointed diamond.[25] The city of Edinburgh showed its loyalty by sending a burgess to Dunfermline with a silver plate and spoon 'for the use of the King's dearest son Duke Robert'.

In spite of all this rejoicing Robert's health was causing grave anxiety. While his elder brother Charles was slowly gaining ground Robert was growing weaker; when he was four months old he died.

Two of Queen Anne's greatest pleasures were fine clothes and expensive jewelry. Unlike her mother, Queen Sophia, she had no idea of the value of money, and although King James had given her a substantial jointure as Queen of Scotland, she was always in debt. Her delight in precious stones was unbounded. She would cover her fingers with rings and her arms with bracelets, and clasp pendants round her neck. This love of jewelry brought her in touch with George Heriot and their relationship continued over many years to their mutual advantage.

George Heriot's career began in quite a small way with the fifteen hundred Scots marks his father gave him 'for the setting up of ane booth' in the north-east corner of St Giles Cathedral.[26] He worked hard both as a goldsmith and a moneylender and he was able to buy larger premises not far from his original shop at the west end of St Giles. Then he had a piece of good luck. Someone mentioned him to the Queen. Anne found him both reliable and discreet and in July 1597 he was appointed goldsmith to the Queen.[27] Heriot's fortune was made. Four years later he became jeweller to King James and was given an apartment in Holyroodhouse where he could carry on his business.

Yet his success was not without hazards, as the unhappy fate of his predecessor showed. He was a Dane, who made jewelry for Queen Anne and was entrusted with the safe-keeping of most of her jewels. Becoming exasperated by the non-payment of his wages, he fled to England, taking some of the Queen's less valuable jewels with him. His wrongdoing was soon detected. He was captured, convicted, executed, as a warning to his fellow craftsmen not to yield to temptation, even when suffering royal injustice.[28]

Generous by nature, Queen Anne would bestow diamond rings on bringers of good tidings or anyone who did her a service, however slight, with the result that she was always in debt. In George Heriot she found a solution to her difficulties, for acting as her banker, he would make her loans, taking her jewels as security and even buying them from her when her finances became desperate. Bills for her purchases of jewels amounted to £50,000 in the ten years before Anne became Queen of England.

The first of Queen Anne's letters which has survived is written to George Heriot, in broad Scots. Probably it dates from the time when she was trying to take Prince Henry from the Earl of Mar. It says:

Ane Precept of the Queen.
Geordg Heriatt

I earnestlie dissyr youe present to send me tua hundrethe pundes with all expidition, because I maun hast me away presentle.

ANNA R.[29]

Transactions between them were frequent. On 23 December 1595 Heriot gave the Queen a receipt for £150 as part repayment of an account of £2,454. In July 1601 Anne's finances were so strained that she had to return 'an emerald set about with diamonds and rubies in the shape of a feather which was engaged by us and delivered to the said George by Alexander, Lord of Fyvie'. In the first ten years of King James's reign Queen Anne spent £48,000 with George Heriot.

7

QUEEN ANNE'S PROGRESS
1603

On 24 March 1603 Queen Elizabeth died and King James VI of Scotland became King James I of England. The way had been carefully prepared by Robert Cecil, who had for many years carried on a secret correspondence with King James. This he had hidden from Queen Elizabeth by having his letters written by Lord Henry Howard and the King's by the Earl of Mar. Even so Cecil was acutely nervous, for he knew that discovery meant ruin, and when Queen Anne, whom he distrusted as a chatterbox, expressed a wish to intercept the packets her husband was sending to England, Cecil's fears, skilfully fanned by Lord Henry Howard,[1] flared into acute anxiety.

So nervous was Cecil that he warned King James to be wary of the Queen, who in his opinion, was weak and might be a source of considerable trouble in the future. He begged that 'Queen Anne may never hear the names of Cecil and Lord Henry Howard so much as sounded with any kind of affection or inclination, from the mouth of King James or any of his elect'.[2]

Cecil's object in promoting the candidature of King James was to obstruct the Infanta Isabel Clara's claim to the English throne[3] and to make sure that King James did not attempt to restore Catholicism. He promised James that when Queen Elizabeth died 'your ship shall be steered into the right harbour, without cross of wave or tide, that shall be able to turn over a cock boat'.

The thought of becoming Queen of England filled Queen Anne with joyous expectation. It would be a welcome change from the penury of the Scottish Court and an escape from the dour invective of the Presbyterian ministers. England seemed to her a land of promise with its riches and fertile fields. King James was even more eager to grasp the prize and he determined to arrive in England without a moment's unnecessary delay.

So twelve days after Queen Elizabeth's death, on 5 April 1603, James took a demonstrative farewell of 'his Annie', as he called his wife, in High Street, Edinburgh, in full view of his loyal subjects. Whatever the rift between them, appearances had to be kept up, and James kissed his wife lovingly, which so moved the spectators that tears poured down their cheeks. Anne was not accompanying him on his journey to England, partly because she was expecting her sixth child and partly because etiquette decreed that the ladies of Queen Elizabeth's Court could not wait in attendance upon her until after the late Queen's funeral. She was to make the journey by easy stages, twenty days after her husband.

Such was James's haste to be acclaimed King of England that he did not even wait to say good-bye to his children. Yet in spite of his haste he did not attend Queen Elizabeth's funeral, but spent the day as Robert Cecil's guest, stag hunting at Theobalds. Much as King James feared Queen Elizabeth in life, in death he felt she could be safely ignored.

As soon as James was on the way to London, Anne put her plan of campaign into action. The long-awaited opportunity had come. James had taken the Earl of Mar with him to England and Anne determined to use his absence to gain possession of her son. But the project proved to be by no means as simple as she had hoped. The Earl might be gone, but his mother, the redoubtable Dowager Countess of Mar, remained as guardian. When Anne arrived at Stirling Castle[4] with a strong body of sympathetic nobles and demanded that her son should be handed over to her, the nobles were refused admission and the Countess declared that she could not deliver up Prince Henry without the King's warrant. A furious quarrel ensued, in which Anne was so carried away by thwarted mother love that she 'fell into such an agony of grief and indignation as threw her into a fever and occasioned her to her miscarry of the child with which she was pregnant'.[5] This added yet another to the disappointing number of the Queen's pregnancies which had ended in miscarriages.

Lord Fyvie, President of the Scottish Council, tried to improve matters by urging King James to use moderation, saying that 'physic and medicine requireth greater place with her Majesty at present than lectures on economics or politics'. He concluded: 'Her Majesty's passions could not be so well mitigated or moderated as by seconding and obeying her directions, which always is subject to your sacred Majesty's anxieties and resolves as answers.'

For several days Anne was so desperately ill that her life was in danger and her almoner Spottiswoode set off for the south to break the bad news to King James. The King realised that steps must be taken to placate Queen Anne, as he had no wish to arrive in London as the husband of an estranged wife. He was also afraid that the succession might be endangered if the Queen continued to bear nothing but dead children and if the weakly Charles were to die. True to form he sent her an admonitory letter, reproving her for 'froward, womanly apprehensions', but at the same time he ordered the Earl of Mar to return to Scotland so that he could escort the Queen to England.[6]

A fresh difficulty now arose. Ill as she was, Queen Anne absolutely refused to see the Earl of Mar when he came to visit her at Linlithgow, nor would she allow him to hand over Prince Henry to her. Angrily she wrote to King James accusing him of preferring the Earl of Mar to herself and of listening to calumnies about her. She refused to leave for Edinburgh unless accompanied by her son and without the Earl of Mar. James sat down and wrote a long letter to his wife, which was a characteristic admixture of unsubtle flattery and barely concealed resentment.

My heart

Immediately before the receipt of your letter I was purposed to have written you and that without any great occasion excepting for to free myself (at your hands) from the imputation of severeness but now your letter has given (me) more matter to write, although I take small delight to meddle in so unpleasant a process, I wonder that neither your long knowledge of my nature, nor my late earnest purgation to you can cure you of that rooted error that any one living dare speak or inform me in any ways to your prejudice and yet you can think them your unfriends, that are true servants to me. I can say no more but protest upon peril of my salvation and damnation that neither the Earl of Mar nor any flesh living ever informed me that ye was upon any Papist or Spanish course or that ye had any other thought but a wrong conceived opinion that he had more interest in your son and would not deliver him unto you. . . . God is my witness that I ever preferred you to all my bairns, much more than to any subject; but if you will ever give place to the reports of every flattering sycophant that will persuade you that when I account well of an honest and wise servant for his true and faithful service to me, that is to compare or prefer him to you, then will neither you nor I be ever at rest or at peace. . . .

Praying God, my heart, to preserve you and all the bairns send me a blithe meeting with you and a couple of them.

Your own

JAMES R[7]

Praise of a detested enemy is seldom palatable and the letter with its laudatory references to the Earl of Mar only served to inflame Anne's indignation. She felt James was absurdly complacent to speak of the Earl of Mar's 'true and faithful service', remembering the part he had played in the Ruthven raid, and she suspected that so long as the heir to the throne remained in Mar's custody the Earl might be tempted to exploit the situation and plot to make Henry king instead of his father.

So Anne remained determined to pursue her feud with the Earl. She insisted that Mar should make a public apology to her. This he flatly refused to do, declaring that he had given the Queen no cause for offence, which made Anne more furious than ever. James thereupon wrote again to his wife, telling her 'she would do wisely to forget all her grudges to the Earl of Mar, and think of nothing but thanking God for the peaceful possession they had got of England, which, next under God, might be ascribed to the wise negotiation of the Earl of Mar'.[8] Anne retorted angrily that 'she would rather never see England than to be in any sort beholden to him for the same'.[9]

Victory lay with Queen Anne. James had to admit defeat. He wrote to the Earl of Mar from Greenwich on 13 May to tell him that as the Queen would not receive the Prince from him nor the King's letter of which he was the bearer, 'It is our will that you deliver the same to any of our council, to be given to her and disposed of as she pleaseth, in case she continues in that wilfulness that she will not hear your credit nor receive the letter from your hands.' He should hand over Prince Henry to the Duke of Lennox who would deliver him to the Council and the Council would hand him over to the Queen. The Queen would bring him with her to Edinburgh.[10] On 19 May Lennox was sent to escort the Queen and Prince Henry to London, and, as a further concession to Queen Anne, the Earl of Mar was not to be one of the noblemen accompanying them.

The 23rd of May 1603 was one of the happiest days of Anne of Denmark's life. She left Stirling Castle accompanied by Prince Henry and entered Edinburgh to a salvo of guns from the Castle[11] and the cheers of the citizens. For in spite of the fulminations of the ministers of the Kirk, Anne was popular with the people. They liked her dignity and affability and felt she was worthy to be their Queen.

Once installed in Holyroodhouse, Anne was busy making preparations for the journey to London. She ordered a new Edinburgh-built coach from George Hendry and gave close attention to procuring new clothes for herself and her children, to do them credit when they entered the promised land. Both she and King James were agreed that her present wardrobe was not worthy of the Queen of England. For herself Anne ordered a gown of figured taffeta and a mantle of white satin and purple velvet, while Henry had a purple satin doublet and breeches and six-year-old Princess Elizabeth, who had been brought from Linlithgow, had a Spanish red taffeta bodice and brown skirt.[12] Even the Queen's jester, Thomas Drury, was not forgotten. He was to have a new green coat.

It was common knowledge that Queen Elizabeth had left an immense wardrobe of over a thousand dresses. In her old age she could not bring herself to part with anything. James, who enjoyed economising at the expense of others, saw in this an excellent opportunity to fit out his Queen at a comparatively small cost. Although Queen Anne declared that she never wore cast clothes, this did not deter King James from asking the English Council 'to forward such jewels and stuffs, with other furniture [as coaches, horses and litters] which had pertained to the late Queen Elizabeth and all things which they might deem fit for the use of Queen Anne'.[13] The English Council were by no means pleased at this request from their new sovereign. They replied coldly that 'they considered it illegal and against their oaths to send any of the Crown jewels out of England'.

This rebuff did not daunt King James. From Topcliffe on 15 April he sent a second letter to the Council explaining that he was not asking for the Crown jewels so far, but he would like the Council in consultation with Queen Elizabeth's ladies in waiting to choose jewels and dresses for Queen Anne's ordinary wear and also 'as soon as Queen Elizabeth's funeral was over, some of her ladies of high degree should journey to Berwick to meet Queen Anne with such usual jewels and dresses as were proper for her appearance in England'. In fact, six ladies of the English Court with an escort of two hundred horse had already arrived in Scotland.

On a day of burning heat, 31 May 1603, Queen Anne drove with Prince Henry in her new coach drawn by six horses, accompanied by the ladies of the English Court, some on horseback, others in coaches, to St Giles Cathedral. Crowds lined the streets, hoping to catch a glimpse of Prince Henry, who had hitherto been hidden from public view by his guardian, the Earl of Mar. They saw a nine-year-old boy, slender, fair-haired, with the Stuart eyes set wide apart, and his mother's long, oval face. They broke into thunderous cheers as he gave them a dignified salute.

Before leaving Scotland Queen Anne summoned the ladies of her household and distributed amongst them her dresses, some jewels and the hangings of her private apartments, declaring with tears in her eyes that 'if she had had more, she would have given it'. Two days later Queen Anne and Prince Henry, accompanied by the Duke of Lennox, set out on their long journey to London. The Prince was mounted on a new French horse and escorted by pages of honour. It had been decided that Prince Charles was to remain at Dunfermline under the care of Lady Fyvie, as he was too delicate to undertake such an arduous journey.

Princess Elizabeth, too, had to be left behind at Holyroodhouse owing to a sudden illness,[14] but she was to follow as soon as she recovered. Queen Anne was going through a difficult time with her daughter. The child had dissolved into floods of tears when she heard that she was to be parted from her governess, Lady Livingstone, to whom she was deeply attached. At six years old such separations can be very stark. Her new guardian was to be Lady Kildare.

Yet Elizabeth need not have worried. Lady Kildare was never to take up her duties. She was Frances Howard, the daughter of the Earl of Nottingham, better known as Lord Howard of Effingham, but this illustrious ancestry did nothing to shield her from the campaign which Cecil launched against her second husband, Lord Cobham, part of the odium of which fell upon his wife. This poisoned King James's mind against her and Lord Harington was chosen as Princess Elizabeth's guardian instead. At least his reputation was unblemished, not only was he descended from an old Rutland family, but amongst his ancestors was Robert Bruce in the female line. His wife, Lady Harington,[15] proved to be both capable and considerate, and Elizabeth lived happily with them at Coombe Abbey.

Mingled exasperation and excitement filled Queen Anne as she started on her journey south. Above all she was determined that it should be a triumphal progress all the way, unimpeded by her husband's dislike of crowds. With all eyes focused on herself and her two attractive children, she could win the goodwill of her new subjects with her gay smile.

Princess Elizabeth rapidly recovered and rejoined the royal party, but when they reached Berwick fresh trouble awaited Queen Anne. There the Earls of Sussex and Lincoln were waiting to greet her, as well as Sir George Carey, whom the King had appointed her chamberlain, and with them were the Countesses of Worcester and Kildare and the Ladies Scrope, Rich and Walsingham. They had brought with them Queen Elizabeth's personal jewels and some of her dresses by King James's orders. But Anne was not in an accommodating mood. She was not going to see her Danish and Scottish ladies, who had been her attendants for the last thirteen years, thrust on one side to have English strangers set in their place.

When King James learnt that Queen Anne had rejected so many of the English ladies and gentlemen that he had selected to attend upon her he was seriously annoyed. With the exception of Lady Bedford and Lady Harington, who had come to Scotland to meet her, she refused to appoint any of them ladies of the bedchamber. James feared that this might damage his popularity with the English officials. He felt that Queen Anne by her loyalty to her friends might even be endangering his hold on the throne of England, for he was fully aware that the English expected to fill all the chief posts in the royal households.

What upset King James far more was the fact that Queen Anne insisted on retaining John Kennedy as her chamberlain. When Kennedy appeared before the King to be confirmed in his office, James flew into a passion and ordered him to get out of his sight, warning him that 'if he should find that she do bring him hither to attend her in that place, that he would break the staff of his chamberlainship on his head and so dismiss him'.[16] The Duke of Lennox, too, who had been entrusted with the formation of Queen Anne's new household, came in for a severe reprimand and was sent north to inform Queen Anne that 'his Majesty took her continued perversity very heinously'.

These harsh words of her husband's did not unduly trouble Queen Anne. She had a royal reception at Berwick, and when she arrived at York on Whitsun Eve, 11 June 1603, the crowds greeted her warmly. Unlike King James, whom the Venetian ambassador had seen in May and remarked 'from his dress he would have been taken for the meanest among the courtiers, had it not been for a chain of diamonds round his neck and a great diamond in his hat',[17] Queen Anne was elegantly turned out and her two lively children added to the enthusiasm of the citizens of York.

The Lord Mayor of York, the aldermen and other civic dignitaries welcomed the Queen and presented her with a silver banqueting cup filled with four score gold angels, while for Prince Henry there was a smaller silver cup with £20 in gold, and little Princess Elizabeth was handed a purse containing twenty gold angels.[18] Presently

the Queen asked the Lord Mayor to let her see something of the country around York, Willingly he took her through Monk Bar to Heworth Moor, and then through Tanghall Lane into the Hull road and back again into the city through Walmgate Bar. When they reached the Lord Mayor's door, near St Crux church, the mayoress and her lady friends were drinking spiced wine and offered some of it to their royal visitor. When the Queen heard what it was, she asked for some beer—a beverage with which she was no doubt more familiar.[19]

For four days the royal guests were fêted and feasted and when they left to continue their journey south, they were escorted out of the city by the corporation in their official robes.

Following in King James's footsteps, they travelled to Worksop, where on 20 June they were sumptuously entertained by Gilbert Talbot, seventh Earl of Shrewsbury, who had married Bess of Harwick's youngest daughter, Mary Cavendish. Gilbert was always lavish with money, and like most reckless spenders he was always on the verge of bankruptcy. His formidable mother-in-law, who was now an old lady of eighty-three, had planned to entertain the Queen at Chatsworth. It was rumoured that she wished to see for herself if Queen Anne's complexion was really as flawless as it was reputed to be. But James declined the invitation. Perhaps the part Bess of Hardwick when Countess of Shrewsbury, had played for fourteen years as custodian to his mother, Mary Queen of Scots, still rankled. However, Gilbert stepped into the breach and entertained the Queen at Worksop on King James's birthday. Queen Anne won all hearts by taking Robert Cecil's little son in her arms, kissing him twice and tying a jewel on his ear, after he had charmed the spectators by dancing a galliard with Princess Elizabeth.[20]

Nor was Sir Henry Pierrepont, who had married Bess of Hardwick's eldest daughter, Frances, less eager in his welcome, as he entertained Queen Anne at Holme Pierrepont, near Nottingham, with great goodwill, if less ostentatiously than the lavish splendour of Worksop.[21]

As the royal party were coming down a hill near Nottingham an unexpected sight met their eyes. A bevy of young girls strewed their path with flowers, while a flock of sheep with dazzlingly white fleeces were driven along the road by young men dressed as shepherds. It made a pretty picture in the June sunshine, for in addition to the shepherds and shepherdesses, a band of huntsmen in gold and silver coats appeared driving a herd of tame deer whose horns were tipped with gold. Then French horns sounded and out of the wood tripped nymphs and dryads. Anne and her children were enchanted with the spectacle.

When they came to Leicester the Lord Mayor and six former holders of the office rode out on horseback to meet them, the aldermen following on foot to escort them to their lodging in William Skipworth's house. No formal speech of welcome was made, doubtless much to the relief of Queen Anne and her children, as the Recorder had fallen sick, but the Queen was presented with a silver standing cup filled with gold nobles worth £14 *6s. 4d.* and Prince Henry with a smaller silver cup valued at £9 16*s.*[22]

From Leicester the royal party made the short journey to Dingley, the seat of Sir Thomas Griffin. By this time the cavalcade had grown enormously, as more and more titled ladies and

English peers hastened to welcome the new Queen, possibly with the hope of becoming members of her household. By the time Anne had arrived at Windsor, she had an escort of 250 carriages and 5,000 horsemen.[23] Here Princess Elizabeth left them for a few days to visit her future residence, Coombe Abbey.

Amongst the newcomers was thirteen-year-old Lady Anne Clifford and her mother, the Countess of Cumberland. They had careered across England in such haste to catch up with the Queen and her children that they had killed three horses in one day. Lady Anne was a precocious young person with an observant eye and a caustic pen. Fortunately for posterity she kept a diary which gives intimate glimpses of Queen Anne and her Court.

High in Queen Anne's favour was Lucy Russell, wife of the third Earl of Bedford and grandniece of Sir Philip Sidney. During the leisurely journey from Scotland Queen Anne had learnt to admire and trust her. Lady Bedford was young and lively with a ready wit which made her a stimulating companion. She had a genius for laying out gardens and revelled in dancing, masques and pageants.[24] In addition to all this, Lucy had literary aspirations. She was the patron of Michael Drayton and both Ben Jonson and John Donne owed much to her encouragement. Above all Lady Bedford was ambitious. She very much disliked seeing anyone else making inroads into the Queen's favour.

Queen Anne received Lady Anne Clifford and her mother most graciously, kissing them warmly. The girl soon noticed that Lady Bedford's star was in the ascendant. She wrote in her diary: 'My Lady of Bedford who was so great a woman with the Queen as everyone respected her.'[25]

During a day of intense heat the Queen rested at Holmby House. In the evening she went by coach to Althorp, where Sir Robert Spencer had devised a masque, written by Ben Jonson, for her entertainment. The Masque *Satyr* was staged in the open air, with the park as the background. It was a light-hearted affair, with satyrs and elves flitting in and out of the woodlands. As at Worksop, the limelight was stolen by a child. This time it was Sir Robert Spencer's eldest son, who, dressed as a huntsman, came on the stage at the end of the play and unleashed two deer. In the hunt that followed Ben Jonson noted that they were fortunately killed, just as they were meant to be, in the presence of Her Majesty, Queen Anne.

In spite of these distractions Lady Anne Clifford found time to note that while the Queen paid scant attention to any elderly ladies who were present, she was most gracious to Lady Hatton and her mother, Lady Cecil. Elizabeth Hatton was gay, self-willed and beautiful. Like the Queen, she delighted in masques and dancing. She was the granddaughter of William Cecil, the first Lord Burghley, and she never forgot her Cecil ancestry. As her second husband she had married Edward Coke, the Attorney-General, but she insisted on retaining her first husband's title, as she did not wish merely to be known as Mrs Coke.[26]

Nor was this Lady Anne's only entry in her diary for that day. With glee she noted: 'Now was my Lady Rich grown great with the Queen in as much as my Lady of Bedford was something out with her and when she came to Hampton Court was entertained but even indifferently.'[27] Penelope, Lady Rich, the sister of Queen Elizabeth's favourite, Essex, was very lovely, with sparkling black eyes, golden hair and an exquisite complexion. She lives in literature as the Stella of Sir Philip Sidney's sonnets. She hoped to marry him, but her guardian, the Earl of Huntingdon, made her marry Lord Rich, many years her senior, whom she detested.[28] This made her life a tragedy.

The real importance of Sir Robert Spencer's ephemeral masque was not the dissensions it caused amongst the Queen's ladies but the fact that it led to the Queen's recognition of Ben Jonson's genius. By employing him to write the Court masques for many years she established his reputation as a playwright, furthered his fortunes and conferred an inestimable gift upon future generations of Englishmen.

By Monday such crowds had flocked to Althorp, in the hope of securing an audience with the Queen, that it was impossible to perform the second part of Ben Jonson's masque. As the Queen drove away drove from Althorp she was greeted at the park gates by 'a morrise of clowns' led by Nobody, a grotesque figure with a cap over his face and breeches reaching to his neck.[29]

On 27 June Queen Anne reached Sir George Fermor's seat, Easton Neston in Northamptonshire. From there she moved to Grafton, the home of Lady Anne Clifford's father, the Earl of Cumberland, where she was entertained 'with speeches and delicate presents'. Lady Cumberland, a domineering, autocratic woman, was on bad terms with her husband. She hurried to Grafton convinced that on a such a memorable occasion her husband would allow her to act as mistress of the house. She was rapidly undeceived. 'My mother', wrote Lady Anne in her diary, 'was there [at Grafton] but not held as mistress of the house by reason of the difference between my lord and her which was grown to a great height.' The Earl was adamant. He would not allow his wife and daughter to sleep at Grafton, so they had spend the night at Doctor Challoner's in Amersham.[30]

By the time Queen Anne met King James at Windsor she was in a more amiable mood. Not only had she two notable victories to her credit—the wresting of her son from the Earl of Mar and the reinstatement of Lady Beatrice Ruthven in her household—but her progress through England had been an outstanding triumph. Everywhere she had been greeted by signs of welcome, rich and poor alike had cheered her. To quote Sir Dudley Carleton, 'she gave great contentment to the world in her fashion and courteous behaviour of her people'.

King James, too, was in an unusually good humour. He wished to present to his new subjects a picture of happy family life, with himself as a devoted husband adored by his wife and children. So he asked his courtiers if they did not think his Anny looked passing well and his little Bessy, too. Then, taking his daughter in his arms, he added, 'She is not an ill-favoured wench and may outshine her mother one of these days', a remark not calculated to endear him to Queen Anne. Lord Southampton, a budding diplomat, hastened to remark: 'If she equals her Majesty some years hence, it will be more, I will be bold to say, than any other princess upon earth will do.'[31]

8

QUEEN OF ENGLAND
1603

The first important event in Queen Anne's life as Queen of England was the investiture of Prince Henry as a Knight of the Garter on 2 July 1603. At nine years old Henry was a well-grown boy, eager, intelligent, not a great lover of books, but fond of all manly sports. It was a proud moment for his mother when Henry came to pay his respects to her wearing his garter robes, and to know that at the ceremony he had won golden opinions from those present by his dignified bearing and the reverence with which he bowed to the altar.[1] The Earls of Nottingham and Northampton were especially loud in their praises.

Other knights receiving the Garter at the same time were the Duke of Lennox, the Earls of Southampton and Pembroke, the Duke of Wurtemburg, and in his absence the Queen's brother, Christian IV of Denmark, King James himself had been made a Knight of the Garter by Queen Elizabeth at the time of Prince Henry's birth.

Unfortunately the better relations between Queen Anne and her husband were not of long duration. The cause of their next quarrel was the Earl of Southampton, a colourful young man, who had just received a special pardon and been released from the Tower by James I. He is best known to later generations as the patron of Shakespeare. The day after the Garter ceremony, in Queen Anne's presence in her private drawing-room, Southampton had a furious altercation with Lord Grey of Wilton. Anne, who was apt to be impulsive, knowing of Southampton's friendship with the late Earl of Essex, unwisely asked him why so many great men did so little at the time of Essex's rebellion. To which Southampton angrily retorted: 'If her Majesty made herself a party against the friends of Essex, of course they were bound to submit; but none of their private enemies durst thus have expressed themselves.'[2]

Lord Grey, a bitter opponent of the rebel Earl, happening to overhear this remark, took it as a personal affront. He broke into the conversation saying that Essex's opponents could have dealt with the situation. Whereupon Southampton 'gave him the lie'.[3] A furious quarrel broke out. Both young men, totally unmindful of the presence of the Queen, stormed at one another until Anne angrily told them to 'remember where they were'. At length they were marched off to their lodgings under guard.

James was highly displeased with his wife, regarding her as the source of the quarrel. He had trouble enough trying to keep the peace between the English and Scottish nobles and now there was this new and quite unnecessary quarrel. He gave Anne a lengthy homily on the iniquity of interfering in matters she did not understand. Next day he summoned both offenders to the Council Chamber in Windsor, and sent them both to the Tower. Anne, for her part, bitterly resented being called to task for a matter in which she did not consider that she was to blame. So she sent a curt note to her husband by Sir Roger Aston[4] saying:

Sir

What I have said to Sir Roger is true. I could not but think it strange that any about your Majesty durst presume to bring near where your Majesty is one that has offered me such a public scorn, for honour goes before life, I must ever think.

So humbly kissing your Majesty's hands, I rest ever yours

ANNA R.

I refer the rest to Sir Roger.[5]

In spite of his annoyance James continued to confer favours on the Earl of Southampton. In July he made him Keeper of the Isle of Wight for life and gave him the monopoly of importing sweet wines, worth £2,000 a year.

Preparations for the coronation were being hurried on, but a dark cloud overshadowed the horizon. No one knew better than King James how necessary it was that he should be crowned with the least possible delay. But the intense heat of the summer of 1603 had swelled the scattered cases of plague in London to such dimensions that it had become an epidemic. There were rumours that some 30,000 Londoners had died of plague.

James, always nervous about catching an infectious illness, decided to postpone the coronation and instead of going to London remained at Windsor. Prince Henry was sent to Oatlands,[6] one of the royal residences in the country. When at length the Court moved to Hampton Court, to the King's dismay, cases of plague broke out amongst the royal servants living in tents near the Palace gates. In view of the seriousness of the situation the Council decided that the customary ride of the new sovereign from the Tower through the streets of the City to Westminster must be abandoned and the number of guests attending the ceremony in the Abbey must be drastically cut. Instead of their usual retinues, earls might only bring sixteen attendants to Westminster and bishops and barons only ten.

There were other changes as well. Instead of the customary dubbing of Knights of the Bath on the eve of the coronation in the Tower of London, King James performed the ceremony in St James's Palace.

On the morning of 25 July 1603, in pouring rain, King James and Queen Anne went by river from Whitehall stairs to the Palace of Westminster and thence on foot to the Abbey.

The first crowning of a Queen Consort since Anne Boleyn was shorn of much of its glory. The Londoners were disappointed and resentful because they were deprived of the pleasure of seeing their new sovereign from over the Border and his Danish wife ride through the City streets; the Abbey was half empty owing to fears of the plague, while rumours of a plot to set Lady Arabella Stuart upon the throne made King James peevish and morose.

Queen Anne had her own procession. Her sceptre and crown were carried before her by two earls. A spectator has given a vivid picture of the scene.

Queen Anne went to her coronation in a robe of crimson velvet with her seemly hair down hanging on her princely shoulders and on her head a coronet of plain gold, followed by the ladies of her household in their crimson velvet robes. She so mildly saluted her new subjects that the women weeping cried out with one voice, 'God bless the royal Queen. Welcome to England. Long to live and continue.'[7]

Even within the Abbey all did not go well. Throughout the service King James showed a lack of dignity and want of reverence which such a solemn occasion warranted. During the paying of homage the reigning favourite Philip Herbert, Earl of Montgomery, had the effrontery to kiss King James on the cheek, but what profoundly shocked the congregation was that the King instead of resenting his insolence, merely laughed and lightly tapped him on the cheek. Nor did Queen Anne improve matters by refraining from taking the sacrament according to the rites of the Church of England, which strengthened the popular belief that she had an 'affection to popery'.

After the coronation the King and Queen moved to Woodstock Palace to avoid the plague, before setting out on a tour of southern England. The Palace was in such a deplorable state of repair that it was quite unsuitable for a royal residence, but the gatehouse where Queen Elizabeth lodged as a prisoner in her sister's reign was still well preserved. For the royal servants the conditions were appalling. Sir Robert Cecil did not exaggerate when he wrote:

The King regardless of the comfort of his courtiers had it roughly fitted up for himself, while the household were compelled to lodge even in tents. The place is unwholesome, all the house standing upon springs. It is unsavoury for there is no savour but of pigs and cows. It is uneaseful for only the King and Queen with the privy chamber ladies and some three or four of the Scottish Council are lodged in the house.[8]

When in August Queen Anne went with her husband on a tour of southern England, she must have found it a bewildering experience to visit so many strange houses, to sleep in so many strange beds, to meet so many strange hosts and hostesses. Above all she was overwhelmed by the luxury of these houses and the seemingly inexhaustible wealth of the English landed classes. After the penury of Scotland, England did indeed seem to her the promised land.

On 11 August the King and Queen left for Loseley Park, the seat of Sir George More, and then they spent three days at Farnham Castle, where Dr Thomson Bilson, Bishop of Winchester, entertained them sumptuously. After a brief stay at Thruxton House, the King and Queen arrived on 29 August at Wilton House, where they were welcomed by William Herbert, third Earl of Pembroke. During their visit King James noted with approval the magnificence of the rooms and earmarked Wilton House for a future and more prolonged visit.

Their next host, Edward Seymour, Earl of Hertford, son of Protector Somerset, was a timid, rather depressed man, whose one romantic adventure, his runaway marriage with Lady Catherine Grey, sister of Lady Jane Grey, had brought such disastrous consequences, not only for himself and his bride, but also for the redoubtable Bess of Hardwick, then Lady St Looe. All three had been sent to the Tower.

From Tottenham Park the King and Queen went to Berkshire, where at Wadley near Faringdon they were entertained by Lady Dorothy Unton, widow of Sir Henry Unton, ambassador to France, and then to Burford Priory in Oxfordshire, where they were hospitably received by Lawrence Tanfield, the eminent lawyer, who was knighted by King James in March 1604 and later became a judge of the King's Bench and Chief Baron of the Exchequer.

After all these visits Anne retired for a rest to Basing House, the home of John Paulet, second Marquis of Winchester, while King James went hunting. Basing House was then at the height of its glory, with spacious rooms and extensive outbuildings, of which only the gateway and the brick barn, used by the Paulets as a riding school, remain. Anne's host was the son of the financial wizard who succeeded in the remarkable feat of weathering the stormy reigns of Henry VIII, Edward VI, Mary and Queen Elizabeth without losing his head.

Anne thoroughly enjoyed herself at Basing House, dancing and playing card games as well as deriving much amusement from the unabashed attentions the sixty-seven-year-old Lord Howard of Effingham, the victor of the Armada, was paying to Lady Margaret Stuart, who was forty years his junior. As Sir Thomas Edmonds told Gilbert, Earl of Shrewsbury, in a gossipy letter,

Since the time that your Lordship left us, we have wholly spent our time in that exercise [hunting]; but the Queen remained at Basing till the King's coming hither and she hath as well entertained herself with good dancing which hath brought forth the effects of a marriage between my Lord Admiral and the Lady Margaret Stuart.'[9]

The Queen herself described this autumn wooing to her husband, camouflaging the couple as Mars and Venus.

Sir,

Your Majesty's letter was welcome to me. I have been as glad of the fair weather as yourself and the last part of your letter, you have guessed right that I would laugh—who would not laugh—both at the persons and the subject but the more at so well chosen Mercury between Mars and Venus? You know that woman can hardly keep counsel. I humbly desire your Majesty to tell me how it is possible that I should keep this secret that have already told it, and shall tell it to as many as I speak with, and if I were a poet I would make a song of it and sing it to the tune of Three Fools well met. So kissing your hands, I rest yours

ANNA R.[10]

On 18 September Queen Anne went to Winchester, where she was joined by King James two days later. Even here they were not safe from the ravages of the plague, so on 6 October they moved to Wilton House, where Prince Henry joined them.

During the weeks from 6 October until 12 December that Queen Anne spent at Wilton House she came to know the Earl of Pembroke well, and a lifelong friendship was formed. William Herbert was gay, courteous, kind-hearted and agreeable. Moreover, he took a lively interest in poetry and the arts. Samuel Daniel had been his tutor since the age of ten, and when Herbert grew up Daniel remained at Wilton, writing many of his best poems there.

Another frequent visitor was Ben Jonson, who knew he would always be welcome at Wilton as a guest and to whom Herbert also gave £20 a year to buy books. Queen Anne's interest in him had already been aroused by the Masque of Flowers and Lady Bedford's enthusiasm, while the fact that he was born in the same year as Queen Anne may have been a further bond. Now closer contact inspired the Queen with the wish to stage bigger and better masques with verse written by poets that was not mere doggerel.

At the same time Queen Anne's sympathy for Sir Walter Raleigh was awakened by the Earl of Pembroke. He was a staunch champion of the Elizabethan seaman, now a prisoner in the Tower, on a charge of treason. So hard did Pembroke work in his defence that in December 1603 Raleigh was released for a time.

Queen Anne was a keen theatre-goer and while they were staying at Wilton House the Earl of Pembroke commanded the Lord Chamberlain's players to come from Mortlake and perform *As You Like It*[11] before Their Majesties. So successful was the performance that Shakespeare received the royal patronage and his company the Lord Chamberlain's Men were known henceforth as the King's Men.

The first Christmas in England was spent at Hampton Court, with festivities on a scale never before seen in London. There were sword dances and masques and on 1 January 1604 a play called *Robin Goodfellow* was performed before a delighted audience. It was all very expensive, but James did not care what he spent. Less than two months after the coronation Cecil was writing to the Earl of Shrewsbury: 'Our Sovereign spends £100,000 yearly on his house which was wont to be but £50,000. Now think what the country feels and so much for that.'

One of King James's first cares after the coronation was to see to what endowments and privileges his wife was entitled, and to settle her jointure as Queen Consort. Sir Robert Cecil set to work to make exhaustive inquiries and in addition to her dowry as Queen of Scotland, Somerset House, Hatfield and the Palaces of Nonsuch and Pontefract were settled on Queen Anne as part of the Queen Consort's dower. Her jointure amounted to £6,376 a year, which, as Cecil remarked, 'was to be expended in wages to her servants, apparel to herself and gratuities, the King charging himself with all other expenses of household and stable'.[12]

King Christian IV also took a keen interest in obtaining a substantial jointure for his sister. Anne was touched by his concern for her welfare. Although she had not seen him for thirteen years, her ties with her family remained very close. She thanked him, saying:

Yet is our bond to you no less for the care you have had concerning our jointure than if there had been cause of mediation wherein because you may be informed how things have proceeded, you shall understand in short that his Majesty hath pleased to pass unto us, under his seal of this crown, such a jointure as King Henry the Eighth, King of England, gave to Queen Catherine, daughter of Spain. In which we have not only had our desire to imitate her that was born a King's daughter, but his Majesty hath ordained in all other things thereunto belonging so as we are satisfied in that point of honour to be used according to our rank.[13]

For a young girl who delighted in rich silks and satins, expensive perfumes and above all precious stones, money meant very little. After a Spartan girlhood in Denmark and her limited resources as Queen of Scotland, such an income seemed inexhaustible. But alas her capacity for spending soon outran all reason. Two years later Cecil noted that her total expenditure amounted to over £50,000 a year.

Anne's passion for masques was the cause of much of the trouble. King James never made any attempt to curb his wife's extravagance, but allowed her free scope in staging masques which, with their floats, rich costumes and elaborate scenery, were extremely costly. In the masque of the *Vision of the Twelve Goddesses* staged in the great hall at Hampton Court on 8 January 1604 Queen Anne and her ladies played the leading parts. The masque was written by Samuel Daniel, whom Lady Bedford 'preferred to the Queen in this employment'.

At the upper end of the hall a wide stairway led to the Cave of Sleep, where Night could be seen arousing her son Somnus with the words: 'Awake, dark sleep, arouse thee from out thy cave.' Lady Suffolk and Lady Walsingham were responsible for the costumes and the goddesses wore petticoats of various colours from Queen Elizabeth's wardrobe, over which were draped loose mantles. Queen Anne, who played the part of Pallas Athene, was a martial figure wearing a tunic embroidered with cannon and other weapons of war, a helmet on her head and a spear in her right hand. She had only these four lines to speak.

Next warlike Pallas in her helmet dressed,
With lance of winning, target of defence,
In whom both wit and courage are expressed,
To get with glory, hold with providence.

The Court rivals Lady Bedford and Lady Rich were Vesta and Venus. 'The parade and intimate movements on the staircase leading to the Temple of Peace were presented with such great majesty and art', and Sir Dudley Carleton thought 'they were the best things that were ever seen'. Only Queen Anne 'had a trick by herself for her clothes were not so much below the knee but that we might see a woman had both feet and legs which I never knew before'.[14] Wilbraham estimated that the masque cost between £2,000 and £3,000 and the Queen's jewels alone were worth £100,000.[15] Wearing masks, the goddesses danced 'their own measures', then they invited the lords to be their partners in 'certain measures, galliards and corantoes'.[16] The dancing became fast and furious and the young Prince Henry was tossed from hand to hand like a tennis ball.[17]

Such amusements did not meet with the approval of some of the elderly courtiers. Arthur Wilson commented acidly on 'the Court being a continued masquerade, where the Queen and her ladies like so many sea nymphs or Nereids, often appeared in various dresses to the ravishment of the beholders'.[18] It was no wonder that Queen Anne was enthusiastic, for she had discovered a medium in which she could indulge her love of dress and jewelry, while at the same time occupying the centre of the stage, without undergoing the tedium of theatrical training or requiring any special talent for acting. Could any Queen ask for more?

As usual, there was friction between the French and Spanish ambassadors. Prudently James decided not to invite them both to the same ceremony, to avoid trouble over the question of precedence. But discord arose from a source which the King had not foreseen. When M. Beaumont was the first to be invited, Queen Anne absolutely refused to dance with anyone unless Señor Juan de Tassis, the Spanish ambassador, also received an invitation. So at the Queen's masque on 8 January James had the annoyance of seeing the Spanish ambassador wearing a red costume and the Queen sporting a red favour in compliment to him.

9

THE ROYAL FAMILY
1603-1605

When King James VI of Scotland became King James I of England he realised that one of his greatest assets was inheriting the services of Principal Secretary Robert Cecil. Cecil might lack the vision of his father, the first Lord Burghley, but he was a very efficient civil servant. Moreover, James knew that Robert Cecil understood the English as he, being a Scot, would never do. Above all, being incorrigibly idle, James was able to leave the affairs of state in the hands of his Secretary and indulge in his passion for hunting. 'Sometimes he comes to Council', commented Thomas Wilson, 'but most time he spends in fields and parks and chases, chasing away idleness by violent exercise.'[1]

If Robert Cecil lacked the political acumen of his father, he was shrewd and industrious, having undergone a long and careful training in state-craft. King James owed him an immense debt, for his peaceful succession to the throne of England was due to Cecil. While Cecil disliked King James's coarseness and slackness, he was prepared to put up with much so long as the real power remained in his hands and he could build up the fortunes of his family. He even endured the incessant travelling necessitated by the King's absence from London due to his fear of the plague and addiction to hunting. But he lamented sadly on the good days of Queen Elizabeth, 'I wish I waited now in her Presence Chamber with ease at my food and rest in my bed. I am pushed from the shore of comfort and know not where the winds and waves of court will bear me.'[2] James rewarded his services by creating him Viscount Cranborne in 1604. The King called him familiarly 'my little beagle', which coming from such a lover of hounds was clearly a term of endearment.

With Queen Anne Cecil's relations varied. When the quarrel with the Earl of Mar was at its height he had tried to ingratiate himself with her by assuring her of his devotion to her service and that 'her interest in him was paramount to that of all others'.[3]

His half-brother Thomas, Lord Burghley, had met Queen Anne at Berwick and he spoke enthusiastically of her, telling Cecil 'she will prove, if I be not decieved, a magnifical prince, a kind wife and a constant mistress'.[4] Cecil was by no means so enraptured. Like King James, he distrusted all women. Perhaps the long apprenticeship he had served in the reign of Queen Elizabeth had helped to embitter him. He looked upon Queen Anne as hopelessly indiscreet, and confided to Mr Bruce that 'the Queen was weak and a tool in the hands of clever and unscrupulous persons'.[5]

As time passed Queen Anne's feelings towards Cecil grew more friendly. She pitied him for his misshapen body and sympathised with his sensitive shrinking from King James's coarseness. They even joked together. When Cecil said 'she loved nobody but dead pictures'—a criticism as wide of the mark as could well be imagined—Anne retorted 'she was more contented with her pictures than he with his great employments'.[6]

One cause of Cecil's distrust of the Queen remained. This was her championship of Spain. Anne admired the Spanish monarchy, and not being English by birth, she did not, like many of her subjects, look upon hatred of Spain as a patriotic duty. Her feelings towards Spain were even more kindly when she received from Philip II's daughter, the Infanta Isabel Clara Eugenia and her husband, the Archduke Albert, their beautifully painted miniatures.[7]

When Juan de Velasco, Constable of Castile, was in London in 1604 to sign an Anglo-Spanish peace treaty, Anne assured him that she would welcome a marriage between Prince Henry and the Infanta Anna, daughter of King Philip III. King James, too, in the early months of his reign was quite in favour of the match until he discovered that the Spaniards were insisting that Prince Henry should become a Roman Catholic and be sent to Spain to be educated. The King knew that the English with their inborn hatred of Spain would never tolerate such conditions. So negotiations were broken off, although they were reopened again in 1605 and 1607.

During the cold weather the virulence of the plague had abated and in March 1604 it was considered possible for the King and Queen to make their long-delayed drive through London. So on 12 March King James and Queen Anne with Prince Henry went to the Tower of London, the traditional starting point. Before setting out the royal party went to see the lions which were kept there and King James asked that a mastiff should be put in the cage of the fiercest lion. The dog was at once seized by the neck and dragged along the floor of the cage by the outraged inmate. When a second dog, and later a third, was thrust in to fight the lion, they suffered the same fate. Then the lion retired sulkily into a corner of its cage. Prince Henry, who showed a sympathy for animals most unusual at that period, made inquiries about the mastiffs, and on learning that the third dog was the sole survivor, sent his servant to bring it to St James's Palace, where he had it carefully tended.

No one looked forward with less pleasure than King James to his state ride through the City of London. He detested crowds and close contact with his loyal subjects did nothing to enhance his popularity. As the Venetian ambassador remarked, the English 'like their King to show pleasure at their devotion as the late Queen knew well how to do; but this King manifests no taste for them but rather contempt and dislike. The result is he is despised and almost hated.'[8]

It was a far more imposing sight than the coronation procession, which fear of the plague had shorn of its glory. Now all ranks of the King's subjects were represented in such numbers that the procession took six hours to pass from the Tower of

London to Whitehall. All the Court was there: the judges, the state officials, the nobles, the bishops, the Knights of the Bath, all in their places according to their rank, each group being of higher rank than the one preceding it. Then came Prince Henry, whose fine horsemanship and erect carriage caused the crowd to break into loud acclamations. It was three-quarters of a century since the English had seen an heir to the throne riding along a London street and in Prince Henry they saw a prince who fulfilled their highest hopes.

Ten paces behind rode King James on a white jennet with a canopy held over his head, by eight gentlemen of his Chamber. Then came Queen Anne in a carriage drawn by two white mules, followed by the King's cousin, Lady Arabella Stuart, and the ladies of her household.

Unlike her husband, Queen Anne enjoyed state occasions. Her progress from Scotland had given her confidence in dealing with crowds. She smiled and bowed so graciously that she won their hearts. A spectator who saw the enthusiasm she aroused wrote: 'Our gracious Queen, mild and courteous, placed in a chariot of exceeding beauty, did all the way so humbly and with mildness salute her subjects, never ceasing to bend her body this way and that, that men and women wept with joy.'

The various spectacles the state drive offered delighted the Queen. Soon after leaving the Tower she heard three hundred boys of Christ's Hospital singing in the churchyard of All Hallows, Barking. Then as she drove down Fenchurch Street beneath the first of the seven triumphal arches she saw a model of the City of London at its apex.[9] But the next arch in Gracechurch Street surpassed it in beauty, for this was the work of the Italian colony. At the Royal Exchange the Dutch merchants had erected an arch representing the seventeen provinces of their country and here, as at the other arches, the procession halted and the King and Queen were entertained with a speech in Latin.

So down Cheapside, where the Fountain of Virtue ran with wine and gold cups were presented to the King and Queen and Prince Henry. As the procession passed old St Paul's, choristers sang an anthem from the lower battlements, but what gave the Queen greater pleasure were the strains of a Danish march played in her honour as she passed under the sixth triumphal arch in Fleet Street. At Temple Bar[10] they paused for the Lord Mayor to surrender the sword of the City to the King, then on again along the Strand, past Queen Anne's residence, Somerset House, to the journey's end—the Palace of Whitehall.

From the day he crossed the Border to become King of England King James felt that there was nothing to be gained by prolonging the war with Spain. It may be that he overestimated the power of Spain and failed to realise that her ecomony was in a state of chaos and that a powerful navy and invincible army were things of the past, but nevertheless he was right in thinking that England needed peace. So James welcomed the arrival of a Spanish mission led by Juan de Velasco, Constable of Castile, in the summer of 1604 to conclude an Anglo-Spanish peace treaty.

Queen Anne was wholeheartedly in agreement with him. She wished for friendship with Spain, and when Juan de Tassis, who was soon to be appointed ambassador for Spain to the Court of St James's presumed to ask for Somerset House, her private residence, as the only place suitable for Juan de Velasco to stay during the negotiations, she good-naturedly agreed and helped to furnish the rooms with rich hangings and furniture from the other royal palaces.

On 14 August 1604 Queen Anne, wearing a mask, in the company of Lady Suffolk, the Lord Admiral and Sir Robert Cecil, watched from a barge as the Spanish envoys in a flotilla of twenty-four covered barges swept up the Thames to Westminster. As King James was away hunting at Royston, the Queen sent the Earl of Suffolk to receive the delegates.

Five days later King James returned to London. In spite of thorny questions such as English aid to Dutch rebels in the Netherlands and English demands for freedom of trade with the Spanish colonies in the New World, the difficulties were ironed out, and on 19 August 1604 the treaty was sworn in the Chapel

Royal at Whitehall. Henceforth England and Spain were at peace.

The King celebrated the making of the treaty by giving a banquet at Whitehall. The Constable of Castile, after drinking a toast to Queen Anne, held up 'a very beautiful dragon-shaped cup of crystal garnished with gold' and asked the Queen to join him in drinking a toast to King James from it. He then placed the cup beside the Queen to show that it was a gift to her.

When the banquet ended there was dancing, and ten-year-old Prince Henry 'danced for the company exhibiting much sprightliness and modesty as he took the floor with the lady whom the King and Queen designed for his partner'.[11] Later, from the windows of the great hall, the company watched the King's bears fight with greyhounds, mastiffs attacking a tethered bull, and displays of horsemanship. Then boylike Prince Henry expressed a wish to see a Spanish horse, and the Constable of Castile[12] at once ordered one to be brought with a gay saddle and bridle which he presented to the Prince.

All this time Queen Anne had been waiting for Prince Charles to join her in England. In many ways he was her favourite child. He had shown such courage and determination in trying to overcome his handicaps and she felt he needed her care and protection more than his brother and sister. Fortunately the reports of the Prince's progress coming from Scotland continued to be encouraging. Lord Fyvie, his guardian, reported: 'Your most noble son Duke Charles[13] continues, praised be God, in good health, good courage and lofty mind; although yet weak in body, he is beginning to speak some words. He is far better as yet with his mind than with his body and feet.'

On 3 July 1604 his doctor, Henry Atkins, told the Queen:

Our noble prince, your Majesty's dear son, daily growing from one perfection of health to another. His Highness now walketh many times in a day all the length of the great chamber at Dunfermline like a gallant soldier all alone. He often talketh of going to London and desireth to see his gracious mother.[14]

At Anne's request a doctor and an apothecary were sent to Scotland to report on the Prince's health. They found that 'his joints were so loose that the ankles seemed dislocated', but they decided that he was strong enough to make the journey to England by easy stages. To Anne's great joy he joined her in August, and although painfully shy and speaking in a high-pitched voice, he was very intelligent. He was placed in the care of Sir Robert and Lady Carey.[15] No better choice could have been made, for they watched over him with loving care and great patience.

Sir Robert Carey has described Charles's early years.

The Duke was of past four years when he was first delivered to my wife, he was not able to go nor scant stand alone, he was so weak in his joints yet God so blessed him both with health and strength that he proved daily stronger and stronger. Many a battle my wife had with the King but she still prevailed. The King was desirous that the string under his tongue should be cut, for he so long beginning to speak as he thought he would never have spoke. Then he would have him put in iron boots to strengthen his sinews and joints but my wife protested so much against them both as she got the victory and the King was fain to yield. My wife had charge of him from a little past four till he was almost eleven years old, in all which time he grew more and more in health.[16]

Queen Anne vigorously supported Lady Carey in opposing the drastic remedies her husband proposed. She believed that gentler methods would produce better results, and events proved that she was right. Prince Henry and Princess Elizabeth were devoted to their little brother, and their infinite patience and understanding played a great part in helping him to overcome his disabilities. Charles had the greatest admiration for his elder brother, looking up to him as the pattern of all the virtues, his determination to be like him a good horseman and a brilliant athlete did much to strengthen Charles's willpower, which enabled him to persevere in his struggle against his handicaps.

The year 1604 brought a welcome visitor to Queen Anne. In November her brother Ulric, Duke of Holstein, arrived in London. During the six years which had passed since Ulric's last visit he had grown from a lumpish boy into a powerfully built young man. Less tall than his brother Christian, he was already showing signs of putting on weight, which his habits as a gargantuan eater and a heavy drinker did nothing to curb. 'He hath twenty dishes of meat allowed every meal,'[17] commented a courtier.

Although the English were shocked at his meagre escort, Ulric was now a well-endowed young man. In 1602 he had become titular bishop of the secularised North German sees of Schwerin and Schleswig and drew a substantial income from them. Both the King and Queen were glad to see him. Queen Anne because he brought recent news of her mother and brother Christian and could tell her about her sister Hedwig's marriage to Duke Christian II of Saxony, which he had attended, and King James because he found in him a congenial companion who shared his tastes in hunting and drinking.

Many entertainments were prepared for Duke Ulric, but Queen Anne was such a confirmed playgoer that it was difficult to find a play she had not seen. Sir Walter Cope reported ruefully to Cecil, who was now Viscount Cranborne:

I have been sent and been all this morning hunting for players, jugglers and such kinds of creatures but find them hard to find. Burbage is come and says there is no new play the Queen has not seen but they have revived an old one called Love's Labour's Lost which for wit and mirth he says will please her exceedingly.[18]

King James lent Ulric his best falcon, and the winter months were spent in hunting, hawking and coursing hares at Royston.

Ulric found life in England very much to his taste. With his growing prosperity he had become increasingly arrogant and his manners left much to be desired. At the dinner after Philip Herbert's wedding Ulric was deeply offended because the Venetian ambassador was given precedence, and in the masque which followed, when he saw that his seat was on the Queen's left instead of being on the King's right, he was so affronted that he remained standing for three hours throughout the performance.[19]

As time went on Ulric became so rude and boorish that he was detested both by the royal servants and the courtiers. He even offended his own sister by bursting unceremoniously into her private apartments. When remonstrances had no effect Anne ordered one of her ladies to lock the door of her apartments and refuse her brother admission.[20] Furious at being denied entry, Ulric hammered on the door, using abusive epithets. Anne was so angry that for two months she refused to speak to her brother. At length King James, who enjoyed playing the part of peacemaker, took Ulric by the hand and led him to the Queen's apartments. Then he persuaded Anne to exchange a few words with him, but the breach was never totally healed.

Weeks passed, yet Ulric showed no signs of departing. His original pretext for coming to England had been to congratulate his sister on becoming Queen of England while at the same time he hoped to recruit six thousand men to take to Hungary. Winwood commented: 'Methinks they should have little to do that would adventure themselves so far with a man able to do them no more good.'[21] Even King James was beginning to tire of his guest's petulance and bad temper. So when Ulric casually remarked, when they were hunting at Royston, that he had attended the King all the winter hunting hares and would go on till Christmas attending him in hunting the stag, his offer was received in such stony silence that Ulric realised he had outstayed his welcome. He made no further efforts to prolong his visit, but sailed from England on 15 June 1605, never to return.

Another member of the royal circle whom Queen Anne found very trying was the King's first cousin, Lady Arabella Stuart. She was the only child of Lord Darnley's younger brother Charles and Elizabeth Cavendish, Bess of Hardwick's daughter. All her life Arabella, or Arbella as her contemporaries called her, was her own worst enemy. She had the Stuart obstinacy coupled with a strange want of balance. Perhaps her upbringing was in part responsible, for as both her parents had died when she was only a child, she was brought up at Hardwick Hall by her grandmother, the dowager Countess of Shrewsbury, who insisted that she should be treated as royalty, waited on hand and foot by the servants and deferred to by her Cavendish cousins. This gave Arabella an exaggerated sense of her own importance. As a young girl of seventeen she had been full of romantic ideas, and when in the closing months of 1602 it was apparent that Queen Elizabeth had not long to live, Arabella as great-granddaughter of Margaret Tudor, Henry VII's elder daughter, and her second husband, Archibald Douglas, was in a position, of possible claimant to the English throne, which made her especially vulnerable.

Old Lady Shrewsbury had no wish to see the tragedy of Lady Jane Grey re-enacted in her own family, so after Arabella had foolishly been drawn into a plot by her uncle, Henry Cavendish, and attempted to escape from Hardwick Hall, her grandmother kept strict control over her, watching her movements, not allowing her to speak to strangers and making her sleep in a small room leading out of her own bedroom.

Arabella rebelled furiously against this curtailment of her liberty, but with the accession of King James happier days dawned for her. The new King and Queen welcomed her at Court and showered gifts upon her. King James gave her a pension of £1,000 a year and her own establishment in Whitehall, but what gave her especial pleasure was permission to have eighteen instead of eight dishes a day from the royal table.[22] The King recognised her position and gave her precedence over all the other countesses. In state processions she came directly after the Queen and she played a leading part in every masque. But upon two points James was adamant. He would allow his cousin nothing which might endanger the crown, and she might only marry someone of whom he approved.

At first Arabella tried to ingratiate herself with Queen Anne, praising her tact and gracious public behaviour. But the two women differed fundamentally. The Puritan strain in Arabella's character did not appeal to Queen Anne, while her intellectual pride made her look upon the Queen as a brainless nonentity.

In 1604 Arabella was appointed carver to Queen Anne. It was not an altogether happy post, as she told her uncle, Gilbert Talbot, in an amusing letter:

After I had once carved, the Queen never dined out of her chambers till my Lady Bedford's return. I doubted my unhandsome carving had been the cause thereof but her Majesty took my endeavour in good part and with better words than that beginning deserved put me out of that error.[23]

Arabella soon became utterly bored with the childish games played by Queen Anne and her ladies. Once again she wrote to her Uncle Gilbert:

Will you know how we spend out time on the Queen's side. Whilest I was at Winchester there were certain child plays, remembered by the fair ladies, viz 'I pray my Lord give me a course in your park'; 'Rise pig and go'; 'One penny follow me' etc. And when I came to Court they were as highly in request as ever cracking of nuts was. So I was by the mistress of the revels not only compelled to play at I knew not what (for till that day I never heard of a play called Fier) but even persuaded by the princely example I saw to play the child again. This exercise is mostly used from ten of the clock at night till two or three in the morning.[24]

King James's many kindnesses to his cousin did not pass unnoticed by the foreign diplomats and the Venetian ambassador reported: 'Lady Arabella who is a regular termagant came to visit the King on Sunday last with a suite of ladies and gentlemen. She has returned to favour; they say should the Queen die, she would be wedded and crowned at once.'[25] This was in May 1603, when Queen Anne had just had her stormy interview with the Countess of Mar and was desperately ill. How far this was mere gossip we shall never knew. Fortunately both for King

James and Lady Arabella, the Queen recovered, so James's intentions were never put to the test.

Philip Herbert was the first of King James's English favourites. He was a graceless young man, ill mannered, with a streak of treachery in his nature, besides being so arrogant that when he first came to Court Rowland Whyte commented: 'Mr Philip Herbert is here and one of the forwardest courtiers that I ever saw in my time, for he had been here two hours but he grew as bold as the best.'[26] To do Philip justice, he took no trouble to retain the royal favour, but remained surly and bad-tempered to his patron. His only interests were hunting and gaming and King James's discourses on theology and witchcraft were entirely wasted on him. As Clarendon remarked, he 'pretended to no other gratifications than to understand dogs and horses very well'.[27] Soon the King was showering honours upon the new favourite. In May 1603 Philip was made a Gentleman of the Privy Council and in July a Knight of the Bath, while in May 1605 he was created Earl of Montgomery.[28]

In the autumn of 1604 Philip Herbert became secretly engaged to Lady Susan Vere, granddaughter of William Cecil, first Lord Burghley, 'without the knowledge of any of his or her friends'. Why it should have been so secret seems quite without rhyme or reason. However, their marriage was celebrated two days after Christmas with the utmost éclat. Prince Henry and Duke Ulric of Holstein escorted the bride to the chapel in Whitehall Palace and King James himself gave the bride away. Great festivities followed the ceremony. There was a banquet in the great chamber and a masque performed by noblemen in honour of the young couple called *Juno and Hymenaeus*,[29] in which the Earl of Pembroke played a leading part. Yet the day did not pass without a regrettable incident. For during the masque, which lasted three hours, 'there was no small loss that night of chains and jewels and many great ladies were made shorter by the skirts and were well enough served that they could keep cut no better'.[30]

Amongst the Christmas festivities was the investiture of Prince Charles on Twelfth Night. The five-year-old prince was too feeble to walk the length of the hall, so from the arms of the Lord Admiral he 'watched a substantial lord take the oath on his behalf', and then after eleven young nobles had been made Knights of the Bath, he was brought back to join in their procession and carried out again by the Lord Admiral.[31]

Queen Anne, so far as lay in her power, had taken infinite trouble in giving her children a happy family life. She tried to teach them to have a sense of pride in their ancestry and she laid great emphasis on the importance of doing their duty. Her children were devoted to one another and most patient with their younger brother. Henry would tease Charles by telling him that as his legs were so weak, he must be 'a bishop, a gown would be fittest to hide his legs'. All the children wrote affectionate little notes to one another. Charles's letters were the most lively and best phrased. A note he wrote to Henry when he was nine years old is a good example of his courage and determination.

Good Brother

I hope you are in good health, merry as I am, God be thanked. In your absence I visit sometimes your stable and ride your great horses that at your return I may wait on you in that noble exercise. So committing you to God, I rest

Your loving and dutiful brother

YORK.[32]

The birth of the Queen's sixth child was expected in March. Over eighty years had elapsed since Jane Seymour had given birth to a son, and owing to the passage of time and the reigns of two childless Queens, many of the customs attached to a royal birth had been forgotten. Naturally there was much competition in Court circles for such perquisites as were going. 'There is much ado about the Queen's lying down and great suit made for the offices of carrying the white staff, door keeping and such like gossips' tricks, which you should understand better than I do', commented Sir Dudley Carleton to his friend Winwood.[33]

The Queen retired to Greenwich Palace and prayers were said daily in all the London churches for her safe delivery. The March days passed and still the expected announcement did not come. At length on 8 April 1605 bonfires were lit and church bells rang to celebrate the birth of a princess who was called Mary after her grandmother, Mary Queen of Scots. Perhaps it was an ill-omened choice, for the baby was so frail that her baptism was postponed until 5 May. It was an impressive ceremony 'with greater state than the memory of any then alive could record'. 'The noble babe was carried under a canopy of cloth of gold in a general silence neither voice nor instrument was heard in the way'.[34] Duke Ulric as godfather and Lady Arabella as godmother played their parts with decorum. The baby was placed in the care of Lord and Lady Knyvett at Stanwell near Staines. Mary, as befitted a royal princess, was allowed £20 a week for her diet. Lord Knyvett was soon to rise even higher in the royal favour, for he was the justice of the peace who uncovered the Gunpowder Plot.

One of the advantages of being Queen of England in Queen Anne's eyes was that she could see more of her children. Prince Henry had reached an interesting age. He was a boy of whom any parents could be proud. He had poise and dignity and an old-fashioned courtesy which delighted those who met him. In addition to this he was intelligent and he had varied interests, especially love of the sea and the building of ships. The idea that he was extremely good-looking may have been inspired by flattery, for a miniature by Oliver painted when he was eleven shows that his features were blunt and rather coarse.

In August 1605 Prince Henry accompanied his parents on a state visit to Oxford University. They came with a great retinue of courtiers and lodged in Christ Church. Oxford had made a special effort to welcome them. The gates, windows and railings of the colleges gleamed with fresh paint and the Mayor competed with the heads of the colleges in delivering a loyal address of welcome, but he was made to retire.

All the route from the north gate of the city to Christ Church was lined with excited citizens shouting their welcome. Outside St John's college the King and Queen paused to see a tableau of the three Sybils greeting Banquo, the legendary ancestor of the House of Stuart, who was 'no king but to be the father of many kings'.[35]

At Carfax they paused again, this time for an oration in Greek by a learned scholar of the University, for which Queen Anne graciously thanked him, artlessly remarking that she had never heard Greek spoken before. So on to Christ Church, where on their first evening a pastoral play was performed for the entertainment of the royal guests, which greatly shocked the Queen, as the actors appeared nearly naked.[36]

The four days of the visit passed quickly. Every hour was filled with dissertations, speeches, tableaux and plays. King James was in his element. He took part in debates on theology and discussed the merits of tobacco—a subject near to his heart, as he had written a treatise on *A Counterblast to Tobacco* in 1604. Prince Henry won golden opinions by listening to a disputation at Magdalen by undergraduates of noble birth. So impressed were the senior members of the University by the Prince's intelligence that they wished to confer an honorary degree of Master of Arts upon him, but King James decided that at eleven years old Henry was too young and the offer was declined.

On the second day, as light relief after the discourses, a Latin play, which had been prepared for Queen Elizabeth's visit thirty years before and never produced, was taken out of cold storage. The royal guests found it extremely tedious. On the last night, 30 August, the undergraduates of Christ Church performed a pastoral play, *Vestuminus*, which was lively and amusing.[37] It was thoroughly enjoyed by Queen Anne and Prince Henry, although as usual King James fell asleep during the performance.

In November 1605 England was shaken by the news that a plot

had been discovered to blow up the Parliament House when King James went to open Parliament on 5 November. The immediate cause of the plot was the King's broken promises to the Roman Catholics. His efforts to play them off against the Puritans had failed, so the penal laws against recusants were more strictly enforced than in Queen Elizabeth's time. The plot was betrayed, the conspirators captured and tortured, and thanksgiving services held throughout England. The plotters had no wish to harm Queen Anne, who was believed to be secretly a Catholic, but the effects of the plot both on King James and Robert Cecil had marked influence on her life. King James had a morbid dread of gunpowder, as his father, Lord Darnley, had been the victim of such an attack at Kirk o' the Field, and the thought of his narrow escape frayed his nerves. Never again, if he could help it, would he allow his subjects free access to him on his progresses.

The person who benefited most from the Gunpowder Plot was Robert Cecil. It established him firmly in the royal favour and he easily obtained the King's consent to pass new anti-Catholic legislation. Fines were levied on households where the servants did not attend Church of England services and all Catholics had to swear that allegiance to the Pope did not absolve them from their allegiance to the King. Queen Anne, for her part, had to redouble her precautions that the services in her private chapel should not become known to the public.

Among the first to send congratulatory messages to King James on his providential escape was King Philip III of Spain. Juan Vlasco de Aragon headed an embassy, which according to the Venetian ambassador was intended to serve a double purpose, for King Philip and his ministers suddenly realised that they had a valuable ally in Queen Anne with her pro-Spanish sympathies. 'In future they intend to make up for their neglect in the past now that they are aware of her great weight with the King.' This was wishful thinking, as King James seldom allowed his wife's wishes to influence him in any way. However, to Anne's delight the Spaniards brought with them as a present for her a dress of murry-coloured satin embroidered with amber leather and a velvet cap with gold buttons.[38] Fortunately Anne's pleasure was not marred by hearing the Venetian ambassador's rather spiteful comment that the presents were more remarkable for the beauty of their design than for the richness of the stuff.

10

KING CHRISTIAN'S VISIT
1606

Queen Anne's religious beliefs were always a subject of speculation. Perhaps the truth was that she was a lethargic Christian with no burning zeal for religion. As a child Anne had been brought up as a Lutheran in Denmark and a clause in her marriage treaty safeguarded her right to worship as a Lutheran.[1] According to her confessor, Father Abercromby, as a young girl Anne fell under Catholic influences and went to Mass when it was celebrated in the household of a German princess.[2] The identity of the German princess has never been satisfactorily explained; nor at what period in Anne's life she stayed in a German household. Certainly it cannot have been while she was living with her grandmother at Güstrow, for Duchess Elizabeth would never have allowed Catholic influences to infiltrate into her Lutheran household.

When Anne went to live in Scotland she found the bleakness of Calvinism intolerable. Her sense of frustration was heightened by the harsh rebukes of the ministers of the Kirk for 'not repairing to the word and sacraments, night walking, and balling',[3] as the Scots called dancing. The Queen had drawn much adverse comment on herself by not having her children brought up as Calvinists, and what was even worse, by having many Catholic friends such as the Duke of Lennox; his daughter, Lady Huntley; Alexander Seton, Prior of Pluscardine, and Lord Elphinstone.

Queen Elizabeth was so disturbed by rumours of Queen Anne's Catholic tendencies that she wrote warning her of the danger. After complaining that Anne was a bad correspondent and 'of late passed under greater silence than we would ever have expected', she added a postscript written in her own hand. Like most postscripts it contained the heart of the matter, touching somewhat obliquely on Anne's rumoured conversion to the Church of Rome. 'Sister, I beseech you let a few of your own lines satisfy me in some one point that is boasted against you.'[4] The bearer was Sir Robert Bowes, the English ambassador to Scotland.

About 1600 the Queen's Lutheran chaplain, Dr Sering, had decided to leave the Lutheran faith and join the Presbyterians. This probably further inclined Queen Anne to Catholicism, as, not without cause, she detested the Kirk of Scotland and its ministers.[5] It so happened that about this time her friend Henrietta Stuart, Countess of Huntley, was recommending Father Abercromby to the Queen as her spiritual adviser and about 1600 or perhaps earlier he received her, with the utmost secrecy, into the Catholic Church.[6] As Father Abercromby wrote:

I was summoned to her and conducted to the palace where I was concealed during the day in a private closet. Every morning she paid me a visit for the purpose of instruction, her ladies meanwhile remaining in the ante-chamber. She made a show of repairing to this room as if to write letters; and in order to deceive the ladies, returned with the papers in her hand. Not until she had on the third day, heard mass and received the Holy Communion did I abandon my hiding place.[7]

In the summer of 1601 she answered, on her husband's behalf, a letter Pope Clement VIII had sent to King James, in which she assured the Pope of her devotion to the Catholic Church. In reply Clement expressed his pleasure at her conversion, and hoped that King James would also join the Catholic Church and that Prince Henry would be educated in the Catholic faith.[8]

While they were King and Queen of Scotland, King James had no objection to Anne's Catholic sympathies. Indeed, he cleverly exploited it for his own advantage. It enabled him to gain the support of the Catholic peers and so play them off against the

Protestants and prevent either party becoming predominantly powerful. But James was careful to keep his support of the Catholic lords a closely guarded secret, for had Queen Elizabeth heard a whisper of what was going on, his hopes of succeeding to the throne of England would have been seriously damaged.

When James became King of England his wife's religion assumed a very different aspect. Anne's refusal to take the sacrament according to the Church of England at the coronation service was seen by many people and caused much unfavourable comment. When later she became an eager advocate of a Spanish bride for Prince Henry, both King James and Robert Cecil were seriously annoyed.

Yet Anne was most careful not to allow her religion to interfere with her husband's policy in any way. In public she attended Church of England services with her husband, but in 'private she observed the Catholic rule'.[9] When Father Abercromby accompanied her to England as her confessor, and said Mass for her in her private chapel, elaborate precautions were taken that he should remain unnoticed in the background. Above all, the Queen was careful never to intervene in Catholic underground movements after she came to England, and she left the religious education of her children entirely to her husband's decision.

Yet in spite of these precautions it was not long before Anne was involved in further trouble with her husband and the Council. Cecil undoubtedly did his best to discredit the Queen in King James's mind and to foment the trouble.[10] Early in 1604 Pope Clement sent Queen Anne a present of a rosary and a small cross, which were delivered by Sir Anthony Standen, the English ambassador in Rome, together with a message that he held her in special regard on account of her piety and profession of the Catholic faith, and hoping that she would strive by all means to bring about the conversion of her husband.[11]

It was the last part of the message which inflamed King James. Standen was arrested on a charge of corresponding with Father Persons and sent to prison, and the Queen's position was seriously compromised. In desperation Anne pretended to be annoyed by the gifts, although earlier she had welcomed presents sent by the Pope. Gradually the scandal died down and Anne was able to intercede for the unfortunate Standen and secure his release from prison.[12]

Once again in the late spring of 1606 Queen Anne retired to the peaceful surroundings of Greenwich Palace to await the birth of her seventh child. Little Mary's health continued to cause anxiety, as she had sudden rises in temperature for which the doctors could not account. On Sunday, 22 June, a daughter was born who was christened Sophia, after the Queen's mother, Sophia of Mecklenberg. Unfortunately baby Sophia was so weakly that a clergyman was hastily summoned to baptise her.[13] She only lived a few hours; and three days later a barge draped in black velvet and escorted by three other black barges bore the tiny body to Westminster Abbey for burial.

One of the most pathetic tombs in the Abbey is Maximilian Colt's monument to Princess Sophia, showing her asleep in an alabaster cradle. The Latin inscription describes her as:

Sophia, a royal rosebud, untimely plucked to death; . . .
Torn from her parents to bloom afresh in the rose garden of Christ.[14]

The death of baby Sophia had a decisive influence on Queen Anne's life. Her health was being ruined by frequent confinements; after Sophia's birth she was so ill that her life was in danger. Although Anne was only thirty-two, she had given birth to seven weakly children and had three or more miscarriages. For years Anne had seen as little of her husband as possible, and now she decided to have no more children. This undoubtedly widened the gulf between them. Henceforth they kept separate Courts, only appearing together on state occasions and for the Christmas festivities.

This decision of Queen Anne's became still more final when in August 1607 her daughter Mary developed a violent fever which lasted twenty-three days. Strangely enough, neither her father, nor her mother came to see her during her illness; James perhaps for fear of infection, but Queen Anne's absence is more difficult to fathom. The child died on 16 September and in the funeral sermon Chaplain Leach gave some details of her last hours.

For the space of twelve or fourteen hours at the least, there was no sound of any word heard, breaking from her lips; yet . . . she sighed out these words, I go, I go, . . . again she repeated, away I go. . . . The more strange did this appear to us that heard it, in that it was almost incredible that so much vigour should remain in so weak a body.[15]

King James sent Robert Cecil, now Earl of Salisbury, to convey his condolences to the Queen. The Earl reported that 'since it was irrevocable, she and the King digested it very well and wisely'. Perhaps Anne's grief was less intense because she had seldom seen Mary since she was born, or it might be that Cecil was strangely imperceptive. Her spirits were not raised by a visit from the jesuit Richard Blount upbraiding her for having had Mary baptised by Protestant rites. In any case, Anne insisted on an autopsy, 'being extremely anxious to know the certain cause of her death'.[16] This was carried out at Stanwell, where Princess Mary had lived, and she was buried in Henry VII's chapel in Westminster Abbey beside her baby sister Sophia. On her monument Maximilian Colt showed her resting on her left arm, wearing a full skirt, a stomacher and an elegant French cap.

Queen Anne's year had now settled into a regular pattern. Christmas and the New Year were spent in Whitehall, for the traditional festivities. In the spring she preferred to stay at Greenwich, Oatlands or Hampton Court. Of all these royal palaces Hampton Court was her favourite residence.

It was within easy reach of London and the Queen liked the lofty rooms, hung with tapestries of golden silk, the great hall with its superb hammer-beam roof, the majestic staircase and Long Gallery. There was the knot garden on which she could look down from her first-floor windows and the amazing astronomical clock in the main courtyard, placed there by Henry VIII in 1540.

In summer Anne usually made a progress in southern England or in the West Country; September was spent at Hampton Court and in October Anne moved to Greenwich, where she believed the milder air would benefit her arthritis.

In the sixteen years that had passed since Anne had seen her brother Christian he had married Anna Catherine of Brandenburg and become the father of a son. He showed promise of becoming the greatest king Denmark had ever known. For Christian had the vision and inexhaustible vitality necessary to make his dreams come true, in addition to which he had a passionate love for his country and a high sense of duty.

When Christian came to the throne he found Denmark poor and almost friendlesss, lacking trade and shipping, with only a small ill-equipped army. One of his most urgent tasks was to stimulate trade by abolishing the oppressive privileges of the Hanseatic League; he also determined to capture the herring trade. Another wise step the King took was to induce expert Dutch horticulturists to settle on the island of Amager[17] so that they could teach the Danes market gardening and help to supply Copenhagen with much-needed vegetables.

When Queen Anne heard that her brother Christian proposed to visit England she was delighted. Fortunately the North Sea held no terrors for him. From boyhood he had been deeply interested in ships; when only nine years old he had filled a sketchbook with drawings of sailing ships. Now he resolved to build a navy which should make Denmark a naval power to be feared. His flagship, the *Three Crowns,* in which he sailed to England, was one of the largest warships of the period and with its seventy-two guns was one of the most heavily armoured in the world, while the costly fittings, fine woodwork and gilded decor made it a delight to the eye.

Like his sister Anne, Christian was interested in building. Of course, he had resources far wider than hers and in his lifetime he transformed Copenhagen from a small walled town of narrow streets into one of the most elegant capitals of Europe. He stamped his genius on its silhouette. Dutch architects were brought in to modernise the fortifications and Flemings to rebuild. Copenhagen. As early as 1602 Christian began to transform his birthplace, Frederiksborg Castle, which in his father's time had been a simple hunting lodge with cramped and old-fashioned rooms, by pulling down the old house and building a romantic three-winged castle, whose walls were mirrored in the lake. The skyline of Copenhagen was beautified by the building of the Exchange with its graceful spire of intertwined dragons' tails, Holmen's church, the tower of St Nicholas Church and, in Christian's old age, Rosenborg Castle—but that lay far in the future.

On that July day in 1606 when King Christian sailed up the Thames to Tilbury in the *Three Crowns*, with his escort of seven warships, Queen Anne, feeble and depressed after the birth of her seventh child, felt a surge of new life. Her brother had come at last after so many hopes deferred. As long ago as June 1597 King Christian had assured his sister 'he would be with her shortly in the next good wind', and begged her to get him lodgings in Killough's house in Holyrood. But Christian had never come. Now nine years later he had said once again that he was coming, but in May there were reports that he was dead—reports so circumstantial that for a week Queen Anne and her ladies went into mourning for him. Even when the rumour had proved to be untrue, there was delay after delay.

Although King Christian went on board his flagship on 12 June, more than a month passed before he landed at Gravesend, owing to unfavourable winds. Unlike his brother Ulric, who had come to England with such a slender retinue that the English concluded that he must be very poor, King Christian arrived in considerable state,

with a gallant fleet appointed with huge ordnance, men and victuals. The courtiers, according to their country's fashion, were richly decked in silk with chains of rare estimation. The pages and guards of blue velvet laid with silver lace for their best suits. The trumpeters were in white satin doublets and velvet hose. The common soldiers were all in cassocks and hose of watchet colour.[18]

King James and Prince Henry were waiting in a royal barge to welcome their visitor and row up the Thames with him to Greenwich. There Christian rushed into the palace, bounded up the stairs to his sister's bedroom, where Anne was slowly regaining her strength, and clasped her in a warm embrace. With his golden hair and beard, deep-set eyes and weather-beaten face, the Danish King appeared a true descendant of the Vikings. A contemporary saw him as 'a man of goodly person in stature of no extremes, in face so like his sister that he who hath seen the one may paint in his fancy the other'.[19] There was something dynamic about Christian; he had such a great zest for life, and such an inexhaustible store of energy. Above all he had the moral strength to rise above disaster. Again and again in his long life Christian was to show his greatness in hours of crisis when all seemed lost.

His enthusiasm infected Queen Anne and gave her the desire to live. The intolerable weight of depression vanished. With her brother she held long conversations in which she learnt the latest news of her mother Queen Sophia who, indomitable as ever in her retirement at Nykøbing, was running her estate with growing efficiency. She was becoming a well-known breeder of horses and Anne seized the opportunity to send her mother a present of some fine bloodstock, gaily caparisoned.

King Christian gave himself no rest. He entered wholeheartedly into all the entertainment prepared for him; playing tennis, running the ring in the tiltyard, jousting, hunting and hawking until King James was worn out. He thoroughly enjoyed his state ride through London, pausing on the way at Somerset House, where Queen Anne held her Court, which in honour of King Christian's visit was renamed Denmark House.[20]

Next day, escorted by King James, the Danish King visited the Tower, where he was shown the coronation robes, the crown jewels and the mint; then to St Paul's, where Christian climbed the steeple,[21] and finally to Westminster Abbey, where the royal tombs had been cleaned in his honour and Queen Elizabeth's funeral effigy redressed in royal garments.

Queen Anne was no more sympathetic to the sufferings of animals than most of her contemporaries. She went to see bear baiting and bull baiting, and when a display of bear baiting was laid on in the Tower to entertain King Christian she not only accompanied her husband and brother but took her three young children with her. It was a very special occasion, as the bear had killed a child which had 'accidently been left in the bear-house'.

How the boy came to be left by accident in such a place had never been satisfactorily explained. King James consoled the bereaved mother with a gift of £20, although a stern reprimand for gross negligence in the care of her child would seem to have been fitting. He sentenced the bear to death. The executioner was to be a large ferocious lion, but when the two animals met they simply looked at one another and turned away. So two mastiffs were released which attacked the bear with little effect. Then six more dogs were sent into the arena, which mangled the bear but did not kill it. Finally a young lion and lioness were loosed to administer the *coup de grâce*, but they took one look at the struggling dogs and bolted back into their den, as did the first lion, one of the dogs accompanying him, and when later an attendant peered into the den he found them both curled up fast asleep. Even then King James's sporting instincts were not sated. He ordered the bear to be publicly baited in ten days' time.

The Danes were reputed to be heavy drinkers. Before disembarking King Christian warned his ship's officers and courtiers to be abstemious while they were in England. Alas for his good intentions! Far from curbing their drunken ways, once ashore his words were soon forgotten, and they infected the English. As Sir John Harington ruefully remarked, 'I think the Dane hath strangely wrought in our good English nobles; for those whom I never could get to taste good liquor, now follow the fashion, and wallow in beastly delights. The ladies abandon their sobriety and are seen to roll about in intoxication.'[22]

The deterioration in the decorum of the Court was seen when King Christian and King James went deer shooting at Theobalds. Queen Anne did not go with them. Perhaps it was as well, for in her absence the revels degenerated into scenes of unparalleled licence.

The sports began each day in such manner and such sort, as well nigh persuaded me of Mahomet's paradise. We had women, and indeed wine too, of such plenty, as would have astonished each sober beholder. Our feasts were magnificent and the two royal guests did most lovingly embrace each other at table.

Worse was to follow.

One day, a great feast was held, and after dinner, the representation of Solomon, his temple and the coming of the Queen of Sheba was made, or (as I may better say) was meant to have been made, before their Majesties, by device of the Earl of Salisbury and others. But alas, as all earthly things do fail to poor mortals in enjoyment, so did prove our presentment thereof. The lady who did play the Queen's part, did carry most previous gifts to both their Majesties; but forgetting the steps araising to the canopy, overset her caskets into his Danish Majesty's lap and fell at his feet though I rather think it was in his face. Much was the hurry and confusion; cloths and napkins were at hand, to make all clean. His Majesty then got up and would dance with the Queen of Sheba; but he fell down and humbled himself before her, and was carried to an inner chamber and laid on a bed of state; which was not a little defiled with the presents of the Queen, which had been bestowed on his garments, such as wine, cream, jelly, beverage, cakes, spices and other good matters.[23]

Clearly Queen Anne's restraining influence was sorely needed at Court.

King Christian's object in coming to England had been to try to persuade King James to join a union of Protestant princes, and as his visit was drawing to a close he felt a deep sense of disappointment at his lack of success. Otherwise he was delighted with all he had seen. Perhaps what gave him the keenest pleasure was his nephew Henry, who was so like his mother that an artist could have used one as the model for the other. He appreciated the boy's interest in ships and seamen, the elegance and grace with which he danced, his courteous manners and his aptitude in all manly sports. He must have wished that he could have had such a son, for his marriage with Anne Catherine was not turning out at all well. She was too colourless and apathetic to be the wife of such a forceful man.

On 10 August 1606 Queen Anne with her brother, husband and elder son went aboard the royal barge and they were rowed down the river to Rochester to attend a service in the cathedral. Then the party went to Chatham to watch 'the proud and glorious sight of the English fleet flying all its standards and pennants'. Two thousand three hundred shots were fired as the royal barge sailed slowly along the fleet, which so delighted King Christian, who liked noise, that he waved his hat and shouted for joy. After reviewing the fleet, the royal party went on board the *Elizabeth Jonas,* which was moored alongside a pontoon bridge. There a farewell banquet was served in the saloon, whose walls were covered with cloth of gold and which was 'perfumed with sweet and pleasant perfume'. Such colossal steaks were served that King Christian expressed his wonder that so much meat could have been brought aboard a ship.[24]

Next day it was the turn of King Christian to play host and Queen Anne with King James and Prince Henry and their attendant courtiers went on board the Danish flagship, the *Three Crowns*, at Gravesend to say good-bye to their guest. King Christian, who was always reckless with money, began to distribute farewell gifts with a prodigal hand. He had already given the English courtiers presents of money, and the gentlemen of the bedchamber received a jewel apiece. For his relations there were more imaginative gifts. He presented King James with a copper cannon embossed with the arms of England, which had been specially cast for him in Halsingborg. Prince Henry's present was even more munificent. Knowing his nephew's passionate interest in ships, Christian handed over to him a Danish warship, fully equipped with armaments 'valued at £25,000 and with quarter galleries and a forecastle such as no English vessel had'. There still remained his sister, and taking Queen Anne by the hand he led her to his private cabin, where he kissed her and gave her his portrait set in diamonds.

As part of the farewell entertainment King Christian had arranged an elaborate firework display, but King James insisted that he must catch the tide at four o'clock to return to Greenwich. So the fireworks had to be let off in broad daylight and the set piece of the English lion holding a chain to which were fastened the Seven Deadly Sins lost much of its significance.

King Christian's visit did not end without involving Queen Anne in fresh trouble. This time at least no one could accuse her of being indiscreet. One of the guests on board was the Lord High Admiral, the Earl of Nottingham. While Queen Anne was standing on deck she noticed he was having a heated argument with her brother. The hero of the Spanish Armada had become a tiresome old man who was both fussy and opinionated. He was trying to tell King Christian that it was time for the royal party to leave the ship. As it was only two o'clock and high tide was not until four, there seemed to be no desperate hurry. Nottingham could speak no Danish and King Christian, who knew very little English, was bewildered to know what all the fuss was about. Queen Anne went up to them and explained to her brother what the Admiral wanted, whereupon King Christian took his watch out of his pocket, pointed to show it was only two o'clock and held up two fingers to his forehead like a pair of horns. Both he and the Queen broke into peals of laughter.[25]

The Lord Admiral was furious. He was very sensitive about his marriage to a lady young enough to be his granddaughter, and he thought King Christian was mocking him by using his fingers to make a cuckold's horns. When the Countess of Nottingham heard what had happened on the *Three Crowns* she was even less amused. In a furious temper she wrote to King Christian's secretary, saying:

It is reported to me, by men of honour the great wrong the king of the Danes hath done me when I was not by to answer by myself; for if I had been present I would have letten him know how much I scorn to receive that wrong at his hands. I need not write the particulars of it, for the King himself knoweth best. I protest to you, sir, I did think as honourably of the King, your Master, as I did of any one prince, but now I persuade myself there is as much baseness in him as can be in any man; for although he be a prince by birth, it seems not to me that there harboureth any princely thoughts in his breast, for either in prince or subject it is the basest part that can be to wrong any woman of honour. . . . So leaving to trouble you any farther, I rest your friend

MARGARET NOTTINGHAM.[26]

King Christian was so angry when he saw the letter that his first impulse was to return immediately to England to refute the charge. He insisted that 'he never thought of making any signs to insult the Lord Admiral; all he wished him to understand was that it was only two o'clock, as he might see by the watch he held in his other hand, and that he ought not to be deprived of his sister so soon'.

This explanation did not put an end to Lady Nottingham's outraged feelings. To Queen Anne's intense annoyance the Lord Admiral brought his wife by the privy way to the Queen's private apartments. When she reproached him for this intrusion on her privacy, 'the Admiral answered with haughty language which the Queen takes ill'.[27] Anne was so angry that she went to the King and, kneeling, implored him to banish Lady Nottingham from the Court. She had long disliked Lady Nottingham and the Countess returned the dislike with added interest, for she suspected Anne of being one of the prime movers in the ribald gossip which had centred round her engagement to the Lord Admiral.

King James was deeply annoyed at being dragged into a

quarrel which did not concern him and as usual the brunt of his anger fell on his wife. Lady Nottingham had married into the Howard family, who formed an all-powerful triumvirate in the early years of his reign, and he had no wish to offend any member of it, but he was even more anxious not to estrange his powerful brother-in-law, the King of Denmark, from whom he hoped to get substantial trade concessions. Much to his relief, the tension died down and the ladies' indignation smouldered away.

This did not end the repercussions from the King of Denmark's visit; another arose, fortunately over a minor matter, to trouble Queen Anne. In a letter to his sister in March 1607 Christian asked her to send one of Lady Arabella Stuart's servants to him in Denmark who could play the lute. The King was fond of music and had brought his own band with him when he came to England the previous year. He must have heard and appreciated Thomas Cutting's skill in playing the lute. The request placed Queen Anne in an awkward dilemma. The last thing she wanted to do was to refuse her brother's request, but she had always found Lady Arabella a discordant element at court and the two ladies were not on the best of terms. So in some trepidation she wrote:

Well beloved cousin

We greet you heartily well. Our dear brother's, the King of Denmark's gentleman servant hath insisted with us for the licensing your servant Thomas Cutting to depart from you but not without your permission to our brother's service and therefore I write these few lines unto you, being assured you will make no difficulty to satisfy our pleasure and our dear brother's desires and so giving you the assurance of our constant favours with our wishes for the continuance and convalescence of your health, expecting your return as we commit your Highness to the protection of God.

ANNA R.[28]

From Whitehall. 9 March 1607.

Queen Anne was by no means certain that her request would meet with success. Lady Arabella, who was very self-centred, had no reason for wishing to do the King of Denmark a favour, and as skilful lute players were much in demand she might find it very difficult to replace Thomas Cutting if she parted with him. So Queen Anne decided to enlist the aid of her thirteen-year-old son. She knew that Arabella was very fond of Henry and at his mother's bidding Henry dutifully wrote to his cousin:

Madam

The Queen's Majesty hath commanded me to signify to your Ladyship that she would have Cutting, your Ladyships' servant, to send to the King of Denmark because he desired the Queen that she should send him one that could play upon the lute. I pray your Ladyship so to send him back with an answer as soon as your Ladyship can. I desire you to commend me to my Lord and Lady of Shrewsbury,[29] *also not to bethink me anything the worse scrivener that I write so ill, but to suspend your judgement until you come hither, then you shall find me as I ever was.*

Your Ladyship's cousin and assured friend

HENRY[30]

In due time a reply came from Arabella granting his request, although she clearly was sorry to part with a favourite musician. Arabella knew she dare not risk offending King James or she might lose the income he allowed her. To Henry she wrote from Sheffield on 15 May: 'Although I may have some cause to be sorry to have lost the contentment of a good lute, yet must I confess that I am right glad to have found any occasion whereby to express to her Majesty and your Highness the humble respect which I owe you.'[31] These were diplomatic words, but it is to be doubted whether Lady Arabella's feelings towards Queen Anne were any more cordial after this episode.

II

THE QUEEN'S MASQUES 1604-1612

Queen Anne was an enthusiastic patron of the theatre. She liked the colour, tension and movement of a play. So when the Tudor fashion for companies of boy players was revived Queen Anne gave her patronage in 1604 to a company of boys who were known as the Children of the Queen's Revels. They started in a small way, giving their performances in a private house in Blackfriars, and their plays were decidedly crude, as they were not censored by the Master of the Revels. In spite of their coarseness, Queen Anne enjoyed the boys' acting and laughed loudly at pointed jokes aimed at her husband.[1] But in 1605 the boys went too far. They fell into disgrace for producing a satire on Scotland and her inhabitants entitled *Eastward Ho*. King James failed to see the humour and greatly against her will Queen Anne was made to cease to be their patron and the company was known in future as Children of the Revels.

When another form of entertainment—the masque—became popular the King and Queen found it even more to their taste. For by the combination of dancing, music, drama and pageantry, the masque became 'the supreme artistic expression of the Jacobean Court'.[2]

Queen Anne had instinctive good taste and what was even more important she could recognise genius when she saw it. The part she played in promoting the fortunes of Ben Jonson and Inigo Jones has never been sufficiently recognised. The open-air performance of Jonson's masque *Satyr*,[3] given in her honour at

Althorp in 1603, had already roused her interest. About the same time her attention was drawn to a young painter and decorative artist who had learnt in Italy from the Medici how to stage spectacles of a richness and beauty hitherto unknown in England. The Queen called upon him to cooperate in producing a masque for her at Whitehall for her second Christmas in England. It was not altogether a happy partnership, as the two men were insanely jealous of one another but from the artistic point of view it was a brilliant success. Jonson's script was outstanding. For the first time he brought 'unity of incident, theme and mood'[4] hitherto unknown in masques, while Inigo Jones added all he had learnt at the Court of Ferdinand I from the masques staged in Pitti Palace and the Palazzo Vecchio in Florence. Moreover, Inigo had a genius for devising scenic effects and in the *Masque of Blackness*, the first he and Ben Jonson produced together, he introduced such hitherto unknown devices as thundering waves and the moon shining upon a lake.

Above all, Inigo Jones was an innovator. He did away with the odd bits of scenery which had cluttered the hall and set it on the stage within a proscenium arch hidden behind a painted curtain until it was time for the performance to begin. He paid great attention to the costumes, making detailed drawings of those of the principal actors. Four hundred and fifty of these drawings can be seen at Chatsworth.[5] With two such craftsmen at her service, Queen Anne's masques reached a standard never seen in England before or since.

The *Masque of Blackness* was a superb spectacle, as a great float, scallop-shaped like a mother-of-pearl shell, came into view drawn by seahorses, rising and falling with the waves. In the centre sat Queen Anne as Euphoria, her corsage blazing with jewels, and beside her the lively Lady Bedford and around them other ladies of the Court with blackened arms and faces as tributaries of the River Niger. Beside the float swam six sea monsters with twelve torch-bearers on their backs.

It was a magnificent sight. Queen Anne hoped to show her English subjects that she could be as regal as Queen Elizabeth and yet at the same time unconventional and *avant-garde*. Never did she make a greater mistake. In spite of the brilliance of the *Masque of Blackness*, it was disastrous for her reputation, for it damaged the public image she was trying to establish. When the Queen and her ladies appeared in scanty attire, with blackened arms and faces, many of the spectators were deeply shocked. As Sir Dudley Carleton told his friend Winwood:

Their apparel was rich but too light and courtesanlike for such great ones. Instead of vizzards their faces and arms up to the elbows were painted black, which was disguise sufficient, for they were hard to be known; but it became them nothing so well as their red and white, and you can not imagine a more ugly sight than a troop of lean-cheeked Moors.[6]

He returned to the subject in a letter written a few hours later to his friend John Chamberlain, commenting 'it was a very loathsome sight' and adding 'he was sorry that strangers should see our court so strangely disguised'.[7]

When the masque ended the Queen and her ladies left the scallop shell and advanced in pairs to choose partners for the dance, waving their fans on which were painted their names and symbols. The Queen danced with the Spanish ambassador, who gallantly bent down to kiss her hand 'though there was danger it would have left a mark upon his lips'.

The evening did not pass without its contretemps. Many ladies never succeeded in getting into the banqueting hall at all, as the narrow passages were choked with guests "who were shut up in several heaps betwixt doors and stayed there till all was ended", but they were more fortunate than those other ladies who had their chains, jewels and purses stolen during the performance as had happened also the year before during the Earl of Montgomery's wedding masque. Manners at public gatherings may leave much to be desired today, but they were worse in Jacobean times. At the banquet which followed there was such a stampede that the table and trestles collapsed 'before one bit was touched'. To add to the calamities the French ambassador, M.

Beaumont,[8] was deeply affronted because he was not invited to the masque, and he had reason to believe that the Spanish ambassador had received a formal invitation. His fears were well founded.[9] Both the Spanish and Venetian ambassadors were there sitting in state beside the King.

On 5 January 1606 no fewer than three masques were staged in the banqueting house in Whitehall in honour of the marriage of Robert Devereux, third Earl of Essex, and Frances Howard, daughter of the Earl of Suffolk. The bridegroom was only fourteen and the bride a year younger. Ben Jonson and Inigo Jones again cooperated in two of the masques. One, the *Masque of Hymen,* was performed on the wedding night. It was a double masque of eight men and eight women. When the curtain went up an altar to Hymen and a great globe of the earth were to be seen, and Juno's priest proclaimed that a bride and bridegroom should be sacrificed to nuptial vision. Before the sacrifice took place the globe opened revealing the men masquers in a grotto, while eight women masquers stepped down from the clouds.[10] Then they did a series of dances 'all notably different, some of them formed into letters very signifying to the name of the bridegroom'. The masque ended with a bridal procession. Sad to relate, the spectators found the lines very long and boring and the whole spectacle extremely tedious. The other masque, *Barriers,* was more lively, for Truth set out to show that the joys of marriage exceeded those of single life.

King James took an interest in masques. He had even tried his hand at writing one himself. He grudged no expense or trouble to make them a success; he even sent to Royston, where he had bought Royston Priory as a hunting box two years before, to order herons' feathers to be sent to Whitehall to adorn the ladies' head-dresses. The masquers glittered with jewels,[11] as every precious stone in the City had been hired for the night.

Queen Anne, however, remained quietly in the background. taking no part in any of the three masques. She had no desire to bring further unfavourable comments on her head. The lesson of the *Masque of Blackness* still rankled bitterly.

These were the last masques held in the old banqueting hall in Whitehall. It was a temporary building of fir and deal which had been erected in Queen Elizabeth's reign when the duke of Alençon's ambassador was expected in 1581. It was far from being the kind of hall James I desired. Even the fact that birds could be heard singing out of doors during the masques did not reconcile him to it. So he had it pulled down in 1606, and the new hall built of brick and stone was completed by Christmas 1609.[12] James told the Venetian ambassador 'he intended this function to consecrate the birth of the Great Hall which his predecessors had left him built merely in wood but which he had converted into stone'.[13] James little knew how shortlived his pride in this new hall was to be, for it was destroyed by fire in 1619.[14]

It was not until 1608 that Queen Anne ventured again to present a masque of her own. This was the *Masque of Beauty* by Ben Jonson. It should have been presented on Twelfth Night in the very new banqueting house at Whitehall, where James complained that 'he could scarce see by reason of certain pillars which are set up before the windows',[15] but it had to be postponed until 10 January because once again the French ambassador was giving trouble. This time he was M. de la Borderie, who was furious because the Spanish and Venetian ambassadors had been invited to the masque and he had not received an invitation. He declared this was the personal act of Queen Anne, and recalled that he had been previously slighted during King Christian's visit and that Henri IV would hold King James responsible. This alarmed the English King and a few days later M. de la Borderie and the Venetian ambassador were invited to dine privately with the King and Queen, but this was a poor substitute for seeing them dine in public and watching the masque. So M. de la Borderie rudely declared that he should have been invited to the masque or that none of the ambassadors should have been asked. Moreover, he hinted that if Queen Anne continued to show her Spanish preferences so openly, King Henri might withdraw his ambassador.

This threat so alarmed the Council that they considered cancelling the performance of the masque, but in the end they decided that it should be staged. James, for his part, was so angry with his wife that he left for Royston next day without speaking to her.[16]

When the *Masque of Beauty* was staged on 10 January the River Niger was again the centrepiece As the curtain went up the sixteen daughters of Niger were seen on a throne, carried on a floating island. It was a dazzling sight, with the daughters of Niger in their orange and silver and green and silver dresses. According to the Venetian ambassador, the stage machinery was a miracle, 'The abundance and beauty of its lights immense, the music and the dance most sumptuous.'[17] John Chamberlain, the gossip-loving, middle-aged bachelor, told his friend Dudley Carleton: 'You should have been sure to have seen great riches in jewels, when one lady and that under a baroness is said to be furnished for better than an hundred thousand pounds and the Lady Arbella goes beyond her and the Queen must not come behind.'[18] The Venetian ambassador confirmed this, saying: 'The Queen wore a wealth of pearl and jewels which eclipsed all others.'

The daughters of the Niger danced four set dances, two of which were encored by King James, in addition to galliardes and corantoes, before returning to their throne. For Queen Anne the height of the evening was the *Queen's Masque*, which she danced with her ladies. Amongst these were Lady Arabella Stuart, Lady Anne Clifford, Lady Walsingham and Lady Hatton, but Lady Nottingham's name is significently absent. It was in some measure a consolation prize for Lady Hatton, as she had not been included in the *Masque of Blackness*, for some reason unknown, much to her annoyance.

Everything went so smoothly that the Venetian ambassador remarked: 'So well composed and ordered was it all that it is evident the mind of her Majesty, the authoress of the whole, is gifted no less highly than her person.'[19]

This was followed in 1609 by another of Queen Anne's masques, the *Masque of Queens*, in which she appeared as Bel-Anna, Queen of the Ocean. Once again Ben Jonson was called in to write the verse. Now the masques were becoming more and more elaborate, and this time an antimasque was introduced with a separate company of maskers in which a dance of witches opened the performance. Naturally this added greatly to the expense. In fact, it was estimated that the *Masque of Queens* cost nearly £5,000.

The masque was staged on Candlemas Day, 2 February 1609, in the new banqueting house at Whitehall. The curtain went up to show Hell with smoke rising to the top of the roof, from which eleven witches, some with rats on their heads, and their dame Ate emerged 'to hollow and infernal music'.[20] The witches danced until suddenly there was a blast of music and they vanished. Instead of Hell the scene changed to the House of Fame, which showed Perseus and twelve masquers seated in the form of a pyramid. After two ceremonial dances they 'took out the men and danced the measures' for nearly an hour. In the third dance they formed the letters of Charles, Duke of York.[21] Then came the *Queen's Masque*, danced by Queen Anne and the Countesses of Arundel, Bedford, Derby, Huntingdon, Essex and Montgomery and four maids of honour. Inigo Jones surpassed himself in the ingenuity of his stage effects and the elaboration of his architecture, besides designing the dresses of the witches.

To avoid trouble with the French ambassador, the masque was postponed from Twelfth Night until Candlemas in the hope that the Spanish ambassador extraordinary[22] would have returned to Spain. Although Anne's Spanish sympathies were as pronounced as ever, she resolved to be tactful and to treat M. de la Borderie with courtesy. For as John Chamberlain noted, 'the French ambassador hath been so long and so much neglected that it is doubted more would not be well endured.'[23] So M. de la Borderie was invited to the masque, and when he would not dance himself, Queen Anne allowed his daughter to take as her partner eight-year-old Prince Charles.

As part of the celebrations in honour of the investiture of Prince Henry as Prince of Wales in June 1610 an even more resplendent masque called *Tethys Festival* was produced. It was the gayest, prettiest sight imaginable, with Tethys and thirteen river nymphs dressed in sky blue and silver cloth. The libretto was written by Samuel Daniel, who now enjoyed the patronage of the Earl of Pembroke whose tutor he had been at Wilton in 1590. Inigo Jones was again responsible for the stage effects and the décor. Queen Anne had asked Daniel to devise something original for the antimasque and he did this by introducing young children. The chief figure in the antimasque was Prince Charles, who, dressed in green satin with wings of silver lawn, was Zephyrus, while eight little girls, the daughters of earls and barons, danced round him as he approached his mother, who handed him gifts to present to his father and brother.[24] These were a trident for King James and a sword studded with jewels for Prince Henry, as well as a scarf embroidered by Queen Anne herself.

Then the main masque followed in which Queen Anne appeared as Tethys, the daughter of Uranus, seated on a throne, and out of caverns came the river nymphs. Princess Elizabeth, taking part in a masque for the first time, was the Nymph of the Thames, while Lady Arabella Stuart was the Nymph of the Trent. This was the last of Arabella's appearances at Court, as soon after she fell into disgrace by making a secret marriage with William Seymour, Earl of Hertford, for which she was sent to the Tower.

Other ladies in the masque were the lively Lady Anne Clifford, who had recently become Countess of Dorset, as the Nymph of Ayr, while the bewitching Lady Frances Howard, now Countess of Essex, was the Nymph of the Lea. Prince Charles knelt before his mother and begged her to come down from the stage and dance. Gladly she yielded to his pleas and danced a quadrille with the river maidens, who sang the charms of the river they represented.

The *Queen's Masque* was performed with great dignity. As Samuel Daniel remarked, 'there were none of inferior sort mixed among these great personages of state and honour (as usually there have been); but all was performed by themselves with a due reservation of their dignity'.[25] When the masque ended Prince

Charles came forward and led the Queen and her ladies back to their niches and caverns.

This time, happily, there were no diplomatic complications. Henri IV had just been assassinated, so the French ambassador was in deep mourning. The Spanish, Venetian and Dutch ambassadors were present; the Venetian, Correr, noted with satisfaction that the Dutch ambassador was given an inferior box.[26] As usual the masque was 'excessively costly'.

On New Year's Day 1611 Prince Henry produced his first masque *Oberon, the Fairy Prince.* Being a brilliant horseman, he wished to have the masquers mounted, which would certainly have produced the novel note so much desired by Queen Anne, but King James vetoed the idea. On 3 February Queen Anne had her own masque, *Love Freed from Ignorance and Folly.* Once again Ben Jonson wrote the script and Inigo Jones was responsible for the décor.

The masque was to have been produced on the night before Prince Henry's, but it was put off until Twelfth Night and finally until Candlemas, 'either because the stage machinery is not in order or because their Majesties thought it well to let the Marshal depart first'.[27] This was the French ambassador extraordinary, Marshal de Laverdin, whose coming was delayed by Marie de Medici, although King James, who was working to discourage the growing accord between France and Spain, wished to receive the Marshal with every honour and invited him to the masques.[28]

As usual Queen Anne played the chief role, appearing as the Queen of the Orient, while the ladies of the Court, whose names have not been preserved, were the eleven daughters of the Morning. In the antimasque which preceded it there were twelve She Follies and a new touch was introduced by a dance of twelve musicians who appeared as priests of the Muses.

This was the last masque Queen Anne initiated. With Prince Henry's untimely death in 1612 the mainspring of her life was broken and in future she left the devising of masques to others.

12

THE RISING FORTUNES OF ROBERT CARR

1607-1612

During a tournament at Whitehall Palace in 1607 an incident occurred which, though trivial in itself, was destined to have a profound effect upon the lives of King James and Queen Anne. The King was seated on a dais, and as the riders filed past, one bearing the shield and device of Lord Hay was thrown from his horse, just in front of where King James was seated. James leant forward to see if the rider was injured, and his interest quickened, for he saw lying upon the ground a fair-haired youth of exceptional beauty. At once he gave orders that one of his personal physicians should attend the injured youth, whose leg was broken, and that he should be taken to Master Rider's house in Charing Cross.[1] There the King paid him frequent visits.

Such solicitude must have surprised both Queen Anne and the members of his Court. Robert Carr was no stranger to the Queen. She had known him years before in Scotland as an incompetent Page of Honour to King James, who was dismissed for his clumsy ways in serving the King and his abysmal failure in saying grace in Latin. Although there is no evidence that Queen Anne was responsible for the dismissal of this inefficient page, Carr was convinced that it was the Queen's doing, and throughout his life he bore her a deep grudge.

After such utter failure, Carr's career seemed in ruins. Fortunately for Robert's future, his family, the Kerrs of Ferniehurst, sent him to France to acquire polish. He returned a much-improved young man; better spoken, better mannered and with sufficient sense to see that to retain the King's favour he must pander to his wishes, even when they ran contrary to his own.

With foreboding Queen Anne noticed how delighted King James was with his new discovery. He had grown tired of the reigning favourite, Philip Herbert, Earl of Montgomery, with his vacuous good looks and surly ways, so that even his addiction to hunting could no longer bind them together. Lord Hay with his senseless extravagance had become equally boring. In young Robert Carr the King found a fellow Scot who was not only better looking and better tempered but far more amenable to the royal will. Even when the King's daily Latin lessons proved a failure[2] because Carr had no aptitude for learning, James was not discouraged. Before long it was clear to Queen Anne and the whole Court that the King had found a new favourite.

As the months passed Robert Carr's power grew. King James was infatuated with him and before the end of 1607 had given him a rent charge of £600 a year and a gold tablet set in diamonds, in addition to making him a Gentleman of the Bedchamber[3] and conferring on him a knighthood. The courtiers noticed that the King could not bear Robert Carr out of his sight for any length of time. If King James delighted in young Robert's company, Queen Anne's feelings were very different. She had to endure the ignominy of seeing her husband embrace Carr in public, fondle him and plant moist kisses on his cheek.[4] Perhaps it may have been some small consolation to her that Carr must have found these royal attentions extremely trying, for as King James seldom washed, his embraces must have been overpowering, while the fact that he constantly dribbled made his kisses most distasteful.

King James's idea was to educate Carr in statecraft and train him to be one of his responsible ministers. But his efforts proved singularly unrewarding. His pupil was too empty-headed, and as the King continued to entrust more and more responsibility to Carr the youth found himself completely out of his depth. Then a stroke of good luck befell him. He met an old acquaintance of his days in Scotland, Thomas Overbury, and managed to enlist his help. Although they had no common interests, for Carr was an athlete and Overbury an Oxford graduate who had studied law and travelled on the Continent as well as being a poet, they had at least one thing in common—they were both overwhelmingly ambitious.

So Carr came to rely on his friend, not only in personal matters but as his political adviser. Thomas wrote his letters for him and drafted minutes to show to King James. Overbury believed that he had made himself indispensable.

With increasing power, Overbury's arrogance grew. A contemporary aptly described him as 'a very witty gentleman but truly insolent'.[5] Inevitably he made many enemies, amongst them the Queen. For if Queen Anne disliked Robert Carr, she detested Thomas Overbury. She found his dry, cold manner and insufferable air of superiority most distasteful. Several small incidents increased the ill feeling between them. In 1609, shortly after King James had appointed Overbury server to the King, Queen Anne was strolling with her husband in their private garden at Hampton Court when James, pointing to Overbury, said, 'Look at my new server', and Anne replied tartly, ''Tis a pretty fellow.'

Later in the summer of 1611, when the Queen was at Greenwich Palace, she happened to glance out of a window and saw Carr and Overbury walking together in the garden. She exclaimed in her loud voice, 'There go Carr and his governor', whereupon Overbury gave a loud laugh, which Anne took as a reflection on herself.

She was so enraged that she went to the King and, falling on her knees, begged him not to permit her to suffer such insults. If he would not protect her, she would go back to Denmark. James in great agitation cried, 'Ah, woe is me, my Queen will go from me', but did nothing. So next day she sent a message to Prince Henry, begging him to come to Greenwich to hear her cause for complaint.[6] Finding herself unable to undermine Carr's position, 'which of all things she desireth most in all the world',

Anne turned her attention to Overbury and demanded his banishment.

This time she appealed to Robert Cecil, Earl of Salisbury, by letter, saying:

My Lord

The King hath told me that he will advise with you and some other four or five of the Council of that fellow. I can say no more, either to make you understand the matter or my mind, than I said this other day. Only I recommend to your care how public the matter is now both in court and city and how far I have reason in that respect. I refer the rest to this bearer and myself to your love

ANNA R.[7]

'That fellow' was the Queen's contemptuous epithet for Overbury, who by now was thoroughly alarmed. In despair he also sought help from Salisbury:

My honourable Lord

As your Lordship was a judge of mine innocence before, so would I now crave that favour that your Lordship would vouchsafe to be a witness of the submission both of myself and cause to the Queen's mercy; which I desire you rather, because as I understand her Majesty is not fully satisfied of the integrity of my intent that way; and to that purpose if your lordship will grant me access and audience, I shall hold it as a great favour and ever rest

Your lordship's to be commanded

T. OVERBURY.[8]

London. 11 September.

With Salisbury's help, Carr and Overbury were able to persuade the King that they were laughing at a funny joke he had recently made and had not even heard the Queen's remark.[9] Queen Anne, however, remained unconvinced.

Robert Carr, Earl of Somerset. After J. Hoskins

Frances Howard, Countess of Somerset. Artist unknown

Queen Anne in mourning for Prince Henry, 1612.
Artist unknown

Prince Charles *circa* 1612. Artist unknown

For a time there was an armed truce between the Queen and Overbury, but the quarrel flared up again in January 1612, when Queen Anne, who was always in financial straits, asked King James to pay her debts by a promissory note under the Privy Seal. When Overbury heard of her request he was so unwise as to boast of the part he played. Queen Anne was furious at his presumption and she was even more annoyed when she found that Sir David Wood, who was indirectly attached to her household, had been obliged to pay Carr and Overbury £1,200 for getting the King's consent to his suit. So Overbury, foreseeing a period of imprisonment in the Tower, prudently retired to the Continent for five months.

As the years passed, so Robert Carr prospered. He became the most powerful subject in the country; indeed, it was whispered more powerful than the King himself. The only hope of gaining a concession or securing a place at Court was to approach the King through the favourite. Thomas Howard, writing to Sir John Harington, said: 'You must see Carr before you go to the King, as he was with him a boy in Scotland, and knoweth his taste and what pleaseth. Carr has all the favours, as I told you before.'[10] Sir Anthony Weldon described the scene at Court: 'Lord, how all the great men then flocked to see him, and to offer to his Shrine in such abundance that the King was forced to lay a restraint, lest it might retard his recovery by spending his spirits.'[11]

In spite of the hostility of Queen Anne and Prince Henry, King James's devotion to his favourite grew greater than ever. He showered gifts and honours upon young Robert. In January 1609 the King gave him Sir Walter Raleigh's Sherborne estate, which not only damaged Carr's image but also the King's, as Raleigh was looked upon by the nation as the last great representative of the glorious Elizabethan age.

The year 1611 saw the height of Robert Carr's glory. He was created Viscount Rochester and given Rochester Castle. In April he was made a Knight of the Garter. Queen Anne, never his friend, was further incensed when King James gave him a house in Scotland which he had already promised to bestow on the Queen's ally, the Chancellor of Scotland. Yet with the public Carr was very unpopular; they believed he was responsible for the forced loans, and for trying to negotiate a Spanish marriage for Prince Henry.

When Salisbury died in 1612 Carr's position seemed impregnable. The old statesman, gauging Carr's abilities, had tried to keep the major offices of state out of his grasp, and only during Cecil's last fatal illness did Carr become a Privy Councillor. With Cecil gone Carr became to all intents and purposes the King's private secretary, with suits of all kinds passing to him for judgment. Soon he was finding the work quite beyond his grasp. Thus he came to rely more and more on his friend Overbury, who, being extremely able, easily coped with these duties. So in the summer of 1612 all seemed set fair and Robert Carr appeared indestructible. Then from a cloudless sky came the bolt which two years later was to lead to his destruction. He fell in love with Frances Howard, Countess of Essex, that *femme fatale* whose evil influence cost Carr King James's favour, sent Overbury to his death and brought about the favourite's ruin.

Behind Lady Frances lay the massive power of the Howards. They formed a triumvirate, which in the early years of King James's reign practically ruled the country. There was Frances's father, Thomas Howard, second son of the fourth Duke of Norfolk (another Thomas, executed by Queen Elizabeth). He was a brave and competent sailor, but no statesman. A pompous man of weak moral fibre who, when temptation came, could not resist resorting to bribery and embezzlement. King James, on his accession, created Thomas Howard Earl of Suffolk.

The second member of the triumvirate was Lord Howard of Effingham, now Earl of Nottingham, who, living on past glories of the Armada, cherished a grievance that he had not been made a duke when he headed an embassy to Spain in 1605. In old age he had become slack and negligent, allowing himself to be duped by unscrupulous timber merchants and letting the Navy fall into a state of sad neglect.

The brains of the triumvirate was Lord Henry Howard, Earl of Northampton, second son of the poet Earl of Surrey. He was extremely able and astute, but utterly devoid of principles. A modern historian has called him probably the most dangerous man in England. His interests were wide, he built Audley End and studied astrology. It was through his machinations that Sir Walter Raleigh was languishing in the Tower. Northampton had no love for his country, only for himself, and he would stoop to any subterfuge to attain his ends. As a friend, as Cecil found, he proved untrustworthy and as an enemy he was capable of any treachery.

The head of the family, Thomas Earl of Arundel, took no part in politics. He was only a boy of seventeen when King James came to the throne and his kinsmen, Northampton, Nottingham and Suffolk, took over his estates. He was a scholar who loved art and architecture, and the long visits he paid to Italy, taking Inigo Jones with him, developed his taste. Unlike his kinsmen, he was a man of integrity and honour.

Frances Howard was the second daughter of the Earl of Suffolk by his second marriage to Katherine Knyvet. She was lovely, with golden hair, sparkling eyes and indescribable grace. As a girl of thirteen she married Robert Devereux, third Earl of Essex, son of Queen Elizabeth's ill-fated favourite. This was a marriage approved of by King James, just as was her elder sister's to the Earl of Salisbury's son. He hoped these alliances would lead to friendly relations with the Howards and put an end to feuds between the English nobility. Frances had an elfin charm which men found irresistible. It seemed impossible that such an exquisite being could harbour an unkind thought, yet Frances was wholly selfish, self-centred and utterly ruthless.[12] She would destroy anyone who stood in her way without the slightest compunction.

She showed this ruthlessness in her treatment of her husband, a stolid, dour young man.[13] They had a brilliant wedding at which the King and Queen were present, and after the ceremony Prince Henry danced with the bride. Then the fourteen-year-old bridegroom was sent abroad to finish his education while Frances led a gay life at Court under the nominal surveillance of her mother. The result was that when Robert Devereux returned home at Christmas 1609 it was to find that his wife would have nothing to do with him.

Nobody was more delighted than Lord Henry Howard, now Earl of Northampton, to see his great-niece's growing interest in the royal favourite. He knew that once married to Frances, Carr would be drawn into the Howard family orbit and his previous Protestant outlook forgotten, while he himself would become the virtual ruler of England. So he looked on blandly while Frances refused to live with her husband, filled him with drugs supplied by Dr Forman,[14] and finally sought the annulment of the marriage on the grounds that he was impotent.

Prince Henry saw the growing ascendancy of Carr in a very different light. He felt a deep dislike for the royal favourite, similar to that felt by Queen Anne. King James, on the other hand, was a wholehearted supporter of Lady Frances. He believed the lies she told him, used his influence to help her and favoured her suit for divorce.[15] Perhaps his inability to refuse Carr anything blinded him to the evil example he was setting.

Another person who shared Prince Henry's alarm and disapproval was Carr's friend and confidant, Sir Thomas Overbury, when he returned from his sojourn on the Continent. At first he did not take the matter seriously, believing it to be but another of Carr's amatory exploits. At this time he could probably have put an end to the entanglement, but his attention was distracted by his own love affair with the Countess of Rutland. When he awoke to the seriousness of the situation it was too late. From the first he had seen Lady Frances Howard in her true light, as a heartless, scheming, utterly selfish woman. Her beauty left him unmoved. He must have regretted that he had encouraged the liaison by writing Carr's love letters for him.[16]

In vain he sought interview after interview with Carr, warning him that marriage with Lady Frances would bring him to ruin, but his friend remained deaf to his pleading. Little though Overbury suspected it, the Howards were working hard to destroy him. Without Overbury, Carr could never transact the nation's business, with which King James entrusted him, and once Carr had gone the Howards would be undisputed masters of the State. Queen Anne approved of these tactics. No one was more determined to secure Carr's downfall than the Queen, but she recognised that he was too firmly entrenched in the King's favour for a direct attack to have any chance of success. The best way lay in alienating him from Overbury.

When Overbury learnt that Lady Essex was seeking a divorce, he awoke to the seriousness of the situation. He was prepared to go to any lengths to stop the case, even to revealing the lady's earlier indiscretions at Hounslow. Not unnaturally this infuriated Carr and from that moment the breach between the former friends was complete. King James, too, played a sinister part. In May 1613 he appointed a commission to hear the nullity suit and interfered when he found that the majority were opposed to granting a decree nisi. 'What a strange and fearful thing it was', said Archbishop Abbot, 'that his Majesty should be so far engaged in that business that he should profess that himself had set the matter in that course of judgment; that the judges should be dealt with beforehand and, in a sort, directed what they should determine.'[17]

James's dislike of Overbury was of long standing. The King, commented Chamberlain, 'hath long had a desire to remove him from about my Lord of Rochester, as thinking it a dishonour to him that the world should have an opinion that Rochester ruled him and Overbury ruleth Rochester'.[18] The King decided to get rid of Overbury by sending him abroad. This had to be done under a plausible pretext, so Lord Ellesmere and Lord Pembroke were sent to offer him the post of ambassador in the Low Countries, France or Muscovy, but owing to the advice of his false friend Carr, Overbury refused the offer in an off-hand, almost insolent way. As Sir Henry Wotton commented: 'Sir Thomas Overbury refused to be sent abroad with such terms as were by the Council interpreted pregnant of contempt in a case where the King had opened his will.'[19] The result was that on 21 April 1613 Overbury was committed to the Tower. There he was cut off from all contact with his family or friends, for five long months, gradually losing all hope, and with declining health as the poison sent to him in tarts and jellies by Lady Frances worked its will.

Overbury had been unwise in allowing his ambition to override his common sense. He believed that he was indispensable to Carr and so the highest offices of state were within his grasp. Even more foolishly he believed in Carr's integrity. Certainly he paid dearly for his error. Yet how could Overbury have foreseen that he would be the victim of a Howard plot and deserted by his false friend Carr; that he would be sent to the Tower on a trumped-up charge, and once there that Lady Frances would see that he never left its walls alive?

It was true that in spite of his considerable ability Overbury was not a lovable man. Chamberlain said: 'He was a very unfortunate man, for nobody almost pities him and his very friends speak but indifferently of him.'[20] The end came on 14 September, just ten days before Lady Frances Howard's divorce went through, while Overbury was still a prisoner in the Tower. Yet had Robert Carr but known it, Overbury's death, far from bringing him security, was the beginning of his downfall.

13

PRINCE HENRY
1606-1612

Queen Anne's affection for her elder son was so great that, to quote a contemporary, she 'could not bear him out of her sight'. Henry, for his part, spent as much time as he could with her. King James regarded his heir in a less favourable light. From birth James had always feared that his son might try to supplant him and his alarm grew when he saw more courtiers flocking to Prince Henry's Court at St James's Palace[1] than to his own Court at Whitehall.

The King realised with dismay that many of his subjects would much prefer to have Henry as their king. For in Henry they saw the qualities they desired in a ruler. He had the advantage of youth, and with his auburn hair, erect figure and winning smile he brought reassurance to all who saw him. Young as he was, Henry was self-confident, with a clear, cool mind and great determination, as he showed when he made the Earls of Pembroke and Southampton remove their households and their horses when he wished to occupy their lodgings himself. The Venetian ambassador remarked: 'This is a great proof of spirit on the part of the prince, who though only fifteen years of age, gives the highest promise in all he does.'[2]

Prince Henry admitted in a letter to the Prince de Joinville:[3] 'You have sent me a present of the two things I most delight in, arms and horses.'[4] He was an energetic young man, running, leaping, swimming, spending four or five hours a day in armour and equally long in the tiltyard, practising running at the ring.

He was a good rider, but did not share his father's passion for hunting. This caused trouble with King James, for when they were both hunting at Royston in May 1611 the Prince became bored and, to his father's intense annoyance, rode away, taking the greater part of his company with him. In his rage King James threatened his son with his cane, but Henry refused to change his mind. Later the Prince became penitent, for however much he disapproved of his father's lack of dignity, his coarse language and disorderly Court, he was always respectful to James as his king, so he went to the King's private apartments and asked his pardon, but all James would say was, 'You are no sportsman.'[5]

What James disliked even more than his son's distaste for hunting was the interest he was showing in seeing state papers. Intelligent young men can be very troublesome to those in authority and Sir Robert Cecil disapproved as strongly as King James of Prince Henry's newly awakened public spirit. As Bishop Goodman saw it, 'I confess the Prince did sometimes pry into the King's actions and a little dislike them. A knight told me the tale that he was privily sent by Prince Henry to see how the royal navy was ordered; what defects there were, and to be a spy upon them and no doubt, but he had others in the Signet Office.'[6] James determined to put an end to this inconvenient zeal on the part of his son by refusing to allow him to have any share in the government.

Fortunately for Prince Henry, he had no lack of other interests. Like his uncle, King Christian, he wanted to see his country become a great naval power. He was specially interested in ships and seafaring men. Love of the sea and the spirit of adventure drew him to Sir Walter Raleigh, a prisoner in the Tower after a trial which was a travesty of justice; so the Prince showed neither the vindictiveness of Sir Robert Cecil and Lord Henry Howard nor the animosity of King James towards the prisoner. Perhaps the contrast with his father increased Henry's admiration for the great Elizabethan seaman. For Sir Walter possessed just those qualities which King James conspicuously lacked. Raleigh was brave, patriotic and daring, and had a deep-seated hatred of

Spain. All this Henry found admirable and when, through the malice of Lord Henry Howard, Raleigh was sent to the Tower, the Prince became his wholehearted champion.

Queen Anne was as dismayed as her son at Sir Walter's plight. She encouraged Henry to visit him in the Tower, where the boy eagerly sought his advice on problems of navigation. Raleigh was not harshly treated as a prisoner. He was allowed to make a laboratory out of a henhouse in the Lieutenant of the Tower's garden where he carried out experiments and entertained visitors, amongst whom was Queen Anne.

In 1609 a further misfortune befell Raleigh. Owing to the careless oversight of a clerk in omitting certain words in copying a deed that Sir Walter made, conveying his lands to his son and heirs male, the bequest was void. So when Raleigh was found guilty of treason, and his lands forfeit to the Crown, he was still the legal owner. Prince Henry's anger can be imagined when in 1609 King James gave Raleigh's Sherborne estate to his favourite Robert Carr.[7] Queen Anne joined with her son in imploring King James not to be guilty of such an act of injustice, but all their pleas were in vain.

It was Prince Henry's love of the sea which led him to seek the friendship of Phineas Pett, master shipwright of Woolwich, and to pay many visits to Woolwich, where he learnt more about naval power and dockyard management than his father ever knew. Henry was only ten years old when Phineas Pett built him a pinnace, 25 feet long and 15 feet wide,[8] which Henry christened *Disdain* with a great bowl of wine.[9] The pinnace was anchored near Westminster and the Prince used to sail about the Thames in her, and visit the ships in the Pool.

One of the proudest days in Queen Anne's life was the investiture of Prince Henry on 16 June 1610. It was a hundred years since there had been a Prince of Wales[10] and King James was determined that the ceremony should be a memorable one. Yet even on this great day in his son's life King James could not contain his jealousy. He would not allow his son to make a state entry on horseback, so Henry came on foot, accompanied by his cousin, the Duke of Brunswick. As the Venetian ambassador remarked, 'James did not desire to exalt him too high'.[11]

Queen Anne's heart must have filled with pride as she watched her son in his mantle of purple velvet as Prince of Wales make his way from Westminster Hall to the Parliament House, escorted by the Earl of Nottingham and the Earl of Northampton. After bowing three times Henry knelt before his father, who girded him a sword, placed a ring on his finger and a coronet on his head; all the time, much to his son's distaste, patting his cheek. Three days of festivities followed and Queen Anne staged a masque, *Tethys Festival*, in honour of the Prince of Wales.

On one point King James and Queen Anne were in agreement. This was in seeking a Spanish bride for their elder son. As long ago as 1604, when Henry was only ten years old, Queen Anne told the Constable of Castile that she would like Philip the Third's eldest daughter, the Infanta Anna, as her daughter-in-law. James supported her until he found that the Spaniards were insisting that Henry should be brought up in Spain, and for a time the matter was dropped. But Spain reopened the marriage project in the hope that James would exert influence with the Dutch to make peace with Spain.

The one person who was not consulted in these negotiations was Prince Henry himself. He had strong Protestant sympathies and the last person he wished to marry was an Infanta of Spain. As events were to prove, Fate was on his side. For when the Spanish reopened negotiations the English ambassador in Madrid, Sir John Digby, discovered that in the interval King Philip had betrothed the Infanta Anna to the boy King of France, Louis XIII. It was the end of a long duel between the Queen Mother of France, Marie de Medici, and King James to win the support of Spain. Philip added fuel to the flame of King James's anger by offering his younger daughter Maria,[12] a mere child, as a substitute bride. Queen Anne was equally annoyed at what she considered the Spanish King's double dealing, and the only person who was pleased was Prince Henry, who declared that he would rather marry a subject than the Infanta.[13] Nor did Marie de

Medici improve matters by offering her six-year-old daughter Princess Christine as a bride. Matters were allowed to rest while negotiations went ahead to find a bridegroom for Princess Elizabeth.

Only intense devotion to her son could have brought Queen Anne to go to the launching of the new warship *Prince Royal* on 24 September 1610. Since her stormy voyage from Denmark as a bride, Anne had shown no wish to encounter the perils of the North Sea. Not even the chance to see her mother could persuade her to sail to Denmark, although she once made plans to meet her mother at Hamburg or some other half-way point.[14]

Evil days had fallen upon Phineas Pett since he built the pinnace *Disdain.* Partly through the enmity of Lord Henry Howard, he was accused of using bad timber in building his ships and frauds in giving receipts for stores. Prince Henry stood by him at his trial and he was acquitted and continued to build the King's ships. Queen Anne with her two young children arrived after dinner for the launching and took her seat in a stand erected in the shipbuilding yard. King James was absent, as he was suffering from eating 'a surfeit of grapes'.

It was a wild, storm-tossed day, and the man-of-war was a proud sight, not for her size alone, but for her décor and lavish use of gold paint. The *Prince Royal* was said to be so seaworthy that even if riddled by enemy guns she would not sink. Prince Henry hoped to sail to Denmark in her to visit his Uncle Christian.

On the fatal Monday of the launching everything went wrong. They had to wait for high tide, and as the hour approached the wind grew stronger. Nautical men could see that there was little hope of launching the *Prince Royal* until the wind dropped. Yet the attempt was made, with the result that as the ship moved, the dock gates which were too narrow, 'pent her in so straight that she stuck fast between them',[15] and she settled in the mud. Hour after hour efforts to move her proved vain and by 5 p.m. it was seen to be hopeless. Queen Anne with Princess Elizabeth and

Prince Charles returned dejectedly by barge to Greenwich.

Only Prince Henry refused to admit defeat. He stayed after the royal party had left, hoping against hope but at length he rode away to Greenwich, promising to return about midnight. The Earl of Nottingham, as Lord High Admiral, remained sitting in his chair until it was high tide again. After midnight Prince Henry reappeared and, standing on the poop, took the great gilt standing cup which was filled with wine, for the christening of the ship, 'threw all the wine forward towards the half deck', and named the ship *Prince Royal*.[16] Then he handed the cup to Phineas Pett and watched the ship leave her moorings.

The year 1611 was a busy time for Queen Anne. On 25 March she was present at a Garter Service in which Prince Charles and Robert Carr, now Viscount Rochester, were made knights of the Garter. Anxiety about her brother Christian had darkened the summer, for he had embarked on a war with Sweden, and before invading the country in person he sent his private band to his sister for safe keeping, together with a jewel forming his monogram in diamonds. Neither Queen Anne nor King James approved of Christian's venture; Anne because she feared for his safety and James because the last thing in the world he wanted was to be dragged into war. Yet when in August King Christian sent a special embassy to England to ask King James to allow him to levy men in England for the Swedish war,[17] Queen Anne set to work to entertain them at Somerset House.

The closing months of the year were darkened for Queen Anne by illness, when she was alone at Hampton Court. It seems to have been arthritis, from which she suffered increasingly. Three weeks later she was reported to be still 'a little lame'.

Relations between Prince Henry and his father had not improved. Indeed, Queen Anne feared the breach between them was growing wider. As Prince of Wales, Henry had an establishment of nearly five hundred persons. He managed his finances so well that, unlike his father, who was falling deeper and deeper in debt, he was actually balancing his accounts. A fresh point of conflict between them arose regarding the appointment of a governor for Prince Charles in 1611. Henry favoured Sir James Fullerton, but King James insisted on appointing Sir Robert Carey, who had been in charge of Princess Elizabeth's upbringing. Henry rushed to Whitehall to protest, but to no purpose.[18]

In the summer of 1612 there were signs of better relations. The royal estate at Woodstock had been given to Prince Henry and to express his thanks he gave a magnificent fête on 30 August. By his orders 'a great summerhouse of green boughs' was erected in the park,[19] and there the King and Queen dined at a table by themselves at the upper end of the bower, while Prince Henry sat with his sister at another table.

Henry was now eighteen and with his increased public appearances as Prince of Wales had less time to devote to his mother, so Anne's affection turned in some degree from him to his younger brother.

In May 1612 Queen Anne was saddened by news of the death of the Earl of Salisbury. He had been in bad health since the previous December, when Sir John More took such a gloomy view that he wrote: 'It is on all hands concluded that his Lordship must shortly leave this world, or at least disburden himself of a great part of his affairs. In the short time of his Lordship's weakness almost all our great affairs are come to a stand and his hand is already shrewdly missed.'[20] But Cecil continued to overwork. He has always been a restraining influence on King James and had to some extent been able to curb his extravagance.

Although Queen Anne's health was far from good in March she had visited Cecil every second day.[21] She felt she owed much to his wise counsel. Indeed, Cecil was now probably more popular in England than he had ever been. As Chamberlain remarked: 'It seems he was never so well beloved as now when they thought him so near lost.'[22] In April he decided to go to Bath to see if the waters would give him relief, but in vain. He was returning home when he became worse and died at Marlborough. King James heard of his death just as he was setting out for a hunting expedition, yet although he owed to Cecil his easy accession to the throne of England, he did not allow it to interfere with his day's pleasure.

Soon another anxiety filled Queen Anne's mind. In the late summer of 1612 she noted with alarm how ill and listless Prince Henry was becoming. He was very pale, tired easily and complained of 'a giddy, lumpish heaviness in his forehead'. Yet although August had brought one of the most intense heat-waves England had ever known, nothing could curb Prince Henry's passion for exercise. He went swimming at midnight and in the August heat rode ninety-six miles in two days to join King James at Belvoir. In October, while entertaining his sister's fiancé, Count Frederick of the Palatinate, he fainted and was obliged to stay in bed.

Queen Anne sent her personal physician, Dr Theodore Turquet de Mayerne,[23] the fashionable doctor of the day, to attend her son at St James's Palace. His rise to fame was the more remarkable as Mayerne was reputed to be 'commonly unfortunate in any dangerous disease'. He promptly diagnosed the Prince's illness as 'a tertian fever' caused by swimming in the Thames and walking late at night. In spite of frequent blood-letting by Dr Mayerne, there was no improvement in his condition.

'The extremity of the disease seemed to lie in his head', reported Chamberlain, 'for remedy whereof they shaved him and applied warm cocks and pigeons newly killed, but with no success.'[24] Dr Mayerne kept a record of the details of the Prince's illness in his journal,[25] and from these it is clear that Prince Henry was suffering from typhoid.

Henry grew steadily worse and by 9 November the doctors admitted that there was little hope of his recovery. Queen Anne was overwhelmed with grief, all the more so because she had no faith in the doctors' treatment of blood-letting and application of newly killed cocks. As a last resource Anne thought of Sir Walter Raleigh, who had sent her a concoction which had proved most effective, so she sent a message to the Tower asking him to send for Prince Henry some of the great cordial 'that had saved her life'. This was a mixture of pearl, musk, hartshorn, bezoar stone (found in the intestines of ruminants), mint, borage, gentian, mace, sugar, aloes and spirits of wine.[26]

Raleigh at once made up the cordial in his laboratory in the Tower, and sent it to the patient. At first it seemed to be having an effect. The Prince opened his eyes and tried to utter a few words. But it was too late. Soon Henry lapsed into unconsciousness again and died on Friday evening, 12 November 1612. His last words were 'Where is my dear sister?'[27] As is often the case, the doctors came in for much blame, especially Dr Mayerne for giving his patient a purge which dispersed the infection throughout his body.

His mother's grief was terrible. For days Queen Anne sat in a darkened room at Somerset House, speaking to no one and weeping uncontrollably. King James, instead of coming to console his wife, remained at Theobalds, and took to his bed 'for fear to refresh the sense of the wound'.[28] Perhaps the most heartbroken of all was Princess Elizabeth. For days she refused to eat and spent the time weeping. Henry had been her joy and her delight and not even the presence of her future husband could comfort her.

To the intense annoyance of King James and the Council the date of Princess Elizabeth's wedding had to be postponed. It was felt it would create a bad impression if foreign envoys coming for the funeral found the wedding guests dancing and revelling. The postponement meant that Count Frederick and his entourage must stay longer, which proved a crippling expense on the Exchequer.

When at length the state funeral took place on 7 December neither King James nor Queen Anne were present. The King, who detested sad occasions, remained at Royston, and Queen Anne was suffering from an attack of gout.

The chief mourner was twelve-year-old Prince Charles, upon whom the burden of affairs of state was already beginning to fall. With him walked his future brother-in-law, Count Frederick of the Palatinate, as the procession slowly wound its way to Westminster Abbey. On the coffin lay a wax effigy of Prince Henry wearing his robes as Prince of Wales. In the cortège walked a hundred and forty poor men in black gowns. Henry was buried in Henry VII's chapel beside his grandmother, Mary Queen of Scots.

The nation was stricken with grief at the loss of the Prince, on whom they had placed such high hopes. As Sir John Throckmorton remarked: 'This lamentable funeral is this day passed, truly with much magnificence but with more grief than any was these many hundred years.'[29] There is little doubt that had Henry lived England would have had the king she needed so much. He would have introduced order into his father's debased, disorderly court and placed the finances of the country on a sound basis. By his popular appeal Henry would have rallied the nation to the Crown, and England might have been spared the miseries of the Civil War and the execution of his brother. But it was not to be.

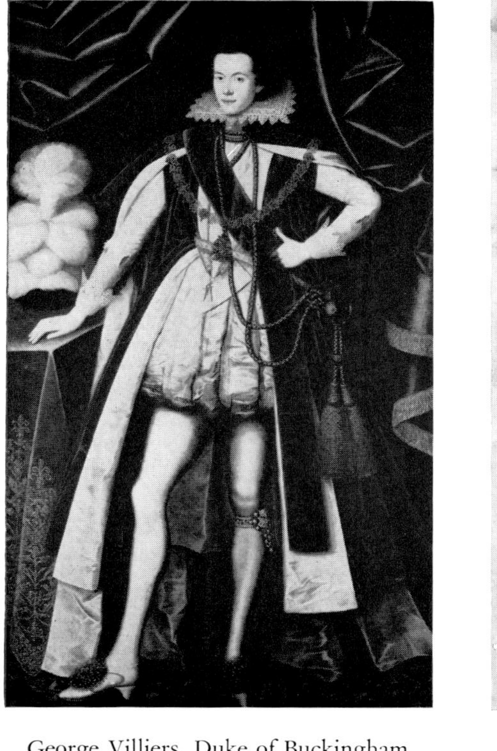

George Villiers, Duke of Buckingham.
Artist unknown

My kind dog, I haue receaued
your letter which is verie well=
com to me yow doe verie well in
lugging the sowes eare, and I
thank yow for it, and would
haue yow doe so still upon con=
dition that yow Continue a
watchfull dog to him and be
alwaies true to him, So wishing
you all happines

Anna R.

An undated letter from Anne to the Duke of Buckingham

Queen Anne at Hampton Court *circa* 1617. Portrait by Van Somer, background by a different artist

14

PRINCESS ELIZABETH'S MARRIAGE 1613

Princess Elizabeth was a lively, buoyant girl with a loud voice and a hearty laugh. She was not beautiful, but with her golden hair and immense zest for life she was attractive. Perhaps because she resembled her mother in her gay nature, her obstinacy and courage in adversity, Queen Anne was less devoted to her daughter than to her sons. Yet Anne gave a great deal of thought to her future, for she was determined that Elizabeth should make a marriage worthy of a king's daughter.

So when a suitor appeared in the person of young King Gustavus Adolphus of Sweden, Anne bitterly opposed his suit, remembering that her brother, King Christian, was Sweden's sworn enemy. For very different reasons she also vetoed the proposal of Duke Frederick Ulric of Brunswick, the eldest son of her sister Elizabeth. In spite of her deep affection for her Danish relatives, Queen Anne did not approve of the marriage of first cousins, and she felt that the young man's father, Duke Henry Julius, had proved sadly lacking in the qualities desirable in a husband, and she feared that the son might have inherited these weaknesses. She knew her sister's married life had been far from happy. However, Duke Frederick Ulric spent the spring and summer of 1610 in England, when Prince Henry had been his tireless companion and guide. He was a spectator of the great aquatic pageant on the Thames staged in honour of Henry's investiture as Prince of Wales. The young Duke thoroughly enjoyed his visit, even if his hopes as a suitor were doomed to disappointment, for on his return to Brunswick his mother wrote to Prince Henry thanking him for being so attentive a host to her son.[1]

Her next suitor was much less attractive in Princess Elizabeth's eyes. He was Prince Maurice of Nassau, and when he arrived in England in May 1611 the Princess saw with dismay that her suitor was a bald, avuncular man, looking much older than his forty-six years. Nor did his portentous manner and materialistic Dutch outlook on life appeal to a lively girl of fourteen. Fortunately for Princess Elizabeth, the negotiations soon faded away, as neither her father nor her mother, nor even the prospective bridegroom himself, showed much enthusiasm. Two other Protestant suitors appeared: Otto, son of the Landgrave of Hesse, and Prince Christian of Anhalt; but neither made any progress.

Then a young man came forward who won favour in Princess Elizabeth's eyes. He was Frederick Henry, Count of the Palatinate. From the first he found an active supporter of his suit in King James, mainly because he would not be called upon to provide a large dowry. Also it fitted in with his policy of holding the balance of power by marrying his son Henry to a Spanish princess and his daughter Elizabeth to a Protestant. He hoped this match would increase his influence in Germany and help him to become the champion of Protestantism in Europe.[2] As a modern historian has described the marriage, 'Elizabeth was sacrificed by her father in the interests of religion and the commonwealth'.[3]

From the first Queen Anne frowned upon the marriage. Like many mothers before and since, she felt that her prospective son-in-law was not a worthy match for her daughter. She had always taught her children to be proud of their royal ancestry and Count Frederick was not a king. He was merely the prince of a small German state, who had been indoctrinated in Protestantism by his mother, the daughter of William the Silent.

Jestingly the Queen would greet her daughter as 'Good wife, Palsgrave'. It was a bitter jest. Elizabeth, who had fallen in love with Frederick as soon as she saw him, retorted angrily: 'I would rather be the Palsgrave's wife than the greatest Papist Queen in Christendom.'[4] Nothing Anne could do made any difference.

When Frederick landed at Gravesend on 16 October 1612 he made a favourable impression. A well-set-up youth with thick curly hair and dark eyes, he had been carefully instructed by his uncle, Prince Maurice of Nassau, to show deference to his future relations-in-law, but from the first glimpse of Princess Elizabeth he knew that she was the only woman in the world for him. Queen Anne was far from sharing their rapture.

Count Frederick must have found his formal introduction to the English royal family a trying occasion. Queen Anne was seated beside her husband on a dais beneath a canopy of gold brocade in the banqueting house at Whitehall with Henry, Elizabeth and Charles standing beside them. Frederick made a speech in French in a very low voice, which left Queen Anne quite unmoved, but King James, although he had probably not grasped a word, exclaimed in a hearty voice, 'Say no more about it. Suffice it that I am anxious to testify to you by deeds that you are welcome.'

Prince Henry, who had no wish to see his sister marry a Catholic prince, at once formed a favourable impression of the young suitor. He thought him 'promising both in wit, courage and judgment'. Queen Anne's opinion was less pleasing. She received the Count coldly, 'with a fixed countenance'.[5] Instead of greeting her future son-in-law with a kiss, she merely allowed him to kiss her hand.

All this time Princess Elizabeth was waiting shyly. It was noticed that until then 'she did not turn so much as a corner of an eye towards him'.[6] As Frederick moved towards her after greeting Prince Henry and bowed low twice, she curtsied and he ventured to kiss her. Whatever misgivings Queen Anne may have had, from that moment Princess Elizabeth had no doubts. Soon the young couple were spending all day together at Denmark House, famous for its waterside garden and luxuriant rosemary hedges.[7] John Chamberlain observed: 'he is every day at court, and plies his mistress hard and takes no delight in running at ring, nor tennis, nor riding with the Prince, (as Count Henry, his uncle, and other of his company do) but only in her conversation.'[8] Such devotion left Frederick's mother-in-law to be completely unmoved. As the days passed she looked upon him with even less favour. Queen Anne was a much shrewder judge of character than modern historians will admit. She saw that Frederick was not very intelligent, but he was intensely ambitious, and she knew only too well that ambition without brains brings disaster. Nor was the position improved when she heard that Colonel Schomberg, steward to the Count Palatine, had said 'his master is a better man than the King of Denmark'.[9] That Schomberg's statement was palpably untrue in no way lessened the offence.

Queen Anne's disapproval was soon submerged by her growing anxiety about Prince Henry's health. At Princess Elizabeth's betrothal the Prince had remained standing by the King's chair and 'stirred not a foot'.[10] He was too ill to attend the banquet at Guildhall. After his death Queen Anne's attitude changed; perhaps because all other matters now seemed of trifling importance. Three days before the wedding John Chamberlain commented: 'The Queen grows every day more favourable, and there is hope that she will grace it yet with her presence.'[11] Another onlooker noted: 'the Queen doth discover her liking of this match over all others and for the more honouring of it she exceedeth the King in new liveries that she giveth to the servants and caresseth the Palsgrave whensoever he cometh to her as if he were her own son.'[12] It is unlikely that Queen Anne was as enthusiastic about her son-in-law as the writer believed, not even the gift to her of a French coach upholstered in rich velvet and gilt ironwork in the wheels could have worked such a change. Probably she saw that the match was inevitable and so she decided to make the best of it.

A severe attack of gout prevented Queen Anne taking part in the betrothal festivities, but she was present on Saint Valentine's Day 1613, when they were married by Archbishop Abbot in the Chapel Royal at Whitehall. In spite of the grief for Prince Henry and a ruinous financial position, King James decided to give his daughter a magnificent wedding.

Dressed in white and wearing jewels valued at £400,000, Queen Anne walked beside her husband, who was strangely attired in a Spanish cape over his black suit, and a cap with a feather. All eyes were centred on the bride and bridegroom, clad in cloth of silver, Elizabeth's long train blazing with diamonds, and a coronet of pearls and diamonds on her head.[13] Unfortunately during the ceremony the bride was overcome with bursts of laughter—it may have been due to nervous strain—but all her former governess Lady Harington's efforts were unable to check them. The bridegroom was radiant, for he felt that the English royal family was now linked with the Protestant courts of Europe. As all could see, the bride was radiantly happy. It was fortunate that they could not foresee the future which was to bring such tragedy into their lives.

Everything was done regardless of expense. At the wedding feast the guests drank hippocras, an aromatic medicated wine, which was traditionally drunk at weddings. In the evening the guests were entertained with the *Lords Masque*.[14] As Ben Jonson was abroad, the libretto was written by Thomas Campion. Inigo Jones surpassed himself in devising stage effects. He divided the stage into two levels which gave more scope for diversity of scenery.[15] The entertainment was 'very rich and sumptuous yet it was very long and tedious with many devices, more like a play than a masque'.[16] Perhaps that was why King James fell fast asleep during the performance.

Next day there were more festivities. Queen Anne and her daughter took their places in a window of the banqueting house at Whitehall and watched Count Frederick, 'mounted up on a high bouncing horse', distinguish himself at running at the ring in the tiltyard. While Princess Elizabeth was radiant, Queen Anne was unutterably sad, for running at the ring had been one of Prince Henry's favourite pastimes.

Much to the relief of King James, who had borne the cost of the wedding, preparations for the departure of the bride and bridegroom were at length under way. With Salisbury's restraining hand removed, expenditure had soared. A sham seafight on the Thames on the eve of the wedding had cost £9,000. By March nearly £50,000 had been spent and the Treasury was empty.

To the annoyance of Count Frederick and his attendants, King James suddenly decided to break up the Palsgrave's household, as a measure of economy, and send them back to Germany. Princess Elizabeth 'took [it] very grievously and not without cause but that necessity hath no law', commented Chamberlain to Winwood. 'We devise all the means we can to cut of expense and not without cause, being come *ad fundum*, and to the very lees of our best liquor.'[17]

Even after the departure of the Count Palatine's retinue there was delay after delay. March the tenth, when the bride and bridegroom were to sail, came and went and their sailing was postponed so that they might have moonlit nights at sea. This romantic reason was by no means the true one, for there was such a shortage of seamen that they could not find enough men to man the King's ships.

At length the day of departure dawned and on 10 April Queen Anne, accompanied by her daughter, went by barge from Whitehall to Greenwich. Guns fired farewell salvoes all along the route. They spent the day at Greenwich and then went together to Rochester. Elizabeth left England with very few attendants, but amongst them was her faithful friend Lady Harington and Alethea, Countess of Arundel. As usual, stormy winds played havoc with the royal plans and the bride and her mother went on board the *Royal Prince* more than once, only to come ashore again. Finally, at the suggestion of Robert Carr, now Viscount Rochester, they adjourned to Rochester Castle, where a farewell banquet was held, and there on 14 April Queen Anne said a sad good-bye to her daughter, whom she was never to see again.

Bereft of her two elder children, Queen Anne made a determined attempt to take charge of her younger son. Prince Charles, now twelve years old, had grown into an intelligent, good-looking boy. Although very small for his age, his erect carriage made him seem taller than he actually was. He had overcome his difficulty in walking, and of his impediment in speech only a slight hesitation remained. As usual, King James turned a deaf ear to his wife's pleading. He merely gave orders that 'the young prince be kept within a stricter compass than the former and not to exceed his ordinary in diet or followers or any other course of show or charge'.[18] It was unlikely that Charles would fall into any of these evil ways. Young as he was, his father's table manners, coarse language and homosexuality filled him with disgust.

Since the death of Prince Henry, Queen Anne's health had seriously deteriorated. Parting from her only daughter further increased her low spirits. Both she and King James suffered from attacks of gout, although like many present day patients the King would not allow his illness to be called by that name. Queen Anne also had arthritis, swollen feet, and a tendency to dropsy. Perhaps the damp climate and the chill of the unheated palaces in which she lived augmented these troubles. Anne herself expressed her dislike of the damp chilly air of Greenwich in December.

Although Queen Anne was putting on weight, she was still a good-looking woman with a fine complexion. She dressed to give dignity to her person, wearing a farthingale,[19] of which for some obscure masculine reason King James disapproved, a low-cut bodice, and instead of the Elizabethan ruff, a highboned lace collar.

On Dr Mayerne's advice Queen Anne decided to visit Bath to try the beneficial effects of the mineral springs. She would make a leisurely journey as she had done ten years before on her way from Scotland to England and see as many friends as possible on the return progress. The Queen travelled in considerable style, taking with her a large retinue, amongst whom were the elderly, learned Lord Chancellor, Lord Ellesmere, and his wife Alice, the daughter of Sir John Spencer of Althorp and widow of the fifth Earl of Derby. She was one of Queen Anne's closest friends, since she had accompanied her on the journey from Scotland, when England was an unknown and terrifying land. Lady Ellesmere was a lively, good-natured woman, with wide interests, who could count many poets amongst her friends.

The doyen of the entourage was Edward Somerset, fourth Earl of Worcester, who had been Master of Horse both to Queen Elizabeth and James I. He was Master of Queen Anne's household. Queen Elizabeth had thought highly of him, declaring in her impetuous way that 'he achieved the impossible for he combined utter loyalty with devout Catholicism'.[20] When the Earl brought a letter of welcome from Queen Elizabeth to Queen Anne and her husband, as they were landing at Leith in 1590, it marked the beginning of a lifelong friendship. Worcester took a lively interest in plays and masques and was the patron of a band of players.

The youngest of Queen Anne's ladies was twenty-three-year-old Lady Anne Clifford, now Countess of Dorset. The Queen had always been attracted to the girl since their first meeting at Althorp, because she was so animated, so strong-willed, and above all so loyal. Her marriage was proving most unhappy. Richard Sackville, Earl of Dorset, left much to be desired. He was utterly self-centred, a compulsive gambler, and as a husband showed no consideration for his wife. Yet had Anne Clifford but known it, her second husband, who was no other than King James's ex-favourite, Philip Herbert, Earl of Montgomery,[21] was to prove infinitely worse. In Anne's words 'the marble pillars of Knole in Kent and Wilton in Wiltshire were to me oft times but the gay arbour of anguish'.[22] Fortunately in 1613 the future was hidden from her, but the present was grim enough.

Bishop Goodman described the Earl of Dorset as 'a little man who played things safe and was willing to sacrifice self-respect for advantage. . . . He was morose and censorious and certainly did not enjoy his situation but because he did not have the courage to snarl, he took refuge in sneers.' In 1616, having already gambled away his own lands and London estates, Dorset tried to compel his wife to sell her lands in Westmorland to pay his debts. King James supported the Earl and in despair Lady Dorset turned for help to Queen Anne. They met in the Queen's withdrawing room and Anne promised to help, at the same time warning the Countess, as she wrote in her diary, 'not to trust my matters absolutely to the King lest he should deceive me'.[23]

No one knew King James and his devious ways better than Queen Anne. So when the King sent for the Countess and suggested that the Earl and his wife should place matters in his hands, and abide by his decision, Lady Dorset was forewarned. She told the King that she 'would never part from Westmorland while I lived upon any condition whatsoever'.[24] The result was deadlock. Anne kept her lands in Westmorland as well as her Yorkshire estates.

Another old friend who accompanied Queen Anne was Lady Jean Drummond, daughter of Patrick, Lord Drummond. Their friendship dated from Anne's early days in Scotland. Jean, like several members of Queen Anne's household, was a Catholic. She was first Lady of the Queen's Bedchamber and was one of the few people whose advice Anne both sought and accepted. At her marriage on 3 February 1614 to Robert Ker, Lord Roxburgh, Queen Anne staged a pastoral masque by Samuel Daniel called *Hymen's Triumph* in the little square-paved court at Somerset House. 'The entertainment was great and cost the Queen, as she says, above £3,000',[25] although a little earlier Anne had declared 'all the charge she means to be at, saving the Bride's wedding gown and the marriage bed, wherein she will not exceed £300, for she saith her maid Drummond is rich enough otherwise as well in wealth as in virtue and favour'. But even royal ladies can change their minds.

The journey was made in easy stages. King James escorted Queen Anne as far as Hampton Court, where she stayed two nights before moving to Windsor. As she passed through Reading, the bells of St Mary's Church rang out in welcome. On arriving at Caversham Park, the seat of Lord Knollys,[26] where the Queen was spending the night, a group of young nobles, amongst whom was the Earl of Dorset, disguised as keepers and Robin Hood's men in green, greeted Queen Anne with songs and dancing.[27]

At the entrance Lord and Lady Knollys were waiting to welcome their royal guest. Lady Knollys was the eldest daughter of Thomas Howard, Earl of Suffolk, and Lady Frances Howard's sister. She was a hard, domineering woman who at the age of nineteen had married the fifty-eight-year-old widower only two months after the death of his first wife. Lord Knollys came completely under the influence of his wife; King James, when depriving him of his post of Master of the Wards, remarked caustically that he had one fault common to him with divers others of his friends and followers, which could neither stand with his service nor of the State, that he 'was altogether guided and overruled by an arch-wife'.[28]

However, on that April day all was harmony. After the Queen had dined quietly with Lord and Lady Knollys, the company adjourned to the great hall, where a masque written by Thomas Campion was staged for her entertainment. It was very much a family affair, as Lady Knollys's four brothers, with the Earl of Dorset, Lord North, Sir Henry Rich and Sir Henry Carey performed a new dance and then led out the ladies. Queen Anne evidently enjoyed herself, as she 'vouchsafed to make herself head of the revels and graciously to adorn the place with her personal dancing; much of the night being thus spent with variety of dances'.[29] When the Queen was leaving next day she was presented with a dainty quilt, a rich carquenet and a curious cabinet valued at £1,500.[30]

The cavalcade arrived in Bath on 30 April and Queen Anne lost no time in taking the waters. Her treatment, however, suffered an unfortunate setback before she had time to feel the benefit. She was taking the treatment in the King's Bath when suddenly 'a flame of fire like a candle . . . spread into a large circle on top of the water'. Anne was terrified. Being superstitious, she believed the light to be 'a supernatural message from the world below and nothing would induce her to enter that bath again'.[31] Much to the annoyance of the municipal authorities, the Queen insisted on using the new bath, which had been built for the poor of Bath, and they never regained the use of it.

For five weeks Queen Anne continued with the treatment and by that time she felt so much better in health and spirits that she was ready for the return journey. She set out on 4 June in a coach drawn by four white horses, while her maids of honour on horseback formed an escort behind it. It was only a short journey to Bristol, where she stayed for four nights. Never was a Queen given a more royal welcome. At the east gate of the city the Queen was met by the Lord Mayor and the civic dignitaries on horseback and presented with an embroidered purse containing a hundred nobles. Then she was escorted to Sir John Young's house, where she lodged, and in the evening the Queen was entertained to dinner by the Mayor. During the dinner Lady Jean Drummond handed Queen Anne a diamond ring which she presented to the Mayor as an expression of thanks for his hospitality. The Queen was always very lavish in her gifts of jewelry.

This was merely a foretaste of pleasures to come. Two days later, on Sunday, 6 June, Queen Anne drove in state to a service in the cathedral with the Bishop of Bath and Wells seated beside her. On Monday she was entertained by a water pageant on the Severn in which an English merchant ship routed two Turkish galleys. There could have been nothing very novel in the spectacle for Queen Anne, as she had watched the same seafight on the Thames as part of the festivities to mark Princess Elizabeth's wedding. Yet Anne, gracious as ever, exclaimed, 'I never knew anything so neatly, so artifically performed', and paid the performers a somewhat ambiguous compliment by adding that 'they were not only like Turks in their apparel but resembled them in their countenances'.[32]

Next day, when Queen Anne left Bristol, the citizens lined the streets and their numbers were swelled by hundreds of countryfolk who flocked into Bristol to catch a glimpse of the royal guest. Queen Anne was so touched by their loyalty that she exclaimed with tears in her eyes, 'I never knew I was a Queen till I came to Bristol.' She was so delighted with all she saw in the countryside that Chamberlain commented: 'She is so pleased with that it is thought she will make many more such progresses.'[33]

Always good-natured, when the Rev. George Ferebi, Vicar of Bishop's Cannings, was presented to Queen Anne and begged her to pause on her way and listen to his choir singing verses he had composed in her honour, she willingly consented. So in one of the wildest parts of Wiltshire, on the downs seven hundred feet above sea-level, at Old Shepherd's Shore, the royal procession halted. There the Rev. George Ferebi, who aspired to write poetry and could at least claim to be a versifier, met the Queen. He was wearing a long white robe, and had a straggling white beard made of sheep's wool and a wreath upon his head. Behind him were ranged his choir dressed as shepherds and shepherdesses. Queen Anne left her coach to greet them and the Vicar recited a poem he had written specially for the occasion beginning:

Stand still, great Queen, amidst your loving people,
And listen to the bells of Cannings steeple.[34]

Then the choir and the musicians broke into a four-part shepherds' song which, according to Aubrey, was well received by the Queen, who 'bounteously rewarded' the singers, while the Lord Chancellor and other members of the royal party 'applauded warmly'.[35] Then came the epilogue, and the long line of coaches moved on slowly towards Marlborough. Perhaps the most tangible sign of the Queen's enjoyment with this rural entertainment was the subsequent appointment of the Rev. George Ferebi as chaplain to the King.

With the improvement in the Queen's health, her feelings towards her husband became more kindly. Then just as their relations were improving an incident occurred which might have made them more estranged than ever. It was one of those accidents which are pure mischance and yet have incalculable consequences. On a July day in 1613 the King and Queen were deer shooting at Theobalds, when Queen Anne, who was by no means a first-class shot, loosed a bolt at what she believed to be a deer but was in reality King James's favourite hound Jewel.

The unfortunate victim was fatally wounded. When the King heard that Jewel was dead he stormed and raged, vowing vengeance on the perpetrator, but when he learnt that it was his wife who had fired the fatal shot he calmed down and assured her 'he should never love her the worse'. Next day to show his forgiveness he gave his wife a superb diamond worth £2,000, saying it was a legacy from his dead dog.[36] Queen Anne could be thankful that her carelessness had not resulted in a worse tragedy. For next year at Basing her friend George Abbot, Archbishop of Canterbury, loosed a shaft which hit and killed a gamekeeper.

15

THE RISING FORTUNES OF GEORGE VILLIERS 1613-1619

In December of the same year which had seen the marriage of Princess Elizabeth to the Count Palatine, Queen Anne, much against her will, was present at another wedding, which was even more distasteful. Frances Howard, Countess of Essex, was marrying the royal favourite Robert Carr, Earl of Somerset. Carr was an empty-headed young man and never more foolish than when he married Lady Frances. The fact that the bride was even more anxious than he was to hasten on the wedding day ought to have warned him of dangers ahead. For the Countess's nullity suit against her husband, the Earl of Essex, had scandalised the nation, and rumours were circulating in London that Lady Frances had tried to destroy the unfortunate Earl by administering potions bought from a certain Mrs Woods.[1]

Against such a background it is little wonder that Queen Anne looked with distaste on the wedding. She believed in decency and decorum, and there was neither in Lady Essex's divorce. So she refused to go to the wedding and was thankful when Court mourning for Prince Henry caused it to be postponed.

King James took a very different view. He would not believe a word against his favourite, declaring he did 'still take more delight in his company and coversation than in any man's living'.[2] When at length the date was fixed, King James induced Queen Anne to agree to be present at the wedding by handing over to her Greenwich Palace.

To Queen Anne, as to many of those packed into the private chapel at Whitehall, it must have seemed that time was in reverse. There they were, as seven years before, sitting in the same building, seeing the same bishop, Dr Montagu, Bishop of Bath and Wells, intoning the same solemn words of the marriage service for the same bride,[3] whose golden hair flowed down over her shoulders, just as it had done at the Essex wedding. Only the bridegroom was different.

In spite of his financial difficulties and debts amounting to over £500,000, King James decided that the wedding should be a memorable occasion. In November he created Carr Earl of Somerset so that Lady Frances should not become a mere Viscountess on her second marriage. The King wished no expense to be spared. He not only paid for the cost of the wedding, but sold crown lands worth £10,000 to provide jewels for the bride and gave the bridegroom a sword whose hilt and scabbard were of solid gold. Chamberlain noted that the wedding presents were more numerous and more costly than at the Essex wedding. The bride, looking more beautiful than ever, entered the chapel, supported by her Howard uncle, the Earl of Northampton, and Queen Anne's brother-in-law, the Duke of Saxony. The congregation gazed in amazement as they saw her hair hanging loose, which was a sign of virginity.[4]

Once she had agreed to attend the wedding, Queen Anne played her part well. She stayed to taste the wafers and sip the hippocras. She also took part in a masque by Thomas Campion, staged on the wedding night in the banqueting house at Whitehall. Four of the twelve young noblemen, who played the parts of disenchanted knights were the same who had danced at Lady Frances's first wedding. After the first antimasque three Destinies brought a golden tree to Queen Anne, from which she tore a branch, which freed the knights from a magic spell.[5] Brilliant though the masque was, it failed to win the approval of John Chamberlain, who wrote: 'I hear little or no commendation of the masque made by the lords that night either for device or dancing, only it was rich and costly.'[6]

Somerset was riding on the crest of the wave. By this marriage he had linked his fortunes with those of the powerful Howard family, and he was more firmly entrenched than ever in the King's favour. Since Salisbury's death he had helped King James in carrying out the duties of Secretary of State, although without Overbury behind him he was incapable of coping with such duties satisfactorily. When crafty old Northampton died, and Somerset was appointed Lord Chamberlain, matters went from bad to worse, yet King James fondly remarked 'no man should marvel that he bestowed a place so near himself upon his friend, whom he loved above all men living'.[7]

With a feeling of security, Somerset's arrogance grew. He had always treated Queen Anne with offhand boorishness; now he became openly discourteous, while the courtiers found his behaviour unbearable. Where he made his fatal mistake was in his treatment of King James. Hitherto Somerset had been companionable, showing himself anxious to please and ready to carry out the King's lightest wish, even when it ran counter to his own desires. Now with his marriage all was changed. Lady Frances was proving a hard task mistress who insisted that her husband should be always at her beck and call. So James began to find himself neglected, with long periods of boredom, and when the favourite appeared he was often disagreeable and ill-tempered. In fact, James, who was never noted for his courage, became afraid of Somerset's furious outbursts of temper. Nor did his integration with the Howards prove as valuable as Somerset had imagined. He had failed to realise that in allying with the Howards he was taking over their enemies as well, and he now found himself allied with a party whose quarrels disrupted the State, and so as the King's confidant he was no longer above party.

It was clear that the government was getting into such a hopeless state that drastic action was needed. The Protestant lords, Pembroke, Bedford and Hertford, decided that Somerset must be removed from the King.[8] It would not be easy, for to quote Sir Thomas Erskine, now Lord Fenton, Somerset 'was more absolute than ever any that I have either heard of or did see myself'.

The dissentient lords decided that the only hope was to provide King James with a new favourite. Their choice fell upon George Villiers, an impecunious young man of twenty-two, but beautiful as a Greek god. Often the project must have seemed hopeless, for King James, in spite of many failings, was always loyal to his friends. Moreover, Pembroke and his supporters had to admit that Villiers had grave drawbacks. He dressed badly,[9] did not know how to ride and had no powerful backers like the Howards.

The conspirators did what they could. After Villiers's good looks had attracted King James's attention at Sir Anthony Mildmay's house, Apethorpe, in August 1614, Pembroke and his friends bought their young protégé the office of cupbearer to the King. It was clear to them that Villiers could never hope to displace Somerset unless he was at Court in close attendance on the King. His progress was disappointingly slow, on 24 November Chamberlain told his friend Sir Dudley Carleton: 'The fortune of Villiers, the new favourite, seems to be at a stand or at least not to go very fast forward, for when it was expected he should be made of the bedchamber, one Carr, a bastard kinsman of the Lord Chamberlain, is stept in and admitted to the place.'[10]

Queen Anne's dislike of the Howards was intensified in July 1614 when Somerset was created Lord Chamberlain, an office she declared the King had promised to bestow on her friend, the Earl of Pembroke. She was even more embittered when in the spring of 1615 the Earl of Suffolk, as Chancellor of Cambridge University, invited King James to pay a state visit, but omitted to include Queen Anne in the invitation. It was a studied insult which she did not forgive.

Clearly the time for action had come. One day when Queen Anne was strolling with her miniature greyhounds in Greenwich Park, the Earl of Pembroke went to see her to beg her help in the overthrow of Somerset. Anne had always made it a rule never to interfere in Court intrigues or between King James and his favourites. She believed George Villiers would be just another in the long line of royal favourites. Although she had no kindly feelings towards Somerset, she did not feel prepared to take an active part in advancing Villiers, so she refused his plea.

It seemed as if deadlock had been reached. Then Pembroke had an inspiration. He sent George Abbot, Archbishop of Canterbury, to plead their cause with the Queen. In spite of differing fundamentally in their religious views, Anne had a great respect for the Archbishop. She believed Abbot to be a man of integrity and one of the few people she could really trust. Yet even with Abbot's advocacy the Queen hesitated to intervene on behalf of Villiers,[11] partly perhaps she had no wish to support a Protestant policy, but also because she feared Villiers would only be another young man to whom her husband was physically attracted. Being a good judge of character, Queen Anne feared that although Villiers had perfect manners, intelligence and great charm he would prove ambitious and headstrong.

So she sounded a note of warning to the Archbishop's pleading.

My Lord [she said], *neither you nor your friends know what you desire. I know your master better than you all; if Villiers get once into his favour, those who shall have most contributed to his preferment will be the first sufferers by him. I shall be no more spared than the rest. The King will teach him himself to despise us and to treat us with pride and scorn. The young proud favourite will fancy that he is obliged to nobody for his preferment.*[12]

Abbot tried to reassure the Queen, saying: 'We were still insistent, telling her Majesty that a change would be for the better. For George was of a good nature, which the other was not, and if he should degenerate, yet it would be a long time before he were able to attain to that height of evil, which the other had.'[13]

These arguments were by no means as reassuring as the speaker meant them to be. The thought of having to endure the reign of another favourite as powerful and as decadent as Robert Carr was more than Queen Anne could contemplate. She realised that something must be done to end the present state of affairs, and rather reluctantly she agreed to ask the King to knight Villiers. It was only years later that Archbishop Abbot with the advantage of hindsight remarked, 'Noble Queen, how like a prophetess or oracle did you speak.'[14]

So on St George's Day 1615 Queen Anne went to the King's bedchamber to beg her husband to make George Villiers a Gentleman of the Bedchamber; a post which would bring him into the inner circle of Court life. Meanwhile Somerset, hearing what was afoot, determined to put a stop to it. When he saw the Queen entering the King's bedchamber he sent a message in his capacity of Lord Chamberlain, urging the King to make Villiers a groom of the bedchamber instead of giving him the more honourable post of Gentleman of the Bedchamber, but Abbot, who was waiting by the door, sent an urgent message to the Queen to insist that Villiers was made a Gentleman of the Bedchamber. Perhaps Somerset's stormy moods and deliberate wounding of the King's feelings had frightened the timid monarch. Whatever the reason, for once James listened to his wife and agreed to do as she wished.

Villiers, who was waiting in an antechamber with Archbishop Abbot, was summoned to the King's bedchamber, and the Queen asked Prince Charles, a shy boy of fourteen, to bring his father's sword.[15] Then pointing to Villiers, she told King James that 'here on the feast of England's patron saint was a young man named George who was a candidate for knighthood worthy of St George himself'.[16] As Queen Anne advanced, holding a drawn sword, King James as always shrank from the sight of bare steel, and when he tried to confer the accolade his hand shook so much that it had to be guided by the Queen. Rather uncharitably Archbishop Abbot ascribed the King's shaking hand to his having 'too powerfully refreshed at the Feast of Saint George'.[17]

So delighted was Villiers at being made a gentleman of the bedchamber and receiving a salary of £1,000 a year that on leaving the royal apartments he embraced the Archbishop and begged him to give him lessons on how to deport himself. At the same time he did his best to disarm criticism and at King James's suggestion he asked Somerset if he might be given a place in his household. He said: 'My Lord, I desire to be your servant and your creature, and shall desire to take my Court preferment under your favour and your Lordship shall find me as faithful a servant unto you as ever did serve you.'[18] But Somerset was always his own worst enemy. He brushed aside the offer in his usual offensive way, retorting: 'I will none of your service and you shall none of my favour. I will, if I can, break your neck and of that be confident.'[19]

After this rebuff George Villiers moved slowly, although as early as 20 May 1615 Chamberlain was referring to him as 'Sir George Villiers, the new Favourite'.[20] He held no public offices made no attempt to influence the King's policy or to exert political power. Yet he must have possessed great personal magnetism to win the undying devotion of three such widely different people as King James, Queen Anne and Prince Charles. With Queen Anne his relations soon became more friendly. She began to write him notes, addressing him by the pet name of 'dog', and as their friendship grew he became her 'kind dog'. For she soon discovered that the new favourite was a salutary influence on King James's unsavoury Court. He tried to curb the King's lapses in decorum, or, as Queen Anne called it, in the idiom she had learnt as a bride in Scotland, 'lug the sow's ear'.

She used the expression in a letter to Villiers which ran:

My kind Dog

I have received your letter which is very welcome to me. You do very well in lugging the sow's ear and I thank you for it and would have you do so still upon condition that you continue a watchful dog to him and be always true to him. So wishing you all happiness.

ANNA R.[21]

Villiers, entering with zest into the role of watchdog, answered 'in obedience to her desire, he had pulled the King's ear, until it was as long as any sow's'.

Queen Anne very seldom dated her letters, so it is difficult to tell when they were written. But the following letter shows that the Queen was placing more and more reliance upon Villiers.

My kind Dog

Your letter hath been acceptable to me. I rest already assured of your carefulness. You may tell your master that the King of Denmark hath sent me twelve fair mares and so the bringer assures me all great with foal which I intend to put in Byfield park, when, being the other day ahunting, I could find but very few deer, but great store of other cattle, as I shall tell your Master myself when I shall see him. I hope to meet you all at Woodstock at the time appointed, till when I wish you all happiness and contentment.

ANNA R.

I thank you for your pains in remembering the King for the paling of my park. Will do you any service I can.[22]

While Queen Anne's relations with Villiers had improved, Prince Charles remained, for the time being, bitterly hostile. Young as he was, he strongly disapproved of his father's favourites. Boylike, he could not conceal his feelings, and once when he had taken a ring from Villiers and failed to return it the favourite complained to King James.[23] Whereupon the King reprimanded his son so harshly that the boy burst into tears. After this Prince Charles was less than ever an admirer of Villiers. So in a spirit of boyish mischief, when he was at Greenwich, in May 1616 Prince Charles turned on a jet of water, which caught Villiers unawares in the face and thoroughly drenched him. This time King James was so angry that he boxed the Prince's ears twice.[24] The coolness between the two young men lasted until June 1619. Then gradually the Prince's hostility faded; Villiers's charm worked and Charles became his devoted friend for the rest of his life.

Undoubtedly Villiers showed great skill in winning golden

opinions. Richard Coke, nephew of Sir Edward Coke, said:

In the beginning of Mr Villiers coming into favour, he was affable and courteous and seemed to court all men as they courted him, he promoted men's suits to the King gratis, which Somerset would not do, but for some great sums of money, and hereby Villiers stole all the hearts of the courtiers and petitioners to the King from Somerset, who was now wholly forsaken by God and all men.[25]

Meanwhile the antagonism of Villiers and Somerset continued, to the great distress of King James. Then in the early autumn of 1615 came a blow which brought ruin to the Earl and Countess of Somerset.

In Flushing an apothecary's boy, William Reeve, knowing he was about to die, sent to the British Embassy saying he wished to make a deathbed confession. So momentous was his statement that the recipient went to the English ambassador, Sir William Trumbull, to tell him what the boy had said. After pondering over the situation, the ambassador took ship for England and sought an interview with Sir Ralph Winwood, now Secretary of State. At the end of August, after making inquiries, Winwood informed King James of what he had learnt. For William Reeve had confessed that in September 1613 he had been ordered by his master, the apothecary Paul de Lobell, to go to the Tower and administer a clyster (an enema) to Sir Thomas Overbury. But it was no ordinary clyster, for it contained a deadly poison—corrosive sublimate. For this the boy had received £20 from Frances, Countess of Essex. Next day Sir Thomas Overbury died in terrible pain.

Sir Ralph Winwood, who had been trained by Robert Cecil, held strongly Protestant views. He longed to see the downfall of the pro-Catholic, pro-Spanish Howard triumvirate. So it was with pleasure that he saw the arrest of the minor people in the plot: Richard Weston, Overbury's personal attendant in the Tower; Mrs Turner, who dispensed the poisons; Dr Franklin who carried messages and advised on poisons; and perhaps most unfortunate of the accused, Sir Gervase Elwes[26] Governor of the Tower of London. They were all in turn, tried, found guilty and executed.

Still the ringleaders seemed to have escaped. It was not until 24 May 1616 that the Countess of Somerset had to stand her trial before the High Steward's Court in Westminster Hall. She had been placed under house arrest at Lord d'Aubigny's house in Blackfrairs, as she was expecting a child, which was born on 9 December. It was a daughter whom the Countess called Anne, in the hope that it might incline the Queen in her favour. As Queen Anne had never had any illusions about Lady Frances, it proved a forlorn hope.

At the trial Lady Frances displayed superb showmanship. Dressed in a simple black woollen gown with white lawn collar and cuffs, and a black cap covering her golden hair, the Countess stood with downcast eyes, and as she pleaded guilty the tears ran down her cheeks. Yet John Chamberlain sensed that there was something spurious in her pose. 'She won pity by her sober demeanour which in my opinion was more curious and confident than was fit for a lady in such distress, yet she shed, or made show of, some few tears divers times.'[27]

When Lord Ellesmere, who as Lord High Steward presided at the trial, pronounced the death sentence, cynics declared that it would never be carried out, just as they did when next day Somerset, pleading 'Not guilty', received the same sentence.[28] The cynics were right. The sentences were commuted and the Earl and Countess lived together in considerable comfort in Raleigh's rooms in the Tower. Londoners were so annoyed at this travesty of justice that when soon after the trial Queen Anne was driving with the Countess of Derby through London a spectator seeing the coach shouted that it was the Countess of Somerset and her mother. A crowd gathered and tried to storm the coach, running after it, shouting abuse, much to the alarm of Queen Anne and her companion, who feared for their lives. It was not until the coach drove up to the Palace of Whitehall that the crowd realised their mistake.[29]

The incident was all the more unfortunate for Queen Anne as her sympathies certainly did not rest with the guilty Countess of Somerset. Indeed, after the trial she sent a ring set with a great diamond to the Chief Justice, Sir Edward Coke, as a mark of appreciation 'for the discovery of the poisoning of Sir Thomas Overbury'.[30]

With the downfall of Somerset came the ruin of the Howards, who had been a dominating force in English politics for many years. Fortunately for himself, their leader, Lord Henry Howard, Earl of Northampton, died in 1616, for the part he had played in ruining Overbury would never have borne public investigation. His elderly kinsman the Earl of Nottingham's long-cherished hopes of being created a Duke were gone for ever. Worse was to follow. In 1618 he lost his office of Lord High Admiral, which passed to Villiers, because due to his incompetence the navy was in a deplorable state, nearly half of the forty-seven ships being unfit to put to sea because of unsound timber which had been bought at a high price.

The fall of the third member of the triumvirate, the Earl of Suffolk, was even more ignominious. His period of office as Lord Treasurer had been disastrous for England. Since taking office in July 1614 he had instituted a wholesale system of bribes, and was accused of embezzlement of public funds, for which he was fined £30,000, ordered to be detained during the King's pleasure, but allowed to retire and live at Audley End.

Villiers's victory was complete. In August 1616 he was created Viscount Villiers and in January 1617 he became Earl of Buckingham. His hold on the King's affection was greater than Somerset's had ever been. 'The King', wrote Chamberlain, 'is never so out of tune but the very sight of my Lord of Buckingham doth settle and quiet it all.'[31]

16

KING CHRISTIAN'S SECOND VISIT TO ENGLAND 1614

While Queen Anne was suffering from deep depression and impaired health, the arrival of an unexpected visitor in the summer of 1614 did much to restore her spirits. She was dining alone at Somerset House when an agitated servant rushed into the great hall exclaiming that the King of Denmark had arrived. Nobody believed him. No news of an intended visit had come from Denmark, and as it was eight years since King Christian had been in England, few of the royal servants would recognise him. So Queen Anne went on with her dinner, only to find herself clasped round the waist and a hearty kiss planted on her cheek. Turning, she saw her brother Christian.[1]

His visit was veiled in the deepest secrecy, for the King had been rowed ashore from his flagship at Great Yarmouth, much to the alarm of the inhabitants, who feared that the Danish ships were a second Spanish Armada. After spending a night at Woodbridge and another at Brentwood, Christian arrived in London on 22 July, and hired a hackney coach to drive to Somerset House. Anne was delighted to see him, all the more so because in May 1612 it had been rumoured in London that King Christian was dead, and Anne and the ladies of her Court wore white taffeta for a week as mourning for him.[2]

Much had happened since Queen Anne had said farewell to her brother on his flagship the *Three Crowns*. Denmark had fought a short war against Sweden, in which King Christian had led his troops in person. His wife, the gentle, colourless Anna Catherine, had died in March 1612, leaving him with two sons. She had never played a significant part in his life. What interested him far more was the progress of his farflung plans to make Denmark a great power.[3] His main interest lay in the Danish navy, for he aimed at making his country lord of the Baltic, in defiance of Sweden, who in 1595 had gained possession of Estonia and Narva from Russia. From his earlier visit to England King Christian had brought back with him David Balfour, a shipbuilder, and this had paid dividends, for by the time King Christian was laying siege to Kalmar, the Danish navy numbered sixty ships, instead of only the nineteen when he came to the throne.

Eagerly Queen Anne listened to the latest news of her mother. Queen Sophie was enjoying the new life she had made for herself at Nykøbing, where she had enlarged the castle and shown herself to be a first-class businesswoman. She ran the estate, bred thoroughbred horses and used her resources so wisely that she had become a rich woman. More than once she was able to come to the rescue of her son with a substantial loan when he was heavily in debt, for, like his sister Anne, Christian was recklessly extravagant.

There was much speculation in London about King Christian's unexpected visit. As Sir Robert Cotton remarked: 'His arrival was so secret that there was no knowledge of him until he came into the presence at Somerset House. He professeth no other occasion than the affection of a brother to see his sister.'[4] This was such an unconvincing reason that rumours began to circulate that there had been a revolution in Denmark and the King was fleeing for his life.

Gradually the true reason emerged. King Gustavus of Sweden had joined an alliance with the Low Countries and Lübeck to oppose the payment of dues to Denmark by ships passing through the Sound. The Swedes also objected to paying an indemnity to Kalmar, which Christian had captured in 1611 when he made war on Sweden. So the Danish King, accompanied by his Chancellor, Christian Friis, and Admiral, Mogens Ulfeld, came to beg his brother-in-law on no account to support the States General and Lübeck in their opposition to Denmark. King Christian had to use Latin as a means of communication while he was in England and he addressed the Privy Council in that language when he made an eloquent plea for help against Sweden, but all he received in reply was a complaint from English merchants about restrictions on their trade.

Messengers were sent post-haste to recall King James, who was on a progress in Bedfordshire. He returned to London and immediately set in train a round of amusements to entertain his brother-in-law. The quiet hours of family reminiscences with her brother were over for Queen Anne. One of the subjects they probably discussed was the headstrong conduct of their nephew, Duke Frederick Julius of Brunswick. The town of Brunswick had joined Lübeck and the other Hanseatic towns and Christian feared that the young Duke would launch an open attack upon the place. In spite of his uncle's efforts to restrain him, Frederick Julius attacked the town with an army of twenty thousand men in 1615, but his attempt proved a failure and he had to raise the siege.[5]

Four days after the Danish King's arrival King James returned to London and two days later, on Saint James's Day, the two went to church, King Christian wearing the Order of the Garter. Then a round of festivities filled the royal guest's days; tilting at the ring, bull and bear baiting and fencing. On the last evening King Christian staged a firework display in honour of his hosts. Then on 1 August, after saying good-bye to his sister at Somerset House, the Danish King, accompanied by King James and Prince Charles, went by boat to Woolwich, where Christian visited the English fleet. He was deeply interested in the ship *Mer Honneur*, then in dry dock, which he saw before going on board his flag-ship, accompanied by King James and Prince Charles.

King James only stayed two hours before going ashore to continue his progress, although the Danish King was not sailing until the next day. This was taken as a sign that King James's feelings towards his brother-in-law were much less friendly than on

Christian's earlier visit. That shrewd observer John Chamberlain noticed a certain coolness:

It is thought the King of Denmark could have been content to have stayed longer but that he was hastened away. . . . There is no other cause of his coming yet discovered than extraordinary kindness . . . some whisper that if the Earl of Northampton had lived,[6] *he would have complained of some hard and unreverent usage and speeches of his touching the Queen, his sister, others that he moved the King to undertake Brandenburg's quarrel for Cleeve with 10,000 men.*[7]

Just before King Christian sailed the Queen's Vice-Chamberlain came on board the flagship bringing a superb diamond ring for the King as a proof of his sister's deep affection for him. It was an afterthought characteristic of Queen Anne's generous nature.

Soon after King Christian's visit Queen Anne decided to commission Inigo Jones to build a new house for her at Greenwich.[8] This is still known as the Queen's House. With her declining health, Anne's interest in masques had slackened. She suffered from ulcers on the left leg and recurrent attacks of gout. In the autumn of 1615, after a visit to Bath to take the waters, she returned 'not so well as when she went'.[9] Inigo Jones, too, had grown tired of designing elaborate stage scenery and devising novel theatrical effects. Moreover, he was finding Ben Jonson more and more difficult to work with. He was anxious to devote himself seriously to architecture, so he was overjoyed when his first important commission came from Queen Anne.

Work on the Queen's House began in 1616. It was classical in style, but the plan was original. The building was in two parts; one within the precincts of Greenwich Palace and the other in Greenwich Park. They were to be linked by a covered bridge crossing the public road. Inigo owed his inspiration to a similar plan he had seen at Lorenzo de Medici's villa at Poggio[10] and he reproduced it at Greenwich to great advantage. There was a colonnaded south front approached by a flight of curved steps. It was the first house in classical style to be built in England. Within there was a forty-foot cubic hall, the forerunner of a number of such halls which became fashionable amongst the nobility in seventeenth-century England, of which there is an outstanding example, known as a double cube, at Wilton House.

Queen Anne was never to live in the Queen's House, or even to see it in all its glory. Probably the first floor was finished at the time of her death; then all work on the building was stopped. It did not begin again until 1630, when the Queen's House was completed for Anne's daughter-in-law, Queen Henrietta Maria. Today the building is but a ghost of its former splendour. The covered way has gone, and the Queen's House is now two separate buildings, one of which contains the National Maritime Museum.[11] In Queen Anne's lifetime the cost of building the Queen's House was estimated to be about £4,000, which was only twice the price of one of the royal masques.

While the work on the Queen's House was proceeding Queen Anne decided to have a full-length portrait of herself painted by her favourite artist, Paul van Somer. She was still good-looking in the style fashionable in her day, and she knew how to dress to enhance her best points. As one of the ladies of the Court noted: 'Her features were not regular but her complexion was extremely fair and she had the finest neck that could be seen, which she took care it should be by the fashions of dress which she from time to time brought up.'[12] This she did by wearing high-boned lace collars, which were disastrous for those with short, thick necks, and by showing her preference for farthingales, which suited her tall figure.

Paul van Somer was born in Antwerp and only settled in London in 1611. He was a skilful portrait painter, and, until the coming of Anthony Van Dyck, the foremost one in England. His portrait of Queen Anne, painted in 1617, was his first important work to bear a date. The Queen is about to go hunting. She is wearing a dark green velvet farthingale, tight bodice and gauntlets as she stands beside her palomino horse. At her feet are five miniature greyhounds, two of which she holds by a crimson cord. All the dogs have ornamental collars with the letters A.R. embossed in gold. In the background is one of her favourite residences, Oatlands, given to her in 1611, which is easily recognisable by the ornamental gateway built by Inigo Jones for Queen Anne.[13]

As has been already shown the Queen was popular with her subjects. The people recognised her courage, dignity and sympathy with those less fortunate than herself. Her contemporaries spoke well of her. To quote Arthur Wilson, Anne was 'a good woman, not tempted to embroil herself . . . content in her own house with such recreations as might not make time tedious to her'.[14] The Venetian ambassador, after remarking that she was passionately fond of dancing, said Queen Anne was of a lively humour, rather good-looking and still more gracious, particularly to those 'who fall in with her humour'; but 'she is terrible proud and intolerable to those she dislikes'.[15] This was true. Anne was an embittered hater. Time did not soften her. To the end of her life she detested the Earl of Mar and Robert Carr, Earl of Somerset.

In spite of the many disappointments and frustrations the Queen had endured, she never lost her kindness of heart and her desire to help those in trouble. This she showed when she invited Pocahontas, the daughter of a Red Indian chief, to come to Court, where she received her graciously and gave her a seat for a masque in 1617. Innate curiosity may have played a part in winning the royal favour, for Pocahontas was an exotic fugure and her romantic story excited much interest in London. The girl had saved the life of Captain John Smith, who later became President of Virginia. Apparently she fell in love with him, but he sailed away and she married John Rolfe. Yet Pocahontas followed him to England, where she fell upon hard times. Her money was exhausted, the climate was too severe after the sunny land of Virginia, and she died on board ship when about to return to America.

A further instance of Queen Anne's essential warmth of heart was shown when she answered Lady Arabella Stuart's appeal for help. For Arabella had an intellectual arrogance which made her treat the Queen with unconcealed contempt as an utterly brainless and frivolous creature. Yet Queen Anne felt sympathy for Arabella, who was thirty-five years of age, still unmarried and with little prospect of finding a husband of whom King James would approve. Not that Arabella Stuart had lacked suitors. Count Maurice of Nassau, Sigismund III, King of Poland, and Ulric, Duke of Holstein, sought her hand, but none of them met with King James's approval. For the King's solution of the marriage problem was a life of perpetual spinsterhood for his cousin.

So the years dragged on and Arabella's claims to beauty continued to fade. Suddenly all was changed. Arabella fell in love with a studious, rather dull young man who was thirteen years her junior. He was William Seymour, grandson of the Earl of Hertford, and a more unsuitable choice it would have been hard to discover. For William Seymour traced his descent from Henry the Eighth's younger sister Mary Tudor and any children of such a marriage would have a formidable claim to the throne. No wonder the mere idea of the possibility of such a union sent King James into paroxysms of rage. Arabella was summoned before the Privy Council and ordered to give up all idea of marrying William Seymour.[16]

Why Seymour wished to marry Arabella will always remain a mystery. He was no gay Lothario and he must have known that his prospective bride was hopelessly extravagant and heavily in debt, besides being the formidable age of thirty-five, an ominous age for an unmarried royal lady. In spite of a generous allowance from King James, Arabella could not live within her means. In 1609 she asked the King for the monopoly of the sale of wine or whiskey in Ireland[17] to pay her debts or the grant of an additional £1,000 a year.[18] When the monopoly was granted she asked to have it exchanged for payment of her debts. Jewels were Arabella's special delight, she tried to wear jewels which outshone even Queen Anne's.

All the initiative for the marriage fell to Arabella. Seymour would never have dared to snatch his bride from the grasp of an outraged monarch. So in great secrecy, while King James was away from London, between four and five in the morning of Friday, 22 June 1610, Arabella was married to William Seymour. Retribution speedily followed. Arabella was placed under house arrest in Lambeth and William Seymour was sent to the Tower.

In despair Arabella turned to Queen Anne for help. It cannot be denied that Arabella had always been a depressing influence at Court. She disapproved of so many things. She made adverse comments on King James's uncouth ways, on Queen Anne's frivolity and on the levity of the ladies of the Court. Nevertheless Queen Anne responded to Arabella's appeal, made through their mutual friend, Lady Jean Drummond, who presented the Queen with a pair of gloves, worked by the ill-fated bride. Anne showed her petition to King James. The result was negative. Lady Jean reported 'he did take it well enough but gave no answer but that "Ye had eaten of the forbidden tree." To soften the blow the Queen sent Arabella 'this little token in notice of the continuation of her Majesty's favour to your Ladyship'.[19]

In the early months of 1611 King James learnt that Arabella had been in secret communication with her husband in the Tower, and fearing that her visits might result in the birth of a son and heir, who would have claims to the throne, he ordered his cousin to be interned in Durham Castle under the custody of the Bishop of Durham. When Arabella learnt of the King's decision she was so distraught that she had attacks of hysteria and incoherent letter writing, as she had done as a young girl at Hardwick Hall when under her grandmother's care. In desperation she resolved to make her escape. Disguised as a man, putting on French-fashioned hose over her petticoats, wearing a man's doublet and with a wig partly hiding her face, she made her way to Blackwall and thence to Leigh, where a French ship was waiting to take her to France. But William Seymour proved to be even more inefficient than his neurotic wife. He made a mistake in the time and failed to arrive at the rendezvous. While Arabella was waiting for him off Calais her ship was captured and brought back to England. Arabella was imprisoned in the Tower. There she pined for four years until death came as a release on 20 September 1615.[20]

Undoubtedly Queen Anne was extravagant. She had no idea of the value of money. Although she had an adequate allowance, she was always in debt. King James treated her generously. In addition to her Scottish jointure, he added £5,000, so that by 1616 her jointure amounted to £24,000 a year. Besides Greenwich Palace and Somerset House, the Queen had been given Oatlands, Hatfield Place, Nonsuch, Pontefract Castle and Havering at Bower.[21] She also had £13,000 a year from duties on sugar and cloth. Queen Anne's habit of distributing diamond rings indiscriminately in return for small personal services did not help her finances. More than once King James had to come to the rescue and pay her debts. He made himself responsible for the cost of her household except the servants and for her stables.[22] This was at a time when his own finances were in a deplorable state.

Even so Queen Anne could not live within her income and she had to turn to George Heriot, her jeweller, for help. Heriot had followed the King and Queen south, and had opened a shop near the New Exchange. Royal messengers often went to his shop to summon him to Somerset House. In the first ten years that Queen Anne was in England she spent £40,000 and was reduced to offering ten per cent interest to anyone who would lend her money to repay Heriot. She also on occasion used him as her pawnbroker. In May 1609 the Queen had recently had goods from him worth a thousand guineas, and as she had not the money to pay for them, and having bought some diamond pendants and a large supply of musk and ambergris worth the same amount, she ordered Heriot to pawn certain of her jewels 'of which she had lost conceit'.[23] Still the Queen could not keep out of debt, and four years later she was owing Heriot a greater sum and he was petitioning for payment.

In spite of the drawbacks involved in the royal connection, George Heriot obtained certain substantial advantages from it. In 1609 his business had grown so large that he was unable to find enough workmen to execute his orders. Probably at Queen Anne's instigation, the Government issued an order calling upon all magistrates to help Heriot to get the workmen he required.[24]

Queen Anne was a devoted mother. Her maternal feelings were so strong that, as we have seen, being deprived of the custody of her children when they were only a few weeks old wrecked her marriage. Of her three children Prince Charles was her favourite. He had shown such courage in overcoming his muscular weakness and difficulty in speech. John Webb had been engaged to teach him tennis, and now he could play a good game; he enjoyed dancing and was an excellent horseman. Moreover, he was highly intelligent, speaking several languages, and deeply interested in music and painting. But what pleased his mother most was that he was a most affectionate boy. As a gentleman at the Court noted, 'the Queen did ever love Charles better than Prince Henry'.[25]

Charles, for his part, was devoted to his mother. He would stay for weeks with her at Greenwich or Oatlands whenever possible. When she was ill Charles wrote affectionate little letters to hasten her recovery, such as this one when she was suffering from an attack of gout.

Most worthy mistress

Seeing I could not have the happiness to see your Majesty, give me leave to declare by these lines the duty and love I owe to you, which makes me long to see you. I wish from my heart that I might help to find a remedy to your disease, the which I must bear the more patiently because it is the sign of a long life. But I must for many causes be sorry; especially because it is troublesome to you and had deprived me of your most comfortable sight and of many good dinners, the which I hope by God's grace, shortly to enjoy and when it shall please you to give me leave to see you, it may be I shall give you some good receips which either shall heal you or make you laugh; the which wishing I may obtain your Majesty's most gracious favour, kissing in all humility your most sacred hands and praying for your health and long prosperity. I end, most worthy mistress, your Majesty's most humble and obedient servant

CHARLES.[26]

It was a deep disappointment to Prince Charles that his mother could not be present at his investiture as Prince of Wales in November 1616. Her absence was partly due to ill health and partly, as John Chamberlain believed, because she feared 'she renew her grief by the memory of the last prince'.[27] The wound caused by Prince Henry's untimely death would never be wholly healed.

Perhaps Queen Anne was fortunate in not being able to attend the ceremony, for it was one of those occasions when everything went wrong. The precarious state of the nation's finances made it impossible to stage the investiture on the lavish scale of Prince Henry's. As Lady Anne Clifford noted in her diary, 'There was running of the ring but not half the pomp as at the creation of Prince Henry'.[28] The day was wet and stormy, the attendance poor, but the worst moment of all came when Lancelot Andrews, Bishop of Ely, made the macabre mistake of solemnly praying for Henry Prince of Wales instead of his brother Charles.[29] It was a superstitious age, and many of those who heard him interpreted it as a portent of the speedy demise of Prince Charles.

In the spring of 1617 King James decided to revisit his native land, which he had not seen for fourteen years. Queen Anne approved of his decision. Not that she had any wish to accompany her husband on the long road to Scotland, but she had high hopes of being appointed Regent in England during his absence. Alas, she was doomed to disappointment, just as her mother Queen Sophia had been when she tried to become Regent of Denmark during the minority of her son King Christian. Much to Queen Anne's annoyance, Lord Keeper Bacon was entrusted with carrying on the government during the King's absence.

However, the Queen dutifully played her part of a loving wife. She accompanied the King to Theobalds on 14 March and went with him as far as Ware. Then she returned with Prince Charles to Greenwich, where most of the Council stayed with her during the months King James was in Scotland. During his absence, mindful of the scoldings she had been given earlier for being a negligent correspondent,[30] the Queen wrote meek little letters to her husband such as the following:

My heart

I crave pardon that I have not sooner answered your Majesty's letter. You shall not fear the pain in my fingers. You shall find them well enough for you when you come home. I think it long to see my gerfalcon fly, which I hope to see when I shall have the honour to kiss your M hands.

Yours

ANNA R.[31]

In May, while thoroughly enjoying her husband's absence,[32] Queen Anne was disturbed by an alarming experience. Always intensely superstitious, she feared the worst when she dreamt that her husband was in acute danger. So terrified was she that she sent a special messenger to Scotland to beg King James to tell her what had happened and to hurry home.[33] However, all was well; the dream proved to be a false portent and no ill had befallen King James.

About the time of the King's return from Scotland Queen Anne's health declined and it was feared that she had not long to live. She removed to Oatlands,[34] one of the largest of the royal houses, built by Henry VIII with materials from Chertsey Abbey, to see if a change of air would do her good. For like all her contemporaries Queen Anne was a firm believer in the beneficial effects of a change of air.

The King's health, too, left much to be desired. The journey to Scotland was a strain. Although he was only fifty-one, he had few teeth, suffered from chronic catarrh, and his legs were so feeble that he had to be tied on his horse when he went hunting. The Spanish ambassador observed: 'The King grows too fat to be able to hunt comfortably, spends much time in reading, especially religious works and eats and drinks so recklessly that it is thought he will not live long.'[35]

Her parents' poor health made their daughter determined to visit England, although she received no encouragement from either her father or her husband. As Chamberlain told Sir Dudley Carleton:

The Lady Elizabeth, we hear, makes great means to come over hither after she is fully recovered of her child-birth and is so bent to it that she will hardly be stayed. I see not to what purpose it is nor what good can come by it to either side. For unless here were a more plentiful world, she will not find the contentment she hath done hitherto and expects.[36]

King James heartily concurred with these sentiments. He had not forgotten the expense of his son-in-law's earlier visit and the delays in his departure, while Frederick, who was busy urging the Protestant princes to elect him King of Bohemia, had no wish to return to a land where he felt he had been slighted. So he insisted that he must be given precedence over the Prince of Wales, a demand which he knew the English would never accept.[37]

Yet nothing damped Elizabeth's determination. It was six years since she had sailed from Margate. Now she was the mother of two sons, of whom the eldest, Frederick Henry, was heir presumptive to the English throne. Queen Anne was never to see any of her grandchildren. She would have been delighted with six-year-old Frederick Henry, who was a spirited boy, with much of the grace and charm which endeared his namesake, the late Prince of Wales, to all who knew him. As it happened, neither King James nor Count Frederick need have worried about the proposed visit to England. Fate took a hand. Suddenly the Electress found that she was pregnant for the third time and all thought of going overseas had for the time being to be abandoned. In spite of her poor health, Queen Anne did not lose her interest in hunting and hawking. While she was at Oatlands she wrote to King James to complain about the state of the park.

My heart

I desire your Majesty to pardon that I have not answered your Majesty sooner upon your letters, because I would know the truth of the park at Ottelands, as I understand there is near forty gross bestiami, of divers kinds that devours my deer, as I will tell your Majesty at meeting. Whereas your Majesty would have me meet you at Whitehall, I am content but I fear some inconvenience in my legs which I have not felt here. So kissing your Majesty's hands, I rest

Yours

ANNA R.[38]

The bestiami were neat cattle, which did not actually devour the royal deer, as the Queen's letter implies, but starved them by eating the grass upon which they fed. This was worrying enough, but an even greater annoyance, during the King's absence, was caused by quarrels which broke out amongst the courtiers. Francis Bacon, who had been appointed Lord Keeper ten days before the King travelled to Scotland, infuriated his contemporaries by assuming almost royal state, occupying the King's private apartments, using the banqueting hall at Whitehall to hold audiences, and worst of all, travelling in such state when he went to preside over the Easter law term of the Court of Chancery that it seemed like a royal progress. The fact that both Queen Anne and Prince Charles sent contingents to march in the procession did nothing to soothe his opponents.

Foremost amongst these was Sir Ralph Winwood, Secretary of State. The two men were temperamentally antagonistic. Winwood was hard-working, conscientious and fervidly Protestant, but his sarcastic tongue and supercilious manner made him many enemies, among them Queen Anne, who never forgave the part he played in promoting the marriage of her daughter to the Elector Palatine.

On the other hand, Lord Keeper Bacon was intensely ambitious, brilliantly clever and utterly ruthless. Queen Anne does not seem to have resented Bacon's encroachment on the royal state, but Winwood viewed his actions very differently. He complained to Queen Anne and wrote to King James 'imploring him to make haste back, for his seat was already usurped, and he verily believed Bacon fancied himself King'.

So outraged were Sir Ralph's feelings that he threatened to resign his office as Secretary of State. Queen Anne did her best to end the quarrel and finally sent for the Lord Keeper and asked him 'Why he and Secretary Winwood could not agree?' to which Bacon replied disarmingly: 'Madam, I can say no more but he is proud and I am proud.'[39] A reply which amused Queen Anne. For a time the two antagonists were mollified, but it was not long before they met again in open conflict.

17

THE CLOSING YEARS 1617-1619

For the third time in her life, in September 1617 Queen Anne was forced to honour with her presence a wedding which she viewed with the utmost distaste. It was a union brought about by the ambition of the bridegroom's mother and the avarice of the bride's father. Neither Lady Compton nor Sir Edward Coke can have felt proud of the part they played.

Since the fall of Somerset George Villiers had gone from strength to strength. King James was so infatuated that he could deny his favourite nothing. In January 1617 Villiers was created Earl of Buckingham. King James would have dearly liked to have made him Duke of Buckingham, as Villiers himself desired, but since the execution of the Duke of Norfolk in Queen Elizabeth's reign there had been no dukes except those of royal birth. King James was afraid of inflaming the Puritan opposition in Parliament still further if he took such a step.

Buckingham's mother, who had married Sir Thomas Compton as her third husband, was a ruthlessly ambitious woman, who was determined to use the meteoric career of her second son to advance the fortunes of his brothers by providing them with wealthy brides. Her eldest son John, a dim-witted youth, was her first concern. Lady Compton was determined, in spite of his disabilities, to advance his interests. Her predatory eye fell on Frances Coke, the only child of the former Chief Justice Sir Edward Coke's second marriage. Sir Edward approved of the match, in the belief that alliance with Buckingham's brother would reinvigorate his flagging fortunes.[1] Even so nearly a year passed while he haggled over the amount of his daughter's dowry. The girl's mother, Lady Hatton, took a diametrically opposite view. On no terms would she give her consent to the match. In her distress she sought the aid of her husband's inveterate enemy, Lord Keeper Bacon, to prevent the marriage.

Determined to have his own way, Sir Edward Coke resorted to battering down the doors of the house where his wife and daughter had taken refuge and abducting the girl. In spite of these scandalous happenings, King James continued to smile upon the match. He could refuse his favourite nothing and he insisted that Queen Anne must attend the ceremony. So in the presence of the Queen on 29 September 1617 in the chapel of Hampton Court Palace, Frances Coke was married to John Villiers.

Not even the most romantic member of the congregation could have felt that it was a happy occasion. The bride was white-faced and trembling, the bridegroom glum, and the bride's mother conspicuous by her absence, while Queen Anne marked her unwillingness to be present by her glacial manner. Anne was beginning to realise that her warning against introducing George Villiers as the new royal favourite had not been without justification. But her resentment was as nothing to that of the bride's mother, who had been compelled to withdraw her opposition by Lord Keeper Bacon's volte-face. He had suddenly realised that his career was at stake and that he was not strong enough to oppose Buckingham. Even the Villiers family were far from happy for Sir Edward Coke had succeeded in whittling down the bride's dowry to a mere £10,000 with no £1,000 a year extra during his lifetime—an action for which Buckingham never forgave him.[2]

Queen Anne's plea of ill health to avoid attending the wedding was no diplomatic illness. Only a fortnight after the ceremony Chamberlain was writing, 'The Queen is somewhat crazy [sickly] again, though they say it is but the gout. She is generally well wished and the care of her welfare makes the world more fearful.[3]

But in spite of being 'well wished', there was no improvement in Queen Anne's condition. 'The Queen continues still ill disposed and though she would fain lay all her infirmities upon the gout yet most of her physicians fear a further inconvenience of an ill habit or disposition through her whole body.[4] 'Nor were reports of King James's health more reassuring, in spite of his unpleasant remedy of plunging his legs into a disembowelled deer which had been recently killed.[5] Ill as she was, Queen Anne travelled several times from Somerset House to Whitehall to see her husband while he was confined to bed. In the end to save the fatigue of journeying across London she accompanied him to Theobalds and stayed there with him.

Theobalds always had a beneficial effect on King James. It was a tangible proof of one of his most successful coups. For it was the wonder house from which Sir Robert Cecil had parted with such great reluctance. Built by his father, the first Lord Burghley, Theobalds was like Hardwick Hall 'more glass than wall'. Built round two courtyards with cupola-capped towers at the corners, the house was even more impressive within. There was a long gallery with the lineage of the kings of England shown in gold leaf, and a great hall with a map of England and artificial trees with natural bark growing up the walls. In addition to a large garden on the south side of the house with a round summerhouse adorned with the busts of twelve Roman emperors, there was a privy garden with a maze on the west side and, what to King James was the greatest attraction, a great park enclosed by a wall, which provided ideal hunting.

Christmas 1617 was a miserable time for the royal family, nor did the New Year bring any brighter hopes. On Twelfth Night the Prince of Wales staged his first masque, *Pleasure reconciled to Virtue*, but Queen Anne was too ailing to be present, much as she admired Ben Jonson's verse, and even when it was repeated at Shrovetide she was not well enough to see it.

Perhaps the melancholy from which the Queen was suffering was the outcome of her anxiety over the fate of Sir Walter Raleigh.

Since 1603 he had been a prisoner in the Tower and just when prospects of release seemed near they were dashed by the death of Prince Henry. Queen Anne had happy memories of visits to Raleigh in his laboratory in the Governor's garden in the Tower of London, and of his kindness in concocting a cordial for her which improved her health. She approved of her son's friendship with the Elizabethan seaman and echoed Prince Henry's oft-quoted remark: 'None but my father would keep such a bird in a cage.'[6] At length it had seemed as if Prince Henry's pleas to his father were having an effect. King James promised that Raleigh should be set free by Christmas. But Henry's untimely death had brought the King's promise to naught.

Sir Walter Raleigh knew that his only hope of freedom lay in appealing to the King's cupidity. So he tried to convince King James that rich stores of gold lay untapped in the mines of Guiana. Indian legends told of El Dorado somewhere in the region of the Orinoco river. It is unlikely that Raleigh really believed in the legends, and he may even have manipulated the evidence for the existence of gold, but he never abandoned his dream of founding an English empire in South America. From the first Prince Charles disapproved of the expedition and persuaded his mother not to visit Raleigh's ship, as she had promised.[7]

King James had debts amounting to over £700,000, so he lent an attentive ear to Raleigh's pleas. At least it offered him a possible release from his financial troubles. Parliament, he knew, would not come to his rescue. So Raleigh was released from the Tower on his promise not to attack any subjects of the King of Spain. He sailed in June 1617 on a voyage to Guiana.

If it be true that nothing succeeds like success, it is equally true that nothing is so disastrous as failure. There is no disguising that Raleigh's last expedition was an abysmal failure. Sir Walter was dogged by bad luck from beginning to end. He never found the goldmine; his exploring party was ambushed in the jungle; his elder son Walter was killed in the attack on San Thomé, and he himself was broken in health.

King James was rabid. Sir Walter had not only antagonised the

King of Spain, and endangered the delicate negotiations for the hand of a Spanish Infanta in marriage for Prince Charles, but what was even worse he had returned without bringing a single piece of Spanish gold. In his rage the King turned to the lawyers for advice. So when Sir Walter Raleigh landed at Plymouth in June 1618 he was immediately placed under arrest on the charge of treason passed on him in 1603. King James dared not risk an open trial, so he had the fifteen-year-old death sentence, which had never been rescinded, confirmed.

At this period of his life King James was completely under the spell of the wily, witty Spanish ambassador, Don Diego Sarmieno de Acuña, later Count Gondomar.[8] 'The King took delight to talk with him for he was full of conceits and would speak false Latin on purpose in his merry fits to please the King, telling the King plainly that he [James] spoke Latin like a pedant but I speak it like a gentleman.' Gondomar played on King James's intense love of peace and of his desire for a Spanish bride for his son, and he insisted that this time there must be no reprieve for Sir Walter Raleigh.

When Queen Anne saw how matters were shaping she became deeply troubled. In spite of a recent attack of hæmorrhage of the lungs and her legs being swollen by dropsy, she determined to do everything in her power to save Sir Walter Raleigh. She decided that the best way to approach King James was through the all-powerful Buckingham, so she wrote imploring his help.

My kind dog

If I have any power or credit with you, I earnestly pray you let me have a trial of it at this time, in dealing sincerely and earnestly with the King that Sir Walter Raleigh's life may not be called in question; if you do it so, that your success answer my expectation, assure yourself that I will take it extraordinarily kindly at your hands, and rest one that wisheth you well, and desires you to continue still as you have been a true servant to your master.

ANNA R.[9]

Queen Anne had made a serious miscalculation. She had not realised that Buckingham had no more desire to offend Count Gondomar than had his master, King James, and that he was advocating the Spanish marriage and acquiescing in Sir Walter's death. When this appeal proved fruitless she made a last desperate plea to the King. Chamberlain commented:

There was great means for his life, and I hear the Queen wrote very earnestly to the king . . . to spare him for that she had received great good by his receipts. I hear not so much of her recovery of late as when I wrote last, but rather that she goes peggiorando insomuch that it is doubted whether the King come hither today from Tiballs or go directly to Hampton Court, where she lies.[10]

It was all in vain. King James was not to be moved either by considerations of justice or pleas for mercy. He had made up his mind. Sir Walter Raleigh was to be sacrificed to placate Spain and keep alive the prospect of a Spanish bride for the Prince of Wales who would bring him a dowry of £600,000 in addition to her jewels. King James offered to send Raleigh to Madrid to be executed, but Philip III preferred to leave the odium to others. So on 28 October 1618 Sir Walter Raleigh was taken from the Tower to the gatehouse at Westminster for the night and next morning beheaded in Old Palace Yard. From that moment 'the people looked upon his execution as a national disgrace and as base appeasement of Spain'.[11] The brilliant comet which appeared in the November sky was regarded as foretelling disaster.

With the coming of the New Year Queen Anne was cheered by the prospect of a visit from her brother King Christian, but he never came and she sank still deeper in a morass of gloom. She had been too ill to take part in any of the Christmas festivities, which she used to enjoy so much, but she had been considering going to Oatlands in the early spring—a move which never materialised.

Unwisely the Queen's doctor prescribed sawing wood as a

remedy to improve her circulation,[12] but this brought on another haemorrhage. King James came three times to visit her at Hampton Court, which John Chamberlain took as an ominous sign.

We begin now to apprehend the Queen's danger [he wrote on 2 January 1619], *when the physicians themselves begin to speak doubtfully; but I can not think the case desperate, as long as she was able to attend a whole sermon on Christmas Day preached by the bishop of London in her inner chamber. Yet I hear the courtiers lay about them already, and plot for leases of her land, for the keeping of Somerset House and the rest, for implements and movables as if they were to divide a spoil. I hope they may come as short as they that made account of the bearskin: yet we can not be out of fear till we see her past the top of May-hill.*[13]

Prince Charles frequently visited his mother at Hampton Court and slept in an adjoining bedroom. In February, when it was known that there was little hope of the Queen's recovery, King James became very worried; not so much about his wife's health but whether she had made a will. He feared that she might leave many of her jewels to her Danish maid Anna, who had been with her since she came as a bride from Denmark, and to the Frenchman whom she called Pierrot. Or what was even worse that she should make her son Charles her sole heir. He distrusted Prince Charles's repeated attempts to persuade his mother to make a will and saw his frequent visits to Hampton Court in a very sinister light.

This troubled Charles and he wrote to Buckingham asking him to use his influence to reassure the King.

There is none that knows me so well as yourself, what dutiful respect and love I have ever and shall every carry to the King and therefore ye may gage what grief it is to me to have the ill fortune as that any of my actions should bear so ill a correspondence as I find by your letter. . . . That which made me think that this message would not displease the King was the command ye know he gave me a good while ago that I should use all the means I could to make the Queen make a will; whereby she should

make over to me her jewels: therefore I sent to have [the] King's approbation of that which I thought he had desired and therefore I thought he would rather be glad than any way displeased with the message; my meaning was never to claim anything as of right but to submit myself as well in this as in all other things to the King's pleasure. It doth grieve me much that the King should be so much moved with it as you say he is, for the least show of his displeasure would make me leave to meddle or think of any such thing any more, without showing himself openly so angry with me. To conclude I pray you to commend my most humble service to his Majesty and to tell him that I am very sorry that I have done anything which may offend him, and that I will be content to have any penance inflicted upon me so that he may forgive me, although I never had a thought nor ever shall have to displease him, yet I deserve to be punished for my ill fortune. So hoping never to have occasion to write to you of so ill a subject again,
I rest

Your true constant loving friend

CHARLES P.[14]

The Court was seething with rumours. Everyone was speculating to whom the Queen would leave her very considerable estate. John Chamberlain as usual was well informed.

The reports ran at first that she had made a will (according to the privilege of our Queens, who as our lawyers say, have potestatem testandi and may dispose of all they have saving lands or jewels belonging to the Crown) that she had set apart a casket of jewels for the Lady Elizabeth . . . But for ought I can learn yet, she made none other than a noncuperative will, or by word of mouth, giving all she had to the Prince with charge to pay her debts or reward her servants and having a grant upon clothes lately given to her to the value of £8,000 a year.[15]

While King James was worrying about the disposal of his wife's temporal possessions, the Archbishop of Canterbury and the bishops were equally troubled about her spiritual welfare. They were determined that the Queen should die a member of the Church of England. Queen Anne had never been a militant Christian. Even the Pope had lamented her lack of zeal. Paul V had expressed his regret in a letter written on 12 August 1612 to the papal nuncio, in which he said: 'Not considering the inconstancy of that Queen and the many changes she had made in religious matters and that even if it might be true that she might be a Catholic, one should not take on oneself any judgment, all the more as the cruelty and pitilessness of that King was increasingly against the poor Catholics.'[16]

With declining health Queen Anne's dependence on Catholic priests deepened. Father Abercromby, her confessor, had gone back to Germany many years before, but during her long illness she had a beautiful little chapel fitted up at Oatlands and she kept Catholic priests always within call at Hampton Court. The Pope noted that she was becoming more earnest in her religious beliefs and in May 1616 he issued a papal brief praising her zeal.[17]

Probably Queen Anne did not realise the serious nature of her illness. When early in 1619 the Archbishop of Canterbury and the Bishop of London visited her to remind her of the fleeting nature of human life and the advisability of putting her affairs in order and making her peace with God; all Queen Anne would say was that she would wait till the morrow, as this was Childermas, 'or as some call it the dismal day'.[18] The Archbishop asked Prince Charles to use his influence to persuade his mother to make a will, but this time he refused to intervene, declaring that it would be most improper.[19]

On Monday, 1 March 1619, the lords and ladies of the household came to Hampton Court to pay their respects to the Queen, but Anne was now so ill that she dreaded crowds of people around her, and by her orders Danish Anna locked the door of her bedchamber. Her friends the Countess of Bedford and the Countess of Arundel took their exclusion in good part, but the imperious Countess of Derby insisted on forcing her way into the royal bedchamber. It was of little avail, for after the Queen had asked her one or two questions she told her to go to her supper.

At midnight the anteroom was cleared of visitors when the Queen's doctors, Dr Mayerne, Dr Atkins and Dr Turner, had paid their nightly visit. Queen Anne was left alone with her Danish maid Anna, who slept in the same room. Anne murmured drowsily: 'Now lay by me to sleep, for in seeing you repose. I shall feel disposed to sleep.'

Suddenly between two and three in the morning the Queen's condition grew worse. Prince Charles, the Archbishop of Canterbury, the Bishop of London and the doctors were hurriedly summoned. In spite of all the pressure brought upon her, Queen Anne had still not made a will. It was too late. Her sight was failing, she could not sign anything, even if her hand were guided. When Charles kneeling by her bedside leant over her and asked 'Your properties, madam. Can I have those?' all she could do was to murmur 'Yea', and again to his further question: 'Your debts and your servants. Am I to take charge of them?' there came a faint 'Yea'.

It was not a satisfactory way of disposing of a large estate. Soon there were critical comments:

The manner of her will was rather in answering questions and saying 'Yea' to anything that was demanded of her than in disposing ought of herself, so that it is doubted by some already how far it will stand good and firm, specially if it fall out that her movables amount to better than £400,000 as is generally reported and her debts not to £40,000.[20]

So the disposal of Queen Anne's earthly goods was settled, but a more important matter still remained. Bishop King of London came to her bedside to try to ensure that she died a member of the Church of England, although he must have known that she had long gone in secret to Mass in her palaces.

'Your soul, madam,' he asked. 'Make a sign that your Majesty is one with God and longs to be with him.'

'I renounce the mediation of all saints and my own merits,' murmured the dying woman and with this the Archbishop was content. Then Queen Anne died, 'having benefited many and injured none. She died most willingly and was more comely in death then ever in life.'[21]

The gift of 'her world of brave jewels' and property to her son occasioned little comment, but the casket of jewels for Princess Elizabeth never materialised. Indeed, the Queen left nothing to her daughter. Six years had passed since Count Frederick had married Princess Elizabeth and he still had not made her a queen.

A week later, on 9 March, Queen Anne's body was brought by water from Hampton Court to Denmark House, as Somerset House was now called, where it was embalmed and lay in state for two and a half months. 'Her corpse was brought to Denmark House and so to be buried at Westminster after Easter . . . with the same solemnity and as much pomp as Queen Elizabeth',[22] wrote Chamberlain. For James never forgot that his wife was the daughter, wife and sister of a king.

The days dragged into weeks and the weeks into months. Still no date was mentioned for the funeral for which all England was waiting. The ladies of the Court came in shifts to keep watch round the dead Queen. Amongst them was Lady Anne Clifford, who wrote in her diary: 'Friday, 23 April, I went to Denmark House and heard prayers there and this night I watched all night by the Queen's corpse.'[23]

The long delay caused much inconvenience not only to the Court ladies but to the Londoners in general. Their pleasures were ruthlessly curtailed. No theatres were allowed to open and no plays might be performed. John Chamberlain put his finger on the cause, when he wrote gloomily:

The Queen's funeral is put off till the 29 of April and perhaps longer, unless they can find out money faster, for the Master of the Wardrobe[24] *is loath to wear his own credit threadbare, or to be so ill an husband as to use the King's credit and so pay double the price, which is now become ordinary, because they stay so long for their money. In the meantime the ladies grow weary of watching at Denmark House, though all the day long there is more concourse than when she was living.*[25]

The continued uncertainty gave rise to two regrettable incidents. One was the violent quarrel between the Countess of Arundel and the Countess of Nottingham for the position of chief female mourner in the funeral procession. Althea Talbot, who had married the Earl of Arundel, the head of the Howard family, had inherited a will of iron from her grandmother Elizabeth, Countess of Shrewsbury, but her antagonist Lady Nottingham had also a will of steel. Queen Anne had encountered her venom during King Christian's visit. It might have been thought that she would have been wise to remain in the background, as her husband had been deprived of his office as Lord High Admiral on the grounds of incompetence. But Lady Nottingham boldly claimed that as her husband was premier earl of England during his lifetime, so she as premier countess must take precedence over all other countesses, including the Countess of Arundel. Another claimant for the honour was the Countess of Northumberland, but she was regarded as a mere featherweight, as her husband was a prisoner in the Tower. In the end it was Althea who proved victorious.

The other incident was even more discreditable. Throughout King James's reign the royal servants had been notorious for their dishonesty. They stole in the most shameless way, taking silver, plate and even vestments from the Queen's private chapel. Indeed, their pilfering reached such a height that an order was issued substituting pewter plates for food carried from the kitchen to the entrance of the dining-room, where it was transferred to silver plates.[26] A preliminary survey of the Queen's property revealed that a quantity of the Queen's jewels was missing. It was discovered that two of her most trusted servants, the Frenchman Pierrot and Danish Anna, had helped themselves to jewels valued at £30,000 as well as a considerable sum of money.[27] King James's fears had proved to be well founded.

At length the date—the thirteenth of May—was chosen for the funeral. To modern superstitious minds it might seem an ominous choice, but at last the Exchequer had sufficient funds to cover the cost. It might be an honour to be invited to walk in

Queen Anne's funeral procession, but as an eyewitness, John Chamberlain, reveals, it was no small ordeal, especially for the ladies.

The funeral which was but a brawling, tedious sight, more remarkable for number than for any other singularity, there being 280 poor women besides an army of mean fellows that were servants to the Lords and others of the train; and though the number of Lords and Ladies were very great, yet methought altogether they made but a poor show, which perhaps was because they were apparelled all alike, or that they came laggering all along, even tired with the length of the way and the weight of their clothes, every Lady having twelve yards of broadcloth about her and the Countesses sixteen. The Countess of Arundel was chief mourner (but whether in her own right or as supplying the place of the Lady Elizabeth I know not); being supported by the Duke of Lennox and the Marquis of Hamilton, as likewise the rest had some to lean on, or else I see not how they had been able to hold out.[28]

The hearse was drawn by six horses and immediately before it walked Prince Charles,[29] for King James, who detested gloomy occasions, was at Theobalds. Behind the coffin on which the Queen's effigy was displayed came Queen Anne's favourite riding horse, led the Master of the Queen's Horse. Then a long line of barons, bishops, viscounts, earls and younger sons of dukes marched in order of precedence. It was late afternoon before the last of the procession had tramped its way into the Abbey of Westminster.

The Earls of Arundel, Pembroke and Oxford and the Marquises of Buckingham and Hamilton carried the coffin through the West door and up the nave to the sanctuary, where it was placed in a catafalque designed by Maximilian Colt. The Archbishop of Canterbury preached the funeral sermon and by six o'clock the Abbey was cleared of visitors.

'When all the company was gone and the church door shut up by the Dean of Westminster, then the prebends and Sir Edward Zouch, who was Knight Marshall, came up the private way and buried the corpse at the east end of Henry the Seventh chapel about 7 o'clock at night.'[30]

Soon the last flicker of the torches faded and the ring of the footsteps on the stone floor died away. After a life of many blighted hopes and bitter disappointments, Queen Anne was left alone in peace in her last resting place.[31]

NOTES

Abbreviations

B.A.A. British Archaeological Association
Cal. Border. Calender of State Papers Border
Cal. Dom. Calender of State Papers Domestic
Cal. Scot. Calender of State Papers relating to Scotland
Cal. Ven. Calender of State Papers Venetian
E.H.R. *English Historical Review*
H.M.C. Historical Manuscript Commission
H.M.C.Sal. Salisbury MSS at Hatfield House
H.M.C. Downshire. Marquis of Downshire's Manuscripts
P.R.O. Public Record Office

1 GIRLHOOD, 1574–1589

1 After the reign of Christian IV the castle of Skanderborg fell into disrepair and was pulled down in 1767. Only the chapel and tower of Frederick II's time remain. The castle as it was at the end of the sixteenth century is illustrated in Bering Lisberg's *Christian IV*, p. 36.

2 Sophie was only fourteen when she married Frederick II, who was twenty-three, on 20 June 1572.

3 J. H. S. Birch, *Denmark in History*, pp. 183–6.

4 The main building of Frederick II's small country seat was pulled down by Christian IV, who built the present imposing castle with three wings, two towers and stone galleries between 1602 and 1620.

5 The present Renaissance building of Frederick II was built by Anthony van Opberger on the site of the old castle of Eric of Pomerania, of which only a square tower on the south side remains.

6 Anna Hardenberg was the niece of Frederick II's tutor, Eiler Hardenberg.

7 Bering Lisberg. *Christian IV*, p. 14.

8 *Ibid.*, p. 26.

9 *Ibid.*, p. 26. The letter is in the original Danish.

10 Ellis, *Original Letters*, ser. 2, III, 149. Daniel Rogers to Burghley.

11 Bering Lisberg, p. 63.

12 Lund, *Christian den Fjerdes Skib paa Skanderborg Sø*, i, 13.

13 *Ibid.*, II, 85–9.

14 Willson, *James VI and I*, pp. 86–7.

2 THE COURTSHIP OF KING JAMES 1589–1590

1 This portrait was long thought to be the miniature attached to the Order of the Thistle in the Scottish regalia in Edinburgh Castle, but expert opinion now believes that the miniature is a likeness of Louise of Stolberg, wife of Prince Charles Edward Stuart.

2 *Cal. Scot.* X, 95: Thomas Fowler to Burghley.

3 Stafford, *James VI of Scotland*, p. 52.

4 *Warrender Papers*, II, 80–1. Catherine of Bourbon married a duke of Lorraine. The letter is printed in full in the original French.

5 Peter Young was granted a pension of £200 a year for his services in promoting the marriage, but payment was often in arrears.

6 B.M. Cotton MSS Caligula D.I., f. 385.

7 H.M.C., *Salisbury MSS*, III, 421.

8 *Ibid*, III, 420.

9 Willson, *James VI and I*, p. 88.

10 *Cal. Scot.*, X, 124.

11 *Ibid*, X, 122: Asheby to Walsingham.

12 Melville, *Memoirs*, p. 369.

13 Norway and Denmark were both ruled by the King of Denmark.

14 Craigmillar was not a royal castle. From the fourteenth century to the eighteenth it was held by the Preston family.

15 Murdin, *State Papers*, p. 637.

16 *Ibid.*

17 For the original French see *Warrender Papers*, ser. 3, XIX, 109–10.

18 Murdin, p. 637.

19 Moysie, *Memoirs*, p. 80.

20 There is some doubt about the date on which James embarked. The books of Session of the Council say 22 October, but according to Fowler it must have been later.

21 The tablet is illustrated in Bering Lisberg, *Christian IV*, p. 71.

22 Moysie, p. 81.

23 Lee, *John Maitland of Thirlstane*, p. 205. *Cal. Scot.*, X, 221–2.

24 Spottiswoode, *History of the Church of Scotland*, II, 406.

25 A morrowing gift was a present given by the bridegroom to his bride, on the day after the marriage. *Marriage of James VI*, p. 17.

26 Calderwood, *The History of the Kirk of Scotland*, VI, 83–4.

27 *Cal. Scot.*, X, 137.

28 *Ibid.*, X, 150.

29 *Letters to King James VI*, Maitland Club, XXXV, facsimile 34.

30 Gade, *Tycho Brahe*, p. 59.

31 These are now in the Nautical Museum in Kronborg.

32 Gade, *Tycho Brahe*, p. 120.

33 Christian IV later deprived Tycho Brahe of his lands and annuity.

3 QUEEN OF SCOTLAND 1590

1 Annabelle, Countess of Mar, was the daughter of William Murray of Tullibardine.

2 Jane Kennedy had attended Mary Queen of Scots in her last hour at Fotheringay. She enjoyed the special respect and favour of King James.

3 Melville, *Memoirs*, p. 370. Andrew Melville was the brother of Sir James Melville, whose *Memoirs* shed much light upon the period.

4 *Letters to James VI from the Queen, etc.*, vol. 35, p. xxi.

5 *Marriage of James VI*, p. 37. Ashton, *James I by his Contemporaries*, p. 90.

6 Douglas Irvine, *Royal Palaces of Scotland*, p. 100.

7 McElwee, *The Wisest Fool in Christendom*, p. 68.

8 The Abbey church or chapel royal is now a ruin. The beautiful Early English west door and great east window still remain.

9 *Marriage of James VI*, p. 53.

10 *Ibid.*, p. 53.

11 Moysie, *Memoirs*, p. 83.

12 *Marriage of James VI*, p. 40.

13 Moysie, pp. 83–4. Calderwood, *Kirk of Scotland*, v, 97.

14 Melville, *Memoirs*, p. 364.

15 Lodge, *Illustrations of English History*, III, 1–2.

16 MacGibbon and Ross Castel, *Architecture of Scotland*, I, 514.

17 Melville, *Memoirs*, p. 372.

18 Fowler said of Lady Maitland 'she is a wise woman and half chancellor when he is at home' *Salisbury MSS* III, 446–7.

19 *Cal. Scot.*, XI, 101. Lee, *John Maitland of Thirlstane*, p. 246.

20 *Ibid.*, p. 279.

21 *Warrender Papers*, II, 179.

22 *Ibid.*, II, 207–9.

23 *Acts of Parliament of Scotland*, IV, 23–7.

24 *Cal. Scot.*, XI, 101.

25 *Register of Deeds of the Scottish Record Office*, XL, 120–2.

26 Melville, *Memoirs*, p. 352.

4 THE EARL OF BOTHWELL, 1590–1593

1 Willson, *King James VI and I*, p. 103.

2 Bering Lisberg, *Christian IV*, p. 78.

3 Spottiswoode, *History of the Church of Scotland*, p. 412.

4 Francis Hepburn, fifth Earl of Bothwell, was the son of Lord John Stuart, an illegitimate son of James V. He was the nephew of Mary Queen of Scots' third husband and stepbrother of the Earl of Moray.

5 Melville, *Memoirs*, pp. 355–6.

6 Calderwood, *Kirk of Scotland*, V, 140–1. Moysie, *Memoirs*, p. 94.

7 Melville, *Memoirs*, pp. 356–7. Calderwood, VI, p. 173–4.

8 Spottiswoode, 421–2.

9 *Ibid.*, 423–4. *King James the Sixth*, p. 25.

10 Not long afterwards Margaret married the laird of Logie.

11 *Salisbury MSS*, XVI, 114.

12 Akrigg, *The Jacobean Pageant*, p. 10.

13 Melville, *Memoirs*, p. 415.

14 *Ibid.*

15 Mathew, *James I*, p. 56. Her sister Marie was the young Countess of Mar.

5 THE BIRTH OF PRINCE HENRY 1594

1 Nichols, *Progresses . . . of Queen Elizabeth*, III, 354.

2 Melville, *Memoirs*, p. 368. Birch, *Life of Henry, Prince of Wales*, p. 2.

3 *Ibid.*, p. 369.

4 *Ibid.*, p. 370.

5 Nichols, *Progresses . . . of Queen Elizabeth*, III, 364–5.

6 Calderwood, *History of the Kirk of Scotland*, V, 345.

7 *Warrender Papers*, 3rd ser. XIX, 266–7. The letter is unsigned.

8 Ashton, *James I by his Contemporaries*, p. 24.

9 *Cal. Scot.*, XI, 580.

10 *Original Letters of John Colville*, ed. D. Laing, 149.

11 Strickland, *Queens of England*, IV, 41.

12 *Cal. Scot*, XII, 18.

13 Halliwell, *Letters of the King of England*, II, 91–2.

14 *Cal. Scot.*, XII, 11.

15 Maitland died on 3 October 1595.

16 Strickland, IV, p. 44.

17 *Cal. Scot.*, XII, 88.

6 LIFE IN SCOTLAND 1596–1600

1 Melville Diary, p. 396.

2 Rait, R. *Five Stuart Princesses*, p. 51.

3 Strickland, *Queens of England*, IV, 44–5.

4 Moysie, *op. cit.*, p. 127.

5 Margaret only lived two years.

6 *Salisbury MSS*, VIII, p. 43.

7 *Cal. Scot.*, X, 272.

8 F. W. Arkbuckle, 'The Gowrie Conspiracy', *Scottish Historical Review*, XXXVI, 89–97.

9 Calderwood, VI, 71.

10 Lang, *History of Scotland*, II, 445.

11 James's official version was stated in a pamphlet sent by Nicholson to Robert Cecil in early September 1600.

12 Ramsay was knighted and later became Earl of Holderness.

13 Melville, *Diary*, p. 326. Mathew, *James I*, p. 92.

14 *Ibid.*, p. 327.

15 *Salisbury MSS*, X, 389.

16 Melville, *Memoirs*, p. 361.

17 *Salisbury MSS*, X, 389.

18 Later Beatrice Ruthven married Sir John Home of Coldingknows.

19 *Cal. Dom. 1603–1610*, p. 43.

20 Winwood, *Memoirs of the Affairs of State . . .*, II, 32.

21 The fireplace and the window of the room in which Prince Charles was born can be seen at the west end of the new wing.

22 Lord Treasurer's Accounts, *Maitland Club*, XXXV, 77.

23 *Ibid.*, p. 78.

24 *Ibid.*, p. 82.

25 *Ibid.*, p. 83.

26 The door with Heriot's name carved over it and his forge, bellows and crucible are now in the museum of Heriot's Hospital.

27 Strickland, IV, 42.

28 *Cal. Border* S.P., I, 538.

29 *Heriot Papers*, II, no. 4.

7 QUEEN ANNE'S JOURNEY TO ENGLAND, 1603

1 Lord Henry Howard was the son of the poet Earl of Surrey who was executed by Henry VIII in 1547. His elder brother, the Duke of Norfolk, was executed by Queen Elizabeth in 1572.

2 Hailes, *Secret Correspondence*, 216–17.

3 The Infanta Isabel Clara Eugenia was descended from John of Gaunt.

4 Calderwood, *History of the Kirk of Scotland*, VI, 230–1.

5 J. H. S. Birch, *Life of Henry Prince of Wales*, p. 29.

6 *Cal. Ven. 1603–1607*, p. 40.

7 Nichols, *Progresses of James I*, I. 153–4.

8 Strickland, *Queens of England*, IV, 65. She says the original letter had disappeared.

9 Spottiswoode, p. 477.

10 *H.M.C. 60. Mar & Kellie*, II, 51.

11 The sum of £90 13*s.* 4*d* was paid for 8 stones weight of gunpowder fired from Edinburgh Castle when Queen Anne and Prince Henry arrived at Holyroodhouse.

12 Lord Treasurer's Accounts, p. 86.

13 *Cal. Ven. 1603–1607*, 64.

14 Calderwood, VI, 282. Oman, *Elizabeth of Bohemia*, p. 14.

15 Lady Harington was the mother of Queen Anne's friend the Countess of Bedford. Sir John Harington was created Baron Harington of Exton by James I as a coronation honour.

16 Lodge, *Illustrations of English History*, III, 164.

17 *Cal. Ven. 1603–1607*, p. 39.

18 House Books of the Corporation of York, No. 52. 1590–1605, f 276. Nichols, *Progresses of James I*, I, 170.

19 R. Raine, York, p. 115.

20 *Salisbury MSS*, XV, 143.

21 E. Carleton Williams, *Bess of Hardwick*, p. 255.

22 H.M.C. *Report VIII*, *Corporation of Leicester*, p. 428b.

23 *Cal. Ven. 1603–1607*, p. 63.

24 Lady Cornwallis, *Private Correspondence*, p. 42.

25 *Diary of Lady Anne Clifford*, p. 8.

26 Coke married Lady Hatton in November 1598. He was not knighted until 1601.

27 *Diary of Lady Anne Clifford*, p. 13.

28 Lady Rich married Charles Blount, who was later created Earl of Devon, as her second husband. She had been his mistress for many years and had five children by him before their marriage.

29 Herford & Sampson, *Ben Jonson*, VII, 90.

30 *Diary of Lady Anne Clifford*, p. 10.

31 Bodl. Vet. A5. C. 899 ff. 56, 57.

8 QUEEN OF ENGLAND 1603

1 Nichols, *Progresses of James I*, I, 194.

2 *Ibid.*, pp. 197–8.

3 A. L. Rowse, *Shakespeare's Southampton*, p. 174.

4 Sir Roger Aston was a popular member of the royal household.

5 *Letters to James VI*, XXXV, facsimile 4.

6 Oatlands was near Weybridge.

7 Nichols, I, 232–3.

8 Lodge, *Illustration of English History.*, III, 186: Robert Cecil to the Earl of Shrewsbury.

9 *Ibid.*, III, 171: Sir Thomas Edmonds to the Earl of Shrewsbury.

10 *Letters to James VI*, XXXV, facsimile 3, p. lxv.

11 Tresham Lever, *The Herberts of Wilton*, p. 77. Shakespeare dedicated his first folio to Pembroke's brother Philip.

12 *Salisbury MSS*, XV, 348. James's expenses for the first year were £76,954 2*s* 5¼*d* and there was also £16,000 for Prince Henry.

13 *Salisbury MSS*, XV, 347.

14 Chambers, *Elizabethan Stage*, III, 280.

15 Wilbraham, *Journal*, X, 66.

16 A coranto was a quick-moving dance like a gallop.

17 Chambers, *Elizabethan Stage*, III, 280.

18 Wilson, *King James I*, in W. Kennet, *Complete History of England*, p. 685.

9 THE ROYAL FAMILY 1603–1605

1 Willson, *King James VI and I*, p. 164.

2 Rowse, *Shakespeare's Southampton*, p. 176.

3 *Cal. Dom. 1603–1610*, p. 12. Goodman, *The Court of King James*, pp. 87–8.

4 *Salisbury MSS*, XV, 133.

5 Hailes, *Secret Correspondence*, 216–17.

6 *Ibid.*, 144. *Cal. Dom. 1611–1618*, p. 96.

7 Lodge, *Illustrations*, III, 177.

8 *Cal. Ven. 1603–1607*, p. 513.

9 The arch at Fenchurch Street is illustrated in Ben Jonson, Herford and Simpson, VII, 83.

10 *Ibid.*, p. 93.

11 Akrigg, *The Jacobean Pageant*, p. 62.

12 In September Queen Anne sent a pearl necklace worth £1,400 to the Constable's wife and a tablet set in diamonds with portraits of herself and King James to the Constable. *Cal. Dom. 1603–1610*, p. 143.

13 Prince Charles was Duke of Rothsay.

14 *Salisbury MSS*, XVI, 163: Dr Henry Atkins to Queen Anne.

15 Sir Robert Carey was appointed Governor to Prince Charles on 22 February 1600.

16 Carey, *Memoirs*, Maitland Papers, xxxiv, 141

17 Lodge, *Illustrations of British History*, III, 244.

18 Rowse, *William Shakespeare*, p. 359. *Love's Labour's Lost* had been performed before Queen Elizabeth as long ago as Christmas 1598.

19 Chambers, *Elizabethan Stage*, III, 377.

20 *Cal. Ven. 1603–1607*, p. 248.

21 Chamberlain, *Letters*, I, 198, no 67.

22 Handover, *Arbella Stuart*, p. 255.

23 B.M. Sloane MSS, 4164, f 190.

24 *Ibid.*, ff 182–3.

25 *Cal. Ven. 1603–1607*, p. 42.

26 Collins, *Sidney Papers*, II, 190. Lever *The Herberts of Wilton*, p. 62.

27 Clarendon, *History of the Great Rebellion*, I. 74–5. Lever, p. 76.

28 Philip succeeded his brother as fourth Earl of Pembroke in 1630.

29 Chambers, *The Elizabethan Stage*, III, 377.

30 *Ibid.*, 377.

31 Winwood, II, 43–4.

32 B.M. Harl. MS, 6986, f 156.

33 Strickland, IV, p. 88

34 *The Old Cheque Book of the Chapel Royal*, Camden Soc, (1872), p. 167.

35 Rowse, *Shakespeare's Southampton*, p. 190.

36 Mallet, *History of the University of Oxford*, II, 231–2.

37 Bodl. Rawlinson MS.D. 1048, ff 66, 69.

38 *Cal. Ven. 1603–1607*, p. 68. Nichols, II, 48. Murray coloured was red-brown, mulberry colour.

10 KING CHRISTIAN'S VISIT, 1606

1 *Marriage, James VI, Papers relative to*, p. 37.

2 Leith, Narrative of the Scottish Catholics, I, 63–5. Archbishop Mathew (*James I*, p. 107) suggests that the 'certain great princess' might have been the dowager Margravine of Baden Rodemunchern, born Princess Cecilia of Sweden, whose sister married Anne's uncle.

3 Calderwood, *History of the Kirk of Scotland*, v. 408–9.

4 Stafford, *James VI of Scotland*, p. 167.

5 Bellesheim, *History of the Catholic Church in Scotland*, III, 347. Ward, *English Historical Review*, III, 796.

6 Bellesheim, III, 450–4. Bliss, 'Religious belief of Queen Anne', *E.H.R.*, IV, 110. Plenkers, *Er Frederick II's Datter Anna, Dronning af Stor Britannien gaaet over til Katholicismen*, *Hist. Tidsskrift*, VI, 403–25. Hicks, 'Embassy of Sir Anthony Standen in 1603', *Recusant History*, v, p. 205, note 6.

7 Ward, E.H.R., III, 796.

8 Willson, *James VI and I*, p. 146. Meyer, 'Clemens VIII und Jacob I von England', *Quellen und Forschungen aus italienischen Archiven*, VII, 273–82; 301–6. Hicks, *Recusant History*, VI, p. 164. Anne's letter to the Pope is lost but one she wrote to Cardinal Borghese on 31 July 1601 is in the British Museum, Add. MSS 37021, 25.

9 *Cal. Ven. 1603–1607*, p. 68.

10 Hicks, *Recusant History*, VII, pp. 60, 76, note 65.

11 Hicks, *ibid.*, VI, I. 4, p. 164.

12 James was afraid of angering the Pope and being excommunicated, so he did not oppose Standen's release.

13 *The Old Cheque Book of the Chapel Royal*, p. 170.

14 Tanner, 'Tombs of Royal Babies in Westminster Abbey', *B.A.A. Journal*, 3rd ser. XVI, 38.

15 *Ibid.*, p. 39.

16 Lodge, III, 323.

17 The Dutch market gardeners had originally been introduced by Christian II.

18 Watchet is pale blue colour.

19 Nichols, *Progresses*, II, 53.

20 Bering Lisberg, *Christian IV*, p. 173.

21 This was old St Paul's, built in Gothic style, which was destroyed in the Great Fire of London.

22 Harington, *Nugae Antiquae*, I, 348. *Salisbury MSS*, XV, 111, 276.

23 Harington, I, 348–9. The unfortunate legend which has grown up about Queen Anne's addiction to drink seems to be based on a mis-reading of this passage. 'The Queen' mentioned was the lady impersonating the Queen of Sheba, not Queen Anne, who was slowly recovering from the birth of Princess Sophia.

24 Bering Lisberg, p. 175.

25 *Ibid.*

26 *Egerton Papers*, Camden Soc., XII, 468 (1840).

27 *Salisbury MSS*, XVIII, 276.

28 Harl. MSS, 6986, 74.

29 Lady Shrewsbury was Arabella's aunt. Before her marriage she was Bess of Hardwick's youngest daughter, Mary Cavendish. Arabella lived with her uncle and aunt at Sheffield Castle.

30 Harl. MSS, 6986, 75.

31 *Ibid.*, 76.

11 THE QUEEN'S MASQUES, 1604–1612

1 Chambers, *The Elizabethan Stage* III, 255.

2 Akrigg, *Jacobean Pageant*, p. 40.

3 Ben Jonson, ed. Herford and Simpson, VII, 121–31.

4 Akrigg, p. 148.

5 Summerson, *Inigo Jones*, p. 22.

6 Winwood, II, 44. Sir Dudley Carleton to Ralph Winwood.

7 Chambers, III, 376.

8 As M. Beaumont had declined an invitation for 27 December on the ground of ill health, the Court took it for granted that he was still indisposed.

9 Winwood, II, 44.

10 Chambers, III, 379. Birch, *The Court and Times of James I*, I, 42.

11 Chambers, III, 379.

12 Summerson, *Inigo Jones*, p. 29.

13 *Cal. Ven.*, XI, 86.

14 The new banqueting house was built in the classical style of architecture with galleries.

15 Summerson, *Inigo Jones*, p. 29.

16 Chambers, III, 381.

17 *Cal. Ven.*, *1607–1610*, p. 86.

18 Chamberlain, *Letters*, ed. N. E. McClure, I, 252–3.

19 *Cal. Ven.*, *1607–1610*, p. 86.

20 Ben Jonson, ed. Herford and Simpson, VII, 283.

21 Chambers, *The Elizabethan Stage*, III, 383.

22 Don Fernandez de Girone was the envoy extraordinary. He asked for an invitation to the masque. He left on 1 February.

23 T. Birch, *The Court of King James*, I, 87.

24 H.M.C., *Downshire MSS*, II, 317. Winwood, *Memoirs*, III, 180.

25 Chambers, III, 282.

26 *Cal. Ven. 1607–1610*, p. 509.

27 Chambers, III, 386.

28 The Marshall was present when the masque was given on 3 Feb., the day after Candlemas.

12 THE RISING FORTUNES OF ROBERT CARR 1607–1612

1 Weldon, *The Court and Character of King James I*, I, 20.

2 Harington, *Nugae Antiquae*, I. 395.

3 Chamberlain, *Letters*, ed. Mc-Clure, I, 249, no 94.

4 Francis Osborne remarked that when King James kissed his favourites in public 'after so lascivous a mode' he was not likely to restrain himself in private. Osborne, 'Traditional Memories' in *Secret Memories of the Court*, I, 275.

5 Goodman, *The Court and Times of James I*, I, 215.

6 *Ibid.*, I, 216. Downshire MSS, III, 83: Taverner to William Trumbull.

7 Goodman, II, 145.

8 *Ibid.*, II, 143–4.

9 Perhaps Arthur Wilson refers to the same incident when he says 'Overbury being a little before his commitment condemned for presumptuous walking with his hat on in her [the Queen's] palace garden, she being at the window', Kennett, *A Complete History of England*, II, 697.

10 Harington, *Nugae Antiquae*, I, 39.

11 Weldon, p. 20.

12 Willson, *James VI and I*, p. 339. Weldon, p. 30.

13 Essex became a leading Parliamentary general in the Civil War.

14 Two letters from Lady Frances to Dr Forman can be seen in the British Museum, Sloan MSS 1002, ff 45–7.

15 Chamberlain, ed. McClure, I, 478.

16 White, *Cast of Ravens*, p. 28.

17 Willson, p. 340.

18 Chamberlain, I, 443, no 172.

19 *Ibid. Life and Letters of Sir Henry Wotton*, p. 19. Although at his trial Carr denied that he had tried to dissuade Overbury from accepting the post, later he admitted that he had done so.

20 Chamberlain, I, 478, no 182.

13 PRINCE HENRY 1606–1612

1 St James's Palace was built by Henry VIII on the site of a leper hospital. The Tudor gatehouse and chapel still remain.

2 *Cal. Ven. 1607–1610*, p. 206.

3 The Prince de Joinville was the brother of the Duc de Guise.

4 T. Birch, *Life of Prince Henry*, p. 100.

5 *Cal. Ven., 1610–1613*, p. 142.

6 Goodman, *The Court and Times of James I*, I, 250.

7 Carr sold Sherborne to Prince Henry, but later bought it back. On his downfall it was given to George Villiers. Nichols, *Progresses of.... James I*, II, 416.

8 *Autobiography of Phineas Pett*, p. 21.

9 *Ibid.*, p. 23.

10 Henry VIII was the last Prince of Wales. His son Edward never held that title.

11 *Cal. Ven. 1607–1610*, p. 507.

12 The Infanta Maria was the object of Prince Charles's romantic journey to Spain with Buckingham in 1623.

13 *Cal. Ven., 1610–1613*, p. 300.

14 *Cal. Ven., 1610–1613*, p. 186.

15 *Autobiography of Phineas Pett*, p. 81.

16 *Ibid.*, p. 83–4.

17 *Cal. Ven., 1610–1613*, p. 162.

18 Akrigg, *The Jacobean Pageant*, p. 133.

19 Nichols, II, 461.

20 Winwood, *Memorials*, III, 338.

21 Chamberlain, I, 338, no 135.

22 *Ibid.*, I, 338, no 135.

23 Dr Theodore de Mayerne was the son of a French Huguenot. He came to England in 1611 and was appointed first physician to King James. He was a great believer in blood-letting, which had unfortunate consequences in his treatment of Prince Henry and Sir Ralph Winwood.

24 Chamberlain, I, 388, no 153.

25 Sloane MSS, 1679. Sir Norman Moore, *Study of Medicine*, p. 96.

26 Chamberlain, *Letters*, ed. E. M. Thomson, p. 195, n. 4.

27 Moore, p. 101.

28 *Cal. Dom. 1611–1618*, p. 155.

29 Downshire MSS, III, 436.

14 PRINCESS ELIZABETH'S MARRIAGE, 1613

1 Harl. MSS, 6986, f 375.

2 Willson, *James VI and I*, p. 280.

3 Davies, *Early Stuarts*, p. 16.

4 Coke, *Detection of the Court and State of England*, I, 73.

5 Oman, *Elizabeth of Bohemia*, p. 62. Ellis, *Original Letters*, III, 170–1.

6 Winwood, *Memorials*, III, 403.

7 Rye, *England as seen by Foreigners in the days of Queen Elizabeth and James I*, p. 204.

8 Chamberlain, ed. E. McClure, I, 381, no 150.

9 *Ibid.*, I, 404, no 159.

10 *Ibid.*, I, 381, no 150.

11 *Ibid.*, I, 421, no 165.

12 *Ibid.*, I, 418.

13 *Ibid.* I 424, no. 166 SP Dom. 14/72/80.

14 *Archaeologia* XXVI, 381.

15 Chambers, *Elizabethan Stage*, III, 242.

16 Chamberlain, I, 428, no 166.

17 *Ibid.*, I, 433, no 169.

18 *Ibid.*, I, 394, no 155.

19 A farthingale was the forerunner of the crinoline. The skirt was distended by whalebone.

20 Willson, p. 178.

21 Philip succeeded his brother as fourth Earl of Pembroke in 1630.

22 *Diary of Lady Anne Clifford*, p. xxxix.

23 *Ibid.*, p. 49. Goodman, *Court and Times of James I*, I, 17.

24 *Ibid.*, p. 49.

25 Chamberlain, I, 507, no 192. Chambers, *Elizabethan Stage*, III, 277.

26 *Ibid.*, I, 446, no 172. Lord Knollys was involved in an attempt to foist Carr's kinsman, young Monson, on the Court as the royal favourite, to displace George Villiers. Lady Knollys imprudently made derogatory remarks about Villiers. This cost them the royal favour.

27 Nichols, *Progresses of . . . James I*, I, 627.

28 Willson, p. 397.

29 *S.P.Dom.*Jac. I, 14/72/120.

30 Chamberlain, I, 450, no 173. A carquenet or carcanet was a collar of precious stones.

31 The appearance of a lunar rainbow over St James's Palace at the time of Prince Henry's fatal illness was regarded by his mother as a sign of his approaching death.

32 Gandy, *Round About the Little Steeple*, p. 140.

33 Chamberlain, I, 457, no 175.

34 Gandy, p. 147.

35 Aubrey, *Natural History of Wiltshire*, Devizes, p. 109.

36 Chamberlain, I, 469, no 180.

15 THE RISING FORTUNES OF GEORGE VILLIERS, 1613–1619

1 Chamberlain, I, 449, no 173.

2 *Ibid.*, I, 444, no 172.

3 *Ibid.*, I, 495, no 188.

4 *Ibid.*, 495, no 188, note 21.

5 Chambers, *The Elizabethan Stage*, III, 245.

6 Chamberlain, I, 496, no 188.

7 *Ibid.*, I, 548, no 209.

8 Pembroke knew that Somerset was working with Gondomar to arrange a Spanish marriage for Prince Charles.

9 D'Ewes, *Autobiography*, p. 86, says Villiers wore old clothes at a horse race meeting.

10 Chamberlain, I, 559, no 213.

11 *Life of George Abbot*, p. 25, note. Beatrice White, *Cast of Ravens*, p. 94.

12 Arthur Wilson, in White Kennet's, *Complete History of England*, II, p. 697. H. Ross Williamson, *George Villiers, first Duke of Buckingham*, p. 39.

13 *Ibid.*, p. 679.

14 Nichols, *Progresses of... James I*, III, 80.

15 *Ibid.* Goodman, *The Court and Times of James I*, I, 224, gives a slightly different account of the incident.

16 Nichols, III, 80. Strickland, *Lives of the Queens*, IV, 120.

17 Nichols, III, 80. Williamson, p. 40.

18 Weldon, *Court and Character of James I*, p. 30.

19 *Ibid.*

20 Chamberlain, I, 597, no 209.

21 Harl. MSS 6986, f 136.

22 *Ibid.*, f 132.

23 Willson, *James VI and I*, p. 407. P.R.O. *S.P. Dom.*, *James I*, 14/76/95.

24 P.R.O. *S.P. Dom.*, 14/87/40.

25 Coke. *Detection of the Court and State of England*, vol. I, p. 79.

26 Bodl. Tanner MSS 299, f 194–6. Defence of Sir Gervase Elwes.

27 Chamberlain, II, 5, no 242.

28 Somerset's estates were confiscated, but he was allowed £4,000 a year and he was not deprived of the Order of the Garter.

29 Chamberlain, II, 17, no 246.

30 H.M.C. 5, *Report*, IV, 323. The ring is listed in an inventory of Holkham Hall.

31 Chamberlain, II, 121, no 280.

16 KING CHRISTIAN'S SECOND VISIT TO ENGLAND 1614

1 Bering Lisberg, *Christian IV*, pp. 246–7.

2 *Cal. Dom. 1611–1618*, p. 128.

3 Gade, *Christian IV*, p. 129.

4 H.M.C., *Buccleuch MSS*, p. 246: Sir Robert Cotton to Sir Edward Montague.

5 Bering Lisberg, p. 249. The quarrel between the town of Brunswick and the Duke of Brunswick was of long standing. In 1605 King Christian had supported the Duke against the townsmen, but in 1615 he remained neutral.

6 Henry Howard, Earl of Northampton, had died on 10 June 1614.

7 Chamberlain, I, 553, no 211.

8 Summerson, p. 40.

9 Chamberlain I, 614, no 236.

10 Summerson, *Inigo Jones*, p. 44.

11 *Ibid.*, pp. 47–8.

12 Bodl. MSS Vet. A 5, f. 13. Memoirs relating to the Queen of Bohemia by one of her ladies. The editor is believed to be Lady Frances Erskine.

13 The building is often described as Theobalds, but the gateway shows conclusively that it is Oatlands.

14 Arthur Wilson in White Kennett's *Complete History of England*, II, 719.

15 *Cal. Ven., 1603–1607*, p. 517.

16 Goodman, *Court and Times of James I*, I, 210–12. Handover, *Arbella Stuart*, p. 259.

17 *Cal. Dom. 1603–1610*, p. 555.

18 *Ibid.*, p. 173.

19 Harl. MSS 7003, f 64.

20 Birch, *Court of King James I*, II, pp. 126–127. Winwood, *Memorials*, III, p. 279.

21 Akrigg, *The Jacobean Pageant*, p. 264.

22 *Ibid.*

23 *Heriot Papers*, III, p. 11.

24 *Ibid.*

25 Goodman, I, 251.

26 Halliwell, *Letters of the Kings of England*, II, 118.

27 Chamberlain, II, 32, no 251.

28 *Diary of Lady Anne Clifford*, p. 41.

29 Chamberlain, II, 32, no 251.

30 *Letters to James VI*, XXXV, facsimile 2.

31 *Ibid.*, facsimile 5.

32 King James was away for six months, going as far north as Perth and Dundee. He returned to Windsor on 12 September.

33 Strickland, *Lives of the Queens*, IV, 124. Letter of Tobias Matthew, Bishop of Durham, 17 May 1612.

34 There is a plan of the house in Nichols's *Progresses of Queen Elizabeth*, III, 598. The palace was destroyed in the Civil War.

35 *Cal. Dom. 1611–1618*, p. 199.

36 Birch, *Court and Times of James I*, I, 359.

37 Oman, *Elizabeth of Bohemia*, p. 155.

38 *Letters to King James*, facsimile 4.
39 Chamberlain, II, 102. no 272.

17 THE CLOSING YEARS, 1716–19

1 Coke had been deprived of the office of Chief Justice of England in November 1616. Bowen, *The Lion and the Throne*, p. 388.

2 *Ibid.*, p. 398.

3 Chamberlain, II, 104, no 274.

4 *Ibid.*, II, 106, no 275.

5 Chamberlain, II, 249, no 282.

6 Coke, *Detection of the Court and State of England*, I, 61.

7 Rowse, *Raleigh*, p. 306.

8 Gondomar came to London in 1613.

9 Bodl. Tanner MSS, lxxiv, f 138.

10 Chamberlain, II, 178, no 302.

11 Willson, *James VI and I*, p. 377.

12 William Harvey, who discovered the theory of the circulation of the blood, was a pupil of Dr Mayerne.

13 Chamberlain, II, 197, no 311.

14 Harl. MSS 6986, f 111. Halliwell, *Letters of the Kings of England*, II, 122–3.

15 Chamberlain, II, 219, no 320.

16 Bliss, E.H.R., IV, p. 110.

17 Cath. Record. Soc. Miscellania, III, 55. *Life and Martydom of Mr Maxwell.*

18 Chamberlain, II, 219 no 320. Childermas was another name for Candlemas Day, 2 February. It was considered a day of ill omen.

19 Strickland, *Lives of the Queens*, IV, 130.

20 Chamberlain, II, 219, no 320.

21 *Cal. Dom.*, 16. p. 25.

22 Chamberlain, II, 220, no 320.

23 *Diary of Lady Anne Clifford*, p. 95.

24 The Master of the Wardrobe was Sir Lionel Cranfield. He was in charge of Queen Anne's funeral. Prestwick, *Cranfield*, pp. 100–1.

25 Chamberlain, II, 224, no 322.

26 Akrigg, *The Jacobean Pageant*, p. 281.

27 Chamberlain, II, 240, no 328.

28 *Ibid.*, II, 237, no 327.

29 Bodl. Rawlinson MS. B138, f 16.

30 *Lady Anne Clifford*, p. 101.

31 No monument was ever erected over Queen Anne's grave. Even the catafalque placed there was destroyed in the Civil War. But the wax head of Queen Anne, which can be seen in the Norman undercroft in Westminster Abbey is a portrait taken from her death mask. It shows her long oval face, high cheek bones, and even the pimple on her left cheek.

BIBLIOGRAPHY

MANUSCRIPTS

Public Record Office

State Papers Domestic: James I.

British Museum

Additional MSS 4160 f 3. Letter of Queen Anne re Overbury.

18738. Letters of King James.

19969. Letter of Queen Anne to Count de Boischot.

21913 ff 11–14. Expenses of Princess Elizabeth.

23240 f 117. Letter of Anne to Queen Elizabeth.

25246 f 57. Letter to Anne from the Lords of the Council.

25707 f 147. Letter to Queen Anne from Sir Walter Raleigh.

27404 ff 35–42. Queen Anne's Receiver General, 1606.

37021 f 25. Letter of Queen Anne to Cardinal Borghese, 31 July 1601.

38189 ff 104–6. Papers of Anne of Denmark's Household.

40079 f 69. Letter of Anne to the Pope, 1612. In Italian.

Cottonan MSS

Caligula D.I. ff 262, 382–3. D.II. f 13.

Vespasian F. IV. f 11b.

Harleian MSS

6986 ff 74–6. Letters of Queen Anne, Prince Henry and Arabella Stuart.

7003 f 64. Letters of Prince Henry.

Sloane MSS

1679 Dr Mayerne's record of the symptoms of his royal patients.

4161 Transcripts of documents made by Thomas Birch.

4164 ff 181–2. Letter of Arabella Stuart about Court Life.

f 190. *Ibid.*

Bodleian Library, Oxford

Vet. A 5.c.899. Memoirs relating to the Queen of Bohemia by one of her ladies.

Ashmolean MSS

1729. Letters of the royal family.

Rawlinson MSS

B. 138 f. 16. Procession at Queen Anne's funeral.

D.1048 ff 66, 69. Queen Anne at Oxford.

Tanner MSS

74 f 138. Letter of Queen Anne to Villiers.

299 f 194. Sir Thomas Overbury.

236 f 80. Offerings at Queen Anne's funeral.

Kongelige Bibliotek, Copenhagen

Ny Kongelige Sammlung. 4. 972b. Lord Willoughby's Embassy to Denmark.

Ny Kongelige Sammlung. 4. 2586. James VI's Journey, 1589.

Thott Sammlung. 4. 1610. Marriage of James VI and Anne of Denmark.

Uldall Sammlung. 4. 365. Anne Queen of Scotland.

PRINTED BOOKS

ABBOT, GEORGE *The Life of Dr George Abbot . . . reprinted from Biographica Britannica, with the character by Arthur Onslow*, 4 vols, London, 1777.

Acts of the Parliament of Scotland, ed. T. Thomson, vols III & IV, London, 1814–16.

AKRIGG, G. P. V. *The Jacobean Pageant*, Harvard U. P., 1963.

AIKIN, L. *Memoirs of the Court of James I*, 2 vols, London, 1822.

ARKBUCKLE, F. W. 'The Gowrie Conspiracy', *Scottish Historical Review*, XXXVI, 89–97.

Archaeologia, XII, XV, XXI, XXXV, XXXVII, XXXIX, XLII, XLVI.

ARUP, ERIK *Danmark's Historie*, 3 vols, Copenhagen, 1925–55.

ASHTON, ROBERT *James I by his Contemporaries*, London, Hutchinson, 1969.

AUBREY, JOHN *The National History of Wiltshire*, London, 1847.

BELLESHEIM, A. *History of the Catholic Church in Scotland*, trans. D. O. Hunter Blair, 2 vols, Edinburgh, 1887–90.

BERING LISBERG, H. C. *Christian IV*, Copenhagen, 1890.

BIRCH, J. H. S. *Denmark in History*, London, Murray, 1938.

BIRCH, T. *The Court and Times of James I*, 2 vols, London, 1849.

BIRCH, T. *The Life of Henry Prince of Wales*, London, 1760.

Buccleuch MSS HM C. 1897–1926.

BLISS, W. 'Religious beliefs of Queen Anne, *E.H.R.*, IV.

BOWEN, CATHERINE. *The Lion and the Throne: Sir Edward Coke*, London, Hamish, Hamilton, 1956.

BOWES, ROBERT, ed. *The Correspondence of Robert Bowes*, Surtees Society, 1842.

BRICKA, C. F. *Dansk Biografisk Lexikon*, Copenhagen, 1887–1905.

Calendar of State Papers, Border.

Calendar of State Papers, Domestic (*Cal. Dom.*)

Calendar of State Papers, Scottish (*Cal. Scot.*)

CALDERWOOD, DAVID *The History of the Kirk of Scotland*, ed. T. Thomson, 8 vols, Woodrow Society, 1842–49.

CAMDEN, WILLIAM *Annales Regni Jacobi* in White Kennet, *Complete History of England*, London, 1706.

CAREY, ROBERT *Memoirs*. London, 1759.

CHAMBERLAIN, JOHN *The Letters of John Chamberlain*, ed. N. E. McClure, 3 vols, Philadelphia, American Philosophical Society, 1939.

CHAMBERLAIN, JOHN *Letters* (selection), ed. E. Mc C. Thomson, London, Murray, 1966.

CHAMBERS, E. K. *The Elizabethan Stage*, 4 vols, Oxford U. P., 1923.

CLARENDON, EARL *The History of the Great Rebellion*, 1704–7.

CLIFFORD, LADY ANNE *Diary of Lady Anne Clifford*, ed. V. Sackville West, London, Heinemann, 1923.

COKE, R. *Detection of the Court and State of England*, 3 vols, London, 1694.

COLVILLE, JOHN *The Original Letters of Mr John Colville*. Edinburgh, Bannatyne Club, 1858.

CORNWALLIS, LADY *Private Correspondence of 1613–1644*, London, 1892.

CORNWALLIS, SIR CHARLES *Life, Death and Funeral of Henry Prince of Wales*, London, 1751.

DAVIES, GODFREY *The Early Stuarts, 1603–1660: Oxford History of England*, Oxford U. P., 1937 (2 vol edn 1959).

Det Danmarks Riges Historie, ed. I. A. Frederica, 6 vols.

D'EWES, SIMON *Autobiography and Correspondence*, ed. J. O. Halliwell, 2 vols, London, 1845.

DONALDSON, GORDON *James V to VII: Edinburgh History of Scotland*, III, Oliver & Boyd, 1965.

DOUGLAS, IRVINE *Royal Palaces of Scotland*, London, 1911.

Downshire MSS H.M.C., 1924–40.

DREYER, JOHN *Tycho Brake*, Copenhagen, 1890.

DUNLOP, I. *Palaces and Progresses of Elizabeth I*, London, Cape, 1962.

DUTTON, RALPH *English Court Life from Henry VII to George II*, London, Batsford, 1963.

Egerton Papers Camden Society, 1840.

ELLIS, SIR HENRY *Original Letters Illustrative of English History*, ser. 2, III, and ser. 3, IV, Camden Soc., 1837.

FLAMAND, L. J. *Christian den Fjerde*, Copenhagen, 1855.

GADE, JOHN *Christian IV, King of Denmark and Norway*, London, Allen & Unwin, 1928.

GADE, JOHN *The Life and Times of Tycho Brahe*, Princeton U. P., 1947.

GANDY IDA *Round About the Little Steeple*, London, Allen & Unwin, 1960.

GARDINER, SAMUEL R. *History of England from the Accession of James I to the Outbreak of the Civil War*, Oxford U. P., 1883.

GOODMAN, GODFREY *The Court and Times of James I*, 2 vols, 1839.

HAILES, LORD (DAVID DALRYMPLE) *Memories and Letters relating to the History of Great Britain in the Reign of James I*, Glasgow, 1792.

HAILES, LORD *Secret Correspondence*, Edinburgh, 1766.

HALLIWELL, J. O. *Letters of the Kings of England*, 2 vols, London, 1846.

HANDOVER, P. *Arbella Stuart*, London, Eyre & Spottiswoode, 1957.

HARINGTON, SIR JOHN *Nugae Antiquae*, ed. T. Park, London, 1804.

HERIOTS HOSPITAL *Inventory of Documents.*

Heriot Papers, 1586–1622, 3 vols.

HERVEY, M. THOMAS *Howard, Earl of Arundel*, Cambridge U.P., 1921.

HICKS, LEO, S. J. 'The Embassy of Sir Anthony Standen in 1603', Parts i–iv, *Recusant History*, V, VI, VII, 1959–64.

JAMES I *The History and Life of King James the Sext*, Bannatyne Club, Edinburgh, 1825.

JAMES I *Papers relative to the Marriage of James the Sixth of Scotland with the Princess Anna of Denmark*, Bannatyne Club, Edinburgh, 1828.

JAMES I *Letters and State Papers during the reign of King James the Sixth*, Edinburgh, 1838.

JAMES I *Letters to King James the Sixth from the Queen, Prince Henry, etc.*, Edinburgh, Maitland Club, no 35, 1835.

JAMES I *Secret History of the Court of James I*, ed. Sir W. Scott, Edinburgh, 1911.

JONSON, BEN *Works*, ed. C. H. Herford and E. Simpson, 11 vols, Oxford U. P., 1925–52.

KENNET, WHITE *A Complete History of England*, 3 vols, London, 1706.

KENYON, J. P. *The Stuarts*, London, Batsford (3rd edn, Collins 1966) 1958.

LANG, ANDREW *The History of Scotland*, London, 1903.

LAURING, PALLE *A History of the Kingdom of Denmark*, N.Y., Heinmann, 1960.

LEE, MAURICE *John Maitland of Thirlstane*, Princeton U. P., Oxford U. P., 1959.

LEITH, W. FORBES *Narrative of the Scottish Catholics*, Edinburgh, 1885.

LEVER, TRESHAM *The Herberts of Wilton*, London, Murray, 1967.

LODGE, EDMUND *Illustrations of British History*, London, 1838.

Lord Treasurer's Accounts in *Letters to James VI*, Edinburgh, Maitland Club, no 35, 1835.

LUND, TROELS *Christian den Fjerdes Skib paa Skanderborg, Sø*, Copenhagen, 1893.

MACKEPRANG, M. 'Dronning Spohia', in *Historisk Tidscrifts*, Copenhagen, 1852.

MALLET, C. E. *History of the University of Oxford*, 3 vols, London, Methuen, 1924–7.

MATHEW, DAVID *Catholicism in England 1535–1935*, London, Longmans, 1936.

MATHEW, DAVID *James I*, London, Eyre & Spottiswoode, 1967.

MATHEW, DAVID *The Jacobean Age*, London, Longmans, 1938.

MCELWEE, WILLIAM *The Murder of Sir Thomas Overbury*, London, Faber, 1952.

MCELWEE, WILLIAM *The Wisest Fool in Christendom*, London, Faber, 1958.

MCGIBBON, and ROSS, T. *Castellated and Domestic Architecture of Scotland*, 5 vols, 1887–92.

Mar & Kellie MSS. H.M.C., 60.

Marriage of James VI: see JAMES I.

MELVILLE, SIR JAMES *Sir James of Halhill, Memoirs of his own Life*, Edinburgh, Bannatyne Club, 1827.

MELVILLE, JAMES *The Autobiography and Diary of Mr James*

Melville, ed. Robert Pitcairn, Woodrow Society, 1842.

MEYER, A. *Clemens VIII und Jakob I von England*, Rome, 1906.

MOORE, SIR NORMAN *The History of the Study of Medicine in the British Isles*, Oxford U. P., 1908.

MOYSIE, DAVID *Memoirs of the Affairs of Scotland, 1577–1603*, Edinburgh, Bannatyne Club, 1830.

MUNCH, P. A. *Samtidig Beretningen om Princesse Annas Giftermaal med Kong Jakob 6te af Skotland og hendes paafolgende Kroning*, Christiana, Norske Samlingen af et historisk Samfund, 1852.

MURDIN, WILLIAM *A Collection of State Papers 1571–1596 transcribed from the original papers left by William Cecil, Lord Burghley*. London, 1759.

NICHOLS, JOHN *The Progresses and Public Processions of Queen Elizabeth*, 4 vols. London, 1788–1821.

NICHOLS, JOHN *The Progresses, Processions and Festivities of King James I, his royal Consort and Family . . .*, 4 vols, London, 1828.

Old Cheque Book of the Chapel Royal, Camden Society, 170, 1872.

OMAN, CAROLA *Elizabeth of Bohemia*, London, Hodder & Stoughton, 1938.

OSBORNE, FRANCIS 'Traditional Memories of the Reign of King James I', in *Secret History of the Court of James I*, Edinburgh, 1811.

PETT, PHINEAS *Autobiography*, Navy Records, London, 1918.

PLENKERS, W. *Er Frederick II's Datter Anna gaaet over til Catholicismen. Hist. Tidskrift 6. Raekkel* I. Copenhagen, 1888.

PRESTWICH, M. *Cranfield Politics and Profits under the Early Stuarts*, Oxford U. P., 1966.

RAIT, ROBERT *Five Stuart Princesses*, London, 1902.

ROBERTS, HENRY *Englands Farewell to Christian IV*, London, 1606.

ROWSE, A. L. *Raleigh and the Throckmortons*, London, Macmillan, 1962.

ROWSE, A. L. *Shakespeare's Southampton*, London, Macmillan, 1965.

RYE, W. B. *England as seen by Foreigners in the days of Elizabeth and James I*, London, 1865.

Salisbury MSS. H.M.C.

Scottish Historical Review, XIII, XIX, XXI, XXVI.

SETON, W. W. 'The Early Years of Henry Frederick Prince of Wales', and Charles Duke of Albany, *Scottish Historical Review*, XIII.

SPOTTISWOOD, JOHN *The History of the Church of Scotland*, 3 vols, Edinburgh, 1847–51.

STAFFORD, HELEN *James VI of Scotland and the throne of England*, New York, American Historical Association, 1940.

STEEHOLM, CLARA *James I of England*, London, M. Joseph, 1938.

STEVEN, W. *Memoir of George Heriot*, Edinburgh, 1845.

STATHAM, E. P. *A Jacobean Letter Writer, The Life and Times of John*

Chamberlain, London, Kegan Paul, 1920.

STONE, L. *The Crisis of the Aristocracy, 1558–1641*, Oxford U. P., 1965.

STRICKLAND, AGNES *Lives of the Queens of England*, 6 vols, London, 1840–8.

SUMMERSON, SIR JOHN *Architecture in Britain, 1530–1830*. Penguin Books, Pelican History of Art, 1958.

SUMMERSON, SIR JOHN *Inigo Jones*. Penguin Books (Pelican), 1966.

TANNER, JOAN 'Tombs of royal babies in Westminster Abbey', *British Archaeological Association Journal*, 3rd ser., XVI.

WARD, A. W. *English Historical Review*, III, 796.

Warrender Papers, ed. A. Cameron and Robert Rait, *Scottish Historical Society*, 3rd ser, vol. XIX, Edinburgh, 1932.

WELDON, SIR ANTHONY *Court and Character of King James I*, London, 1650.

WELSFORD, E. *The Court Masque*, New York, Russell, 1962.

WHITE, BEATRICE, *Cast of Ravens: (Sir Thomas Overbury)*. London, Murray, 1965.

WILLIAMS, E. CARLETON *Bess of Hardwick*, London, Longmans, 1959.

WILBRAHAM, SIR ROGER *Journal of Sir Roger Wilbraham*, Camden Miscellany, X, 1902.

WILLIAMSON, HUGH ROSS *George Villiers, first Duke of Buckingham*, Duckworth, 1940.

WILLIAMSON, HUGH ROSS *King James I*, London, Duckworth, 1936.

WILLSON, D. HARRIS *King James VI and I*, London, Cape, 1955.

WILSON, ARTHUR *The Life and Reign of James I*, in White Kennett, *Complete History of England*, London, 1706.

WINWOOD, SIR RALPH *Memorials of the Affairs of State in the Reigns of Queen Elizabeth & James I*, ed. E. Sawyer, 3 vols. London, 1725.

WOOTTON, SIR HENRY *Life and Letters*, ed. L. Pearsall Smith, 2 vols, Oxford U. P., 1907; reprint 1966.

ZINZERLING, JUSTIN *Description of England*, London, 1610.

INDEX